Advance Praise for *Thriving at College*

"Most Christian young people go to college without specific goals and are unprepared for the challenges that await them. While some prosper spiritually, most get derailed, and an alarming number abandon their faith. Alex has written an insightful and useful book to help college-bound people know what to expect, how to ~~~~ ~~~~ to do to avoid the pitfalls."

RANDY ALCORN, best-selling author of *Heaven*

"Written by an 'insider'—a former student, now a professor—this book addresses all the issues a student might face. It will be an excellent gift for all high school seniors."

DR. JERRY BRIDGES, best-selling author of *The Pursuit of Holiness*

"College represents one of the most strategic transitional moments in the lives of most young Christians. In this book, Alex provides good wisdom and sound, practical advice to young Christians seeking to navigate the world of higher education while simultaneously maturing into faithful Christians."

DR. R. ALBERT MOHLER JR., president of the Southern Baptist Theological Seminary

"Writing from the perspective of both a parent and a professor, Alex presents a practical guide on how students can spiritually and intellectually thrive during their college years. This book will be required reading for all three of my children."

TULLIAN TCHIVIDJIAN, senior pastor of Coral Ridge Presbyterian Church

"*Thriving at College* is a significant how-to volume to help new college students and their families prepare for and adjust to the numerous transitions that accompany the college experience."

DR. DAVID S. DOCKERY, president of Union University

"Many in my generation look back on their college years with regret, wishing we had been more intentional and focused during our time on campus. Before you invest four years of your life and tens of thousands of dollars, spend a few dollars and a few hours to read this book."

BOB LEPINE, cohost of *FamilyLife Today*

"A commonsense approach to ten common mistakes concerning time management, sex, grades, relationships with parents, and other things that might seem simple but rarely are."

DR. MARVIN OLASKY, editor in chief of *World* magazine

"Alex's goal is to spare college-bound young people from entering college thoughtlessly and then drifting after they are there. The book has all the right ingredients to meet that goal."

DR. LELAND RYKEN, professor at Wheaton College

"All the things I speak to college students about are here: maintaining your faith, developing nurturing friendships, having wisdom in relationships, becoming mature, finding balance, growing in spiritual maturity, seizing opportunities. A must-read for kids headed to college and those already there."

TEDD TRIPP, best-selling author of *Shepherding a Child's Heart*

"When Alex talks about thriving at college, he speaks from experience. He has spent a lot of time on campus: from undergrad to professor. Put all of that together, along with a wide knowledge of Scripture, and you have the ideal author of a really helpful book."

DR. MICHAEL HORTON, professor at Westminster Seminary California

"I've been a campus pastor for the last seventeen years and have seen a lot of excellent books on how a Christian student should go about being a truly Christian student. Chediak's book is the best I've seen."

BEN PATTERSON, campus pastor at Westmont College

"A handbook of practical wisdom for the would-be college student. Essential summer reading for every incoming freshman."

DR. GENE VEITH, provost of Patrick Henry College

"Alex cuts through the nonsense to tell you exactly what you need to know: college is a pivotal season that carries great promise, but you have to take specific steps *now* to thrive. *Thriving at College* is a cheat sheet, a strategy session, and a pep talk rolled into one."

LISA ANDERSON, host of Focus on the Family's *The Boundless Show*

"It would be hard to find a better book for the new college student than *Thriving at College.*"

MARK COSGROVE, professor at Taylor University

For more endorsements, see www.alexchediak.com.

THRIVING AT COLLEGE

✓ Make Great Friends,
✓ Keep Your Faith, and
✓ Get Ready for the Real World!

Alex Chediak

Tyndale House Publishers, Inc.
Carol Stream, Illinois

Visit Tyndale online at www.tyndale.com.

TYNDALE and Tyndale's quill logo are registered trademarks of Tyndale House Publishers, Inc.

Thriving at College: Make Great Friends, Keep Your Faith, and Get Ready for the Real World!

Copyright © 2011 by Juan Alexander Chediak. All rights reserved.

Cover and author photographs by Stephen Vosloo copyright © 2010 by Tyndale House Publishers, Inc. All rights reserved.

Designed by Jessie McGrath

Published in association with the literary agency of Wolgemuth & Associates, Inc.

Unless otherwise indicated, all Scripture quotations are taken from *The Holy Bible,* English Standard Version,® copyright © 2001 by Crossway Bibles, a publishing ministry of Good News Publishers. Used by permission. All rights reserved.

Scripture quotations marked NASB are taken from the New American Standard Bible,® copyright © 1960, 1962, 1963, 1968, 1971, 1972, 1973, 1975, 1977, 1995 by The Lockman Foundation. Used by permission.

Scripture quotations marked NIV are taken from the Holy Bible, *New International Version,® NIV.*® Copyright © 1973, 1978, 1984, 2010 by Biblica, Inc.™ Used by permission of Zondervan. All rights reserved worldwide. www.zondervan.com.

Scripture quotations marked NKJV are taken from the New King James Version.® Copyright © 1982 by Thomas Nelson, Inc. Used by permission. All rights reserved. *NKJV* is a trademark of Thomas Nelson, Inc.

Scripture quotations marked NLT are taken from the *Holy Bible,* New Living Translation, copyright © 1996, 2004, 2007 by Tyndale House Foundation. Used by permission of Tyndale House Publishers, Inc., Carol Stream, Illinois 60188. All rights reserved.

Library of Congress Cataloging-in-Publication Data

Chediak, Alex.
 Thriving at college : make great friends, keep your faith, and get ready for the real world! / Alex Chediak.
  p. cm.
 Includes bibliographical references.
 ISBN 978-1-4143-3963-4 (sc)
 1. Christian college students—Religious life. 2. College student orientation. I. Title.
 BV4531.3.C483 2011
 248.8´3—dc22   2010054362

Printed in the United States of America

17 16 15 14 13 12 11
 8   7   6   5   4   3

To my students:

May your hearts be steadfast, trusting in the Lord. May you be zealous for good deeds. May you live godly, pure, fruitful, and productive lives that make Jesus look beautiful to others.

Contents

Foreword

COLLEGE CAN BE a wonderful and a dangerous place. We've seen some of our peers flourish and find their identity at school, and we've seen others completely lose their way—or even self-destruct. Is the college experience inherently bipolar, good for some and unavoidably bad for others? Or is there another possibility: that each outcome is a path we can choose to take? In this terrific book, former college student and current college professor Alex Chediak says the answer to that last question is "Yes!"—and we wholeheartedly agree.

For most high school graduates today, going to college is the default. As a result, a lot of teens end up drifting from high school into college without any clear plan in mind. Maybe you are going to make your parents happy or to get away from somewhere or someone, or maybe college just sounds like a fun, new experience. Whatever your motivation, entering college without a sense of purpose is dangerous.

Why? Because for most young adults, college provides at once more freedom and more responsibility than you've ever had before. Whether you choose to focus on the freedom or the responsibilities of college will determine whether you thrive—or just survive. At college there are no parents to make you read your Bible, do your homework, get sleep, eat well, or do laundry. At college—even at Christian universities—there are "friends" who are willing to support whatever lifestyle you choose to engage in: from bookworm to party animal.

So college is both a crisis and an opportunity. A crisis, because while embracing the *freedom* of campus life can lead to temporary fun, the end result can be a lifetime of regret. An opportunity, because embracing the *responsibility* of college can result in incredible intellectual, spiritual, social, emotional, and physical growth.

The student who thrives at college—the student who glorifies God with his or her college years—is the one who sees it as a great opportunity that requires great responsibility. Alex Chediak understands this better than most, with the experience and heart to help students reach their full God-given potential. *Thriving at College* will help you navigate the common pitfalls relating to faith, relationships, academics, and extracurricular activities.

There is no better guide to college than this.

—Alex and Brett Harris, Patrick Henry College,
cofounders of TheRebelution.com and coauthors
of Do Hard Things *and* Start Here

Preface

I MADE THE decision to go to college almost by accident. What else was I supposed to do after high school? I was a fairly good student, but I lacked the maturity to make that really huge decision in a constructive, sensible manner. Frankly, my college years could have been better. Today, I look back on my younger self in college and wish I could have a cup of coffee with him. I wish I could give him some hard-earned advice.

That's why I'm writing this book. I can't take my younger self out to coffee. There's no time machine for that. But as a college professor today, I have the chance to observe students and how they live their lives. I'm amazed at how many of them remind me of my former self. This book is, in essence, an attempt at taking you out to Starbucks and telling you what I've learned about the college years—and, most important, telling you how to make your college season the best years of your life (so far). I cannot tell you how much I wish someone had told me these things when I was in college.

Our culture has a definite perspective on what college

should involve. If you follow it, you'll throw your best years away, chasing experience after experience, mastering video games, hanging out at the mall, watching movies, and generally delaying responsibility. They'll tell you that college is about having fun, living it up. And they'll say that avoiding true adulthood doesn't need to end at graduation. Last year four out of five graduates moved back in with Mom and Dad. Seven in ten did not have a job lined up when they walked the stage on their big day, having just spent $100,000 and 20 percent of their lives. True, some of these factors were influenced by a weak economy. But the fact remains that our culture promotes the idea of prolonged adolescence.

Did you recently graduate from high school? Not sure what you'll do next? You are not alone. I've been there. It's one of the biggest decisions you'll ever make. But high-school graduation is also a milestone toward something else. It's a step toward functional independence from Mom and Dad—a big step. If your parents love you, they established rules in your household. But at almost any college you can name, I guarantee you that nobody will tell you when to go to sleep, when to wake up, when to do your homework, when to turn off your PlayStation, and when to say no to another late-night donut or movie.

What do you want to be when you graduate? I'm not asking what you want to *do*, but what you want to *be*. A typical twenty-two-year-old in our day is unstable, uncertain, and unrealistic. I was, too, and not that long ago. College students tend to have a million ideas for what they want to do and no idea how to get there or if they're even good at it. Our society tends to make people feel so "affirmed" all their lives that they lose the proper, objective basis for affirmation: a gift, a talent, a skill, as demonstrated by some accomplishment. Instead, everyone gets a trophy in Little League for showing up. When people are regularly reminded how special and talented they are, they're shocked when they're shuffled off the stage of their latest obsession, like another failed *American Idol* contestant.

It doesn't have to be that way. You don't have to fritter away your college experience, going from parties to cramming sessions week in and week out without any overarching purpose. You don't have to experience "failure to launch." You can be a productive, fruitful, godly adult at an early age. You can avoid "think[ing] of [yourself] more highly than [you] ought" and instead think of yourself "with sober [realistic] judgment" (Romans 12:3). And if you are a Christian, a life of fruitful obedience—a life devoted to good works—is the only appropriate response to what God has done for you (Titus 3:8). Let's look at a pair of examples.

In 1924, a young boy named John moved with his family to Martinsville, Indiana, just when he was starting high school. John was strongly influenced by his father, who raised him to work hard at school and on the farm and gave him mottoes like these: *Don't whine, don't complain, and don't make excuses.* When the chores and homework were done (and only then), John found time for basketball—and for leading his team to the state championship finals for three consecutive years.

But John's father wasn't very interested in basketball. He was far more interested in his son's character. He wanted his son to never stop striving to develop his full, God-given potential and to give maximum effort in the classroom, on the farm, and on the court. By example he taught long-suffering and faithfulness. At one point Dad lost the family's farm because of some freak illness that spread among the animals, killing them. Dad never complained or whined, not even to the banker who took the property. How different from the entitlement mentality of our day.

John worked his way through college at Purdue University. While he studied English, a field in which he later taught, he also played basketball and helped his team win a national championship in 1932. Later that year, with the events of the Great Depression, John lost his life's savings less than a week before he was supposed to marry Nell, his high-school sweetheart. Like his dad, John never whined, complained, or made excuses. A friend of the family heard about his loss and gave him a small loan. The day after his wedding, John left town for a weeklong job. He had to start paying the bills and paying back that loan.

John's age in 1932? Twenty-two years old. John was more mature, hardworking, and responsible at twenty-two than most young men today are at thirty-two.

Why? John thought that doing his very best at everything was *just the normal thing to do*. He later coached at the college level and taught his players nuggets of gold:

- "Don't try to be better than someone else. But never stop trying to be the best you can be."
- "When you blame others, you are trying to excuse yourself."
- "No one is an overachiever. How can you rise above your level of competency? No, we're all underachievers to different degrees. . . . Don't measure yourself by what you've accomplished, but rather by what you should have accomplished with your abilities."
- "Failing to prepare is preparing to fail."

Not surprisingly, this man went on to become the most successful, most accomplished basketball coach in the history of the sport, winning ten national championships in his last twelve years at UCLA. His name was John Robert Wooden, and he died in the summer of 2010, just a couple of months shy of his one-hundredth birthday.

But basketball wasn't John's life, and winning wasn't everything to him. John told others, "There is only one kind of life that truly wins, and that is the one that places faith in the hands of the Savior."[1] He was a deeply humble man, often avoiding the spotlight and living far below his income potential, even until his last days. John had character and principle and even as a young man was wise beyond his years. He forfeited championship opportunities in the 1940s because African American players weren't allowed to compete for the national title (and his team was racially integrated, even in that day). You see, by every indication John was a Christian above all else. Christianity gave him the grounding, and the perspective, to live a life of incredible fruitfulness and productivity and to embrace adulthood without going through a lengthy period of irresponsible living.

John isn't just some throwback. No, there are John Woodens in our own day. Meet Nick Vujicic, a young man born inexplicably without arms or legs, just one foot to help him motor around. Think you've got it bad? You can only imagine how he got mercilessly teased and bullied in school. Nick began to struggle with suicidal thoughts at the age of eight. Yet he ultimately found hope in the gospel of Jesus Christ, in knowing that Christ provides amazing freedom from both sin and despair and gives amazing hope both in heaven and on earth. Nick took comfort from passages like John 9, which speaks of a man being born blind so that God's glory might be displayed in his life.

Nick learned to see that God had a plan for him, and that through faith in Christ he could triumph in the midst of any adversity. At age seventeen, Nick began sharing his testimony at Bible studies. He received one invitation, then another, and then another, as many lives were deeply impacted by his story. At the age of twenty-three he founded a charitable organization called Life Without Limbs, having already earned a double bachelor's degree in accounting and financial planning from Griffith University in Logan, Australia.

Today, Nick is twenty-eight years old, and he travels all over the world seeking to motivate others and share Christ. He's also been able to live on his own, a long-time dream of his. He's developed creative, ingenious ways for turning on the lights, combing his hair, and brushing his teeth. He even puts his college degrees to work, investing in real estate and other industries.

How about you? What's your dream? How do you hope to make a difference? Most of you know, instinctively, that a life of goofing around and hanging out is unfulfilling. I hope you also know that self-centered, workaholic professionalism can't satisfy you, either. Chasing money and prestige is a fool's errand. Its pleasure is fleeting, leaving you with an empty, gnawing hunger for more.

No, you want to be a part of something great. College is about finding your place in God's world—not fitting God into your plans, but finding your place in his—so that you can be a blessing to others. That's what this book is about: *thriving at college*. It's about how to get there, how to avoid getting distracted along the way, how to launch in an awesome way, how to live with maximal impact, and how to change the world in whatever little corner you find yourself. This book is about making your college years the best you've ever had and a launching pad for all that goes with responsible Christian adulthood.

Perhaps you already have a few years of college under your belt. Your college experience has been good, but you want it to be great. You want to make the most out of the semesters left before graduation. You want to launch out of college in a way that really honors God and everyone who's helped you get there. If that's you, stay tuned. I pray this book will spark a new beginning.

I'll talk about what makes college different from high school, about the importance of developing your mind and your character, and about the importance of your relationships with different types of people, including your peers, your professors, your pastors, and your mentors. I'll talk about the value of forming the right kinds of friendships, both with the same sex and the opposite sex. And I'll talk about relating to your parents in this in-between stage when you're out on your own but still under their dime.

It is my prayer for you, the Christian student, that you won't just survive college but thrive in college. That you will not just keep the faith, but dig deeper than you thought was ever possible. That you will not just choose an academic pursuit, but discover your calling. That you will not just have fun with friends, but cultivate lifelong relationships of substance with those who most provoke you to trust and love God, to put away childishness, to make wise choices, and as missionary William Carey once said, to "expect great things from God and attempt great things for God."[2]

Mostly I pray that you will not just memorize facts and figures, but increasingly love God with all your heart and mind, seeing the connections between assorted truths in the academic world and the God of truth, and seeing the entire world as the theater of God's glory.

You ready? Let's get after it.

Introduction

*Surviving or Thriving? Making College
the Best Years of Your Life (So Far)*

MIKE AND CHRIS were freshmen at a Christian college. They were assigned as roommates by a more or less random process and had not previously known each other. Mike was going to that school because his parents made it clear that it was the only school for which they'd pay tuition. He figured going to college was better than getting a job after high school or sitting around the house. Besides, being away from home would give him more freedom, fewer household chores, and a greater variety of new diversions (not to mention the girls in the dorm across campus who had already caught his eye). However, Mike found his roommate, Chris, to be a bit different.

Chris really enjoyed his orientation day, everything from the community feel of the campus to the interesting, personable faculty. He particularly enjoyed conversing with the professors in the humanities department, the area he was planning to pursue. In fact, the professors he met had done some really interesting work outside the classroom, and one of them was the coach of the debate team, for which Chris was planning to try out. He had met a few members of the team during his campus orientation day and had enjoyed hanging out with them. Chris had also been an Eagle Scout and had led wilderness trips the past summer. Through Facebook, he had connected with some of the guys in the school's wilderness club and was looking forward to getting to know them better.

On the other hand, Mike's extracurricular activities in high school were bagging groceries at a nearby food store and playing sports and video games with his friends.

As Mike and Chris started to get to know each other during move-in day, they began to realize that their perspectives on college were quite different. Mike had already figured out who in the dorm had brought the most up-to-date Xbox system and where a few under-the-radar first-weekend parties were being held. And those girls I mentioned? Ever resourceful, Mike had already found many of them on Facebook.

Meanwhile, Chris was setting up his desk and books so that his living situation would be most conducive to keeping track of his classes. Books? That's right. Chris had *already* purchased his textbooks and, after setting up his laptop and printer, had printed out an Excel version of his academic schedule for the fall semester. He had even (get this) built in planned study times between classes and jotted down the library's hours. (In case you're worried, Chris also set up two-hour blocks for dinner breaks and extended time on the weekends to connect with new friends.) While chatting with Mike, he tacked a copy of his schedule above his desk, next to his bed.

Mike couldn't believe his bad luck. He thought about how annoying it was going to be to educate Mr. Organized on the finer points of college life.

COMPETING VISIONS

We all have a worldview—a "mental map" of reality, a set of assumptions or beliefs.* Your parents have one. Your friends have one. I have one. And you have one. Your mental map informs your expectations about high school, college, friends, guys, girls, church, sports, weekends, and everything else. It informs you of what to expect not just of others but of yourself.

What, then, informs this all-informing mental map? Whatever you let shape your mind and heart—your parents, your values, your pastors, friends, what you listen to on your iPod, who you follow on Twitter, your movies, shows, magazines, and all the rest.

What, then, informs this all-informing mental map? Whatever you let shape your mind and heart.

What does your mental map say you are as a young adult? Are you "just" a teenager or early twenties adolescent

---

* Our worldview is also shaped by our religious perspective—that is, our beliefs about God, the spiritual world, and the basis (if any) for morality, sin, judgment, grace, what happens after death, etc. The key differences between the Christian and the atheistic worldviews will be explored a bit in the next chapter.

who, because you're still trying to figure out who you are, isn't capable of doing much? Rather than setting high goals and working toward them, do you need to simply experience whatever your heart fancies at the moment in order to ensure you aren't suppressing healthy self-expression or somehow missing out? Or are you a young adult, capable of delaying gratification and working steadily for meaningful, significant goals, with talent, strength, and vigor on loan from God? Do you see yourself in a season of diligent preparation for becoming the kind of man or woman who can embrace greater responsibilities down the road (job, marriage, family, ministry), even as you do good and bring God glory now?

Broadly speaking, those are the two visions competing for your heart as a young man or woman in the twenty-first century. According to one perspective, school is about just getting by, keeping your parents happy so you can enjoy *your* time between the drudgery of classes. According to the other perspective, college is about glorifying God with every aspect of your week, loving him with all your mind, and training hard for the good works that he has prepared for you (Ephesians 2:10), while developing relationships that will reinforce your convictions and propel you in a God-ward direction. And while there might be some intentional downtime, there's no "*your* time." You are someone who takes care of the time, gifts, and talents that God has entrusted to you.

YOUTH CULTURE

These days the entertainment and leisure industry is aggressively marketing its vision of youth culture to you. That's right, lots of people have a vested interest in making you believe that being young is all about having fun, partying, and more or less ignoring life's responsibilities for as long as possible. It's a culture of low expectations and endless amusement.

In a former era, people moved directly from childhood to adulthood without a long season of adultlike freedoms and opportunities without the associated responsibilities and commitments. Young adults Alex and Brett Harris, authors of *Do Hard Things*, tell on their blog of David Farragut, the U.S. Navy's first admiral, who became a midshipman on the warship *Essex* at the age of ten. By the age of twelve he was given command of his first ship. George Washington, the first president of the United States, mastered geometry, trigonometry, and surveying at about the age of twelve, though folks in his day did not consider him particularly bright. At the age of sixteen he was named official surveyor for Culpepper County, Virginia, and would earn the equivalent of $100,000 in today's dollars per year for his three-year term. After citing these examples, the Harris brothers write:

> *These examples astound us in our day and age, but this is because we view life through an extra social category called "adolescence," a category that would*

*have been completely foreign to men and women just
100 years ago. Prior to the late 1800s there were only 3
categories of age: childhood, adulthood, and old age. It
was only with the coming of the early labor movement
with its progressive child labor laws, coupled with
new compulsory schooling laws, that a new category,
called adolescence, was invented. Coined by G. Stanley
Hall, who is often considered the father of American
psychology, "adolescence" identified the artificial zone
between childhood and adulthood when young people
ceased to be children, but were no longer permitted by
law to assume the normal responsibilities of adulthood,
such as entering into a trade or finding gainful
employment. Consequently, marriage and family had to
be delayed as well, and so we invented "the teenager,"
an unfortunate creature who had all the yearnings and
capabilities of an adult, but none of the freedoms or
responsibilities.*

*Teenage life became a 4-year sentence of continuing
primary education and relative idleness known as "high
school" (four years of schooling which would later be
repeated in the first two years of college). Abolished by
law were the young Farraguts and young Washingtons,
who couldn't spare the time to be children any longer
than necessary. Cultivated instead was the culture
we know today, where young people are allowed,
encouraged, and even forced to remain quasi-children
for much longer than necessary.[1]*

Is that what high school was for you? Getting A's and B's, but never having to work too hard? If so, maybe that wasn't such a good deal after all. Maybe you were robbed of the requirement—the *opportunity*—to more fully develop your academic abilities. Are you thinking college will be just as easy? If you are, boy, are you in for a surprise, especially if you are in one of my classes! If that's you, stay tuned, because unless your attitude changes, college academics just might blow you away.

You see, God has a completely different idea for your college years, which he reveals in several places in the Bible:

- "Let no one despise you for your youth, but set the believers an example in speech, in conduct, in love, in faith, in purity." (1 Timothy 4:12)
- "Whatever your hand finds to do, do it with your might." (Ecclesiastes 9:10)
- "Whatever you do, work heartily, as for the Lord and not for men." (Colossians 3:23)
- "Whether you eat or drink, or whatever you do, do all to the glory of God." (1 Corinthians 10:31)
- "You shall love the Lord your God with all your heart and with all your soul and with all your strength and with all your *mind*." (Luke 10:27, emphasis added)

And when our past sins seek to lure us back or haunt us with guilt, God's Word answers with "therefore, since we are surrounded by so great a cloud of witnesses, let us also lay aside every weight, and sin which clings so closely, and let us run with endurance the race that is set before us, looking to Jesus, the founder and perfecter of our faith" (Hebrews 12:1-2; see also Philippians 3:13-14).

We also see it exemplified in men like Daniel, who went to "college" in Babylon and "resolved that he would not defile himself" (by disobeying God's commands) and at the end of three years was found to be "ten times better" than his classmates in "every matter of wisdom and understanding" (Daniel 1:8, 18-20).

When our past sins seek to lure us back or haunt us with guilt, God's Word answers with "therefore, since we are surrounded by so great a cloud of witnesses, let us also lay aside every weight, and sin which clings so closely, and let us run with endurance the race that is set before us, looking to Jesus, the founder and perfecter of our faith" (Hebrews 12:1-2).

We see it in Joseph—a young guy who certainly had his fair share of hard times, and then some—yet never grew bitter, never gave up, and never betrayed God. Because he was diligent, his responsibilities in Potiphar's house grew (Genesis 39:2-4). When tempted by sexual immorality, Joseph reasoned, "How then can I do this great wickedness and sin against God?" Instead of moving closer, Joseph consciously moved away from the danger (Genesis 39:9-10). And after that obedience was rewarded with prison time, Joseph went from being a model employee to a model prisoner (Genesis 39:21-23). But even as a prisoner, his responsibility and authority were increased, as his superiors couldn't help but recognize his extraordinary capability and faithfulness. Is *that* your vision of young-adult life?

How will things go for Mike and Chris? The proof will come over time. But for now, know this: When Mike and Chris were packing for college, the most significant thing they brought with them didn't need to fit in their luggage. It didn't have to fit because it was invisible. Invisible, yet all-controlling. Mike and Chris brought contrasting worldviews with them—and those worldviews were influencing their attitudes and behavior as they arrived on campus.

There's actually a second invisible friend that Mike and Chris both brought to college with them: their *character*. By "character" I don't just mean "personality." God-given personality differences, as we'll see, are *amoral*—they are not intrinsically good or bad. Character, on the other hand, has moral degrees to it. Character is measured by qualities like honesty or dishonesty, industriousness or laziness, responsibility or irresponsibility, kindness or selfishness, hastiness or self-control, etc.

Put simply, the kinds of people Mike and Chris had become through their decisions and responses to life's circumstances (along with their worldviews) will shape their ongoing attitudes and behaviors. Their character differences help explain why Mike has gone on Facebook to look for the girls but doesn't yet know where his classes are, let alone what books he needs. And they explain why Chris printed out his schedule, even though classes don't start until next week. Here's the principle:

Worldview & Character → Attitude & Behavior

In other words, our worldview (how we think) and our character (who we are) impact our attitude (what we think) and our behavior (what we do). We've looked at worldview (how we think). Let's turn our attention to character (who we are). For studying the subject of character, we can't do better than the book of Proverbs. There we meet three interesting characters: the fool, the sluggard, and the wise. Now chances are, there's a little of all three in each of us. But if we're ever going to be characterized as wise, we'll need to set our sights on understanding wisdom.

THE FOOL, THE SLUGGARD, AND THE WISE

The first attribute of the fool in Proverbs is *simplicity*. Not simplicity in the sense of don't-worry-be-happy and living off the land. No, the word refers to *gullibility*, moral irresponsibility, and lacking *sense* (the knowledge to live well): "O simple ones, learn prudence; O fools, learn sense" (Proverbs 8:5). The "simple" lack sense. Whatever they may know, they haven't translated that knowledge into an ability to make choices that exhibit good judgment.

They are also gullible: "The simple believes everything, but the prudent gives thought to his steps" (Proverbs 14:15). Once again, simplicity is contrasted with prudence. But the simple are also willful and irresponsible: "The prudent sees danger and hides himself, but the simple go on and suffer for it" (Proverbs 22:3; 27:12). They're morally suspect.

The third attribute of the fool is *dullness* or *obstinacy*. He already thinks he's going the right way, so he has no need to receive advice (Proverbs 12:15), as he's far too busy dispensing it (Proverbs 10:8; 12:23). He disregards wisdom and instruction (Proverbs 1:7) and does not learn even when he's corrected (Proverbs 17:10). Instead, he returns to folly (Proverbs 26:11), though it leads to his own destruction (Proverbs 1:32).

Okay, on to the sluggard. You'll meet plenty of these in college, so be alert. The word *sluggard* is interesting: It appears only fourteen times in the English Standard Version of the Bible, all in the book of Proverbs. Sluggards are lazy: They don't attend to their responsibilities and so are ultimately overwhelmed by them (Proverbs 6:9-10). It isn't that sluggards lack aspirations—they definitely have desires, but they lack the discipline to work at making them a reality. They rationalize their laziness (Proverbs 20:4) and have a generally high and unsubstantiated view of themselves (Proverbs 26:16). It is difficult for them to learn and grow since they think they're already awesome. Because they lack diligence, they are a nightmare as employees: "Like vinegar to the teeth and smoke to the eyes, so is the sluggard to those who send him" (Proverbs 10:26). These people simply do not get stuff done, and they're full of bizarre excuses (Proverbs 26:13).

As students, sluggards don't work hard but expect to do well. Before tests they feel confident, even though they haven't spent much time studying. Why bother when they already know the stuff? Other hardworking students spend hours studying for tests, agonizing over the few concepts they have not yet fully mastered, not content with the 90 percent they already understand backward and forward. Oh, these students may be a bit more miserable; they are far less pleased with themselves. They're too busy striving to get better. But after the test, it's the other way around. The ones who lacked confidence now have the wind at their backs. And the ones who *were* confident are now in despair, wondering how they could have been so misguided. But for some the deception continues: They tell themselves that they *knew* the material; it was the *exam* (and the professor) that were unfair. Hint: Don't do that. Chances are your teacher's tests and assignments are a better indication of your true abilities than your own estimation.

Finally, the wise. These are the ones who *actively* and *vigorously* give themselves to instruction—not just in classes, but in life. Wisdom begins with the fear of God and a desire to be taught by him (Proverbs 1:7). Wisdom is for anyone who wants it (Proverbs 1:20, 23), but it is hard won (Proverbs 2:1-4). It requires the acceptance of correction, even rebuke (Proverbs 3:11-12). It gives rise to a heart knowledge, not just a head knowledge, which means that the wise know in the core of their being the difference between right and wrong. And they have the discretion and discernment to choose the good path (Proverbs 2:9-11, 20).

How do you recognize the wise? They are good listeners (James 1:19). They are slow to share their opinions, preferring to understand a situation first (Proverbs 18:13, 17). And since they are humble, they are not motivated to speak by a desire to impress others, pontificating about things on which they are ignorant, or making commitments that they cannot possibly keep. The wise guard their tempers (Proverbs 16:32). They are disciplined; they can delay gratification, knowing that the best enjoyments come at their

Wisdom is for anyone who wants it.

appointed times, and in their appropriate, limited doses. So while they *can* have fun, they are not *ruled* by the desire to have fun. And they care about others, knowing that loving others is the natural manifestation of love for God (Luke 10:27). Wisdom has more to do with the disposition of your life than with the facts and figures you know in your head.

During college, you'll want to grow in wisdom. This will require regularly praying for wisdom, acknowledging that it comes from God. And it comes from God in two ways: directly from the Bible, by reflecting on passages and the overarching themes of Scripture, and also from the hardships of everyday life. Listen to how Derek Kidner describes it in his commentary on Proverbs:

If we could analyze the influences that build up a godly character to maturity, we might well find that the agencies which we call natural vastly outweighed those that we call supernatural. The book of Proverbs reassures us that this, if it is true, is no reflection on the efficacy of God's grace; for the hard facts of life, which knock some of the nonsense out of us, are God's facts and his appointed school of character; they are not alternatives to his grace, but means of it; for everything is of grace, from the power to know to the power to obey.[2]

In addition, growing in wisdom requires walking with the wise (Proverbs 13:20). We'll talk about the importance of good companions in chapter 3. In short, whether you are growing in wisdom or not will have a big influence on whether you *thrive* in college or merely *survive*.

SURVIVING VS. THRIVING

Whether you survive or thrive has everything to do with the worldview and character that you bring into college. These will shape your attitude and behavior (as we saw with Mike and Chris), which will soon give rise to *habits*. We reap what we sow (Galatians 6:7). Over time, our habits shape our destiny.

Worldview & Character → Attitudes & Behaviors → Habits & Destiny

Within the first month of college, Mike and Chris will be forming habits—some for good, some for bad. Bad habits come naturally. Good habits, like finishing your homework before socializing, will probably need to be intentionally developed—unless you are on the neurotic end of the scale, which we'll get to in due course. For most of us, they don't come naturally. So you'll need to identify a few crucial habits and then actively establish them into your routine so that they *become* your default response.

But you may be wondering, *Hey, what's wrong with having fun at college? If all Chris does is study, he's going to really miss out.* We'll get into this a lot more in future chapters. For now, consider the wisdom of my sixth-grade teacher. Whenever we were being rambunctious (and yes, I was generally guilty), she'd say, "Alex, there's a time and place for everything." It sounded trite at the time.

I did not yet know that the writer of Ecclesiastes actually gives us a similar perspective (Ecclesiastes 3:1-8). Briefly, there's nothing wrong with a healthy dose of recreation and relationship building. God intends these to bring helpful refreshment to us in our daily labors.

But Mike's problem is that he seems to be building his life around amusement, which sooner or later will result in life's responsibilities raining on his parade (Proverbs 24:33-34). Chris is setting himself up to be productive, which will allow him to later enjoy recreation and friendships—and even to derive greater strength from them.

Though worldview and character are large topics (entire books have been written on each of them), let's spend some time on a specific area relevant to success in college: the *assumption* of responsibility. This attribute is crucial in the college years in large part because, for most of you, it is the first time you have stepped out from under the umbrella of your parents' watchful protection and care. Unless you are in a strict military boarding school, nobody is going to tell you when to go bed.

Or when to turn off the PlayStation. Or when to quit chatting on Facebook. So you are living in a glorious, crucially significant in-between stage: What kind of kid/teen you have been has brought you to where you are, but what you will become as an adult remains to be seen.

Whether you thrive or merely survive at college will depend to a large degree on the extent to which you *assume responsibility*.

ASSUMING RESPONSIBILITY

Let's start with the first word: *assume*. To "assume" anything is to consider it a given—right from the start.

In my freshman year, I had a first-semester lab course that was an introduction to the field of ceramic engineering, and we made all kinds of ceramic bowls, plates, and cups, as well as studied the science behind these products. I chose the one graduate student who I knew was a Christian to be my teaching assistant (TA), figuring that she might have more slack in her grading standards. (TAs actually do a lot of the grading at college, especially for lab courses.) After all, Christians are supposed to be loving and merciful, right?

I remember writing my first of many lab reports. I sent her a draft to ask her if it was okay (hint: never do this unless the professor or TA invites you to). I figured she had extra time to read it, and besides, it was her job to care. In addition, I was uncertain about a number of the things I said in the report, but rather than go to my textbook or the library to try to find the answers, I figured I'd just ask her (since she was all-knowing). I also didn't bother to spell-check what I sent her. I figured even if I misspelled a few words, she'd get the drift.

Her reply was terse: "Do your own research. And spell-check your own work, or it will negatively impact your grade." That was it! She gave me nothing in the way of help that I was hoping for. There went my semester of Christian mercy.[†]

Factoid

Did you know that a typical class average GPA in college, especially for larger courses commonly taken by freshmen and sophomores, is about a 2.65/4.00 (about a B-)? And it's not uncommon for about 30 to 40 percent of such a class to earn a C+ or lower.[3] Yet, when surveyed at the beginning of the semester, about 90 percent of students think they'll get a B or an A. Think some folks might be disappointed?

Yet what she *did* give me was priceless: the assumption of responsibility. I learned from her that it was *my job* to make sure the content of my report was factual. It was *my job* to check for spelling and grammatical mistakes. It was *not* her job to grade my work multiple times (so that I could blame her if I got a bad grade). It took a while, but I learned

---

[†] I later read in my Bible that my attitude was not uncommon. In his letter to Timothy, Paul spoke about slaves serving Christian masters. Slaves in that day were in many ways like employees or servants in our day. He said, "Those who have believing masters must not be disrespectful on the ground that they are brothers; rather they must serve all the better since those who benefit by their good service are believers and beloved" (1 Timothy 6:2). In other words, don't slack off just because the boss is a Christ follower.

to be resourceful, going after answers in the textbook and the library and respecting the time of my superiors when I did need to ask questions. By the way, a great way to do this is to approach professors, during their scheduled office hours (which you underlined on the syllabus), in this way: "Dr. Smith, I did the assigned reading, underlined key concepts, and took notes. May I please ask you a few clarifying questions?"

The assumption of responsibility starts with the recognition that, whatever the assignment, it is *mine, not someone else's. I* own it. It is not someone else's job to do it for me. This means, for example, reading the syllabus or a particular assignment before asking questions that may already have been answered. If you have a course schedule, then you already know where the professor is going in the course, so you can prepare for class. You may even know what each exam will cover.

But the assumption of responsibility is not just being resourceful. It is the fundamental recognition of the fact that you own your decisions. Other people aren't responsible to do what only you can and must do. If you have a homework assignment, get it done. If you need to write a paper, go to the library and get the necessary background information. You have the God-given faculty of initiative and the responsibility to make things happen. God will hold you accountable. Like I said earlier, you *will* reap what you sow—there is no getting around that principle (Galatians 6:7).

If you assume responsibility, you have the right frame of

mind for developing your talents and reaching your potential. This is true whether you go to college or choose another path after high school. But to thrive at college requires more, not less, than the assumption of responsibility. It requires knowing the purpose of college.

THE PURPOSE OF COLLEGE

In addition to providing a rigorous, well-rounded education, college should be a launching pad into all that goes with responsible Christian adulthood. Most of you will enter college under your parents' care and financial support. But you'll graduate a man or woman ready to assume your adult role in an interdependent society and a particular local church.

Factoid

Did you know that according to Monster's 2009 "Annual Entry-Level Job Outlook," about 40 percent of 2008 grads still live with their parents? And 42 percent of the 2006 graduates surveyed said they're still living at home.[4]

At least you *ought* to. It's shameful that one in every three men of ages twenty-two to thirty-four is still living at home with Mom and Dad.[5] Don't join that statistic. Avoid that destiny by growing up—now. We'll talk more about this in future chapters. And, hey, if you are living with your folks, pay rent like you would to any other landlord. That'll get you going in the right direction.

Though you may feel on top of things, most of you have not yet proven yourself in the world. If you've always gone to school a quick drive from home, college is probably the longest you've ever been away from home at one stretch. You'll be tested and tried. How you respond will determine the sort of man or woman you'll become. In this book, I'll break down the challenges and opportunities of college into foundational matters (chapters 1–2), significant relationships (friends and mentors, guy-girl, and Mom and Dad, chapters 3–5), issues of character (chapters 6–7), and academics (chapters 8–10).

Are you ready to launch into all that goes along with responsible Christian adulthood? Do you want to make college the best years of your life (so far)? Are you ready to cultivate relationships of eternal significance? Are you eager to grow in wisdom, leaving behind the ways of the fool and the sluggard? Are you ready to develop your academic gifts, honing the talents God gave you into strong, useful skills?

Then let's get started.

DISCUSSION STARTERS

1. Why did you choose to go to college? What were your motivations? Your goals?

2. Describe your worldview. What do you think has been most formative for your worldview?

3. What would your close friends say are the strengths and weaknesses of your character?

4. What are some practical things you need to do to become wiser?

5. List two ways in which you are currently assuming responsibility. Is there an area you need to claim?

PART 1
COLLEGE MATTERS

COMMON MISTAKE #1:
Chucking Your Faith

> *Thrive Principle: Grow Closer to God*

THE DAY BEFORE you entered college, you were a kid in your parents' home. But you'll hopefully exit college as an *adult*, fully owning your life, your choices, and the consequences of those choices. If you started college as a Christian, you probably did so because your parents raised you in a Christian home. Thank God for that blessing; chances are it has helped you more than you know.

But college is a season in which you can—and must—really take ownership of your faith. You can't truly grow in the Christian life on borrowed faith, and most find college to be a season in which their Christian faith is put to the test. Even at a Christian college, you'll probably experience some influences that could draw you away from God. At non-Christian colleges and universities, the pull away from Jesus Christ often comes from every angle and can be quite fierce.

So Mistake #1 is abandoning the Christian faith. In fact, even to *neglect* your Christian faith is to commit Mistake #1 because a Christianity not practiced today becomes a Christianity that is absent tomorrow. To thrive in college you'll need to spread your wings *from* the firm foundation of your Christian faith. Let's unpack what you don't want to do (abandon or neglect your faith) and what you do want to do (grow closer to God).

> *A Christianity not practiced today becomes a Christianity that is absent tomorrow.*

INTELLECTUAL CHALLENGES TO CHRISTIANITY

There are basically two lines of attack that your Christian faith may encounter in college: intellectual attacks and moral attacks. Let's take a look at them one at a time.

Particularly if you are at a non-Christian campus, here's the sort of thing you can expect to hear:

- "The Bible is mythology."
- "Christianity, in claiming to be the only way, is intolerant."
- "Morality is relative, not absolute."
- "Truth is subjective. What's true for you does not have to be true for me."
- "Jesus was a great moral teacher, nothing more."

Q: *Do you recommend revealing one's faith in a classroom setting? I've found that thus far, I've kind of downplayed or checked myself when participating in discussions in my sociology class because I don't want to be scoffed at.* —KATE, FRESHMAN, Creative Writing

A: It is wise to be cautious. The extent to which a classroom allows for a fair-minded exchange of ideas depends largely on the professor. Professors set the rules for group dialogue and the extent to which any ideas or beliefs are disregarded or mocked. The best approach is to seek to understand the perspectives of others by asking simple, reasonable questions with a humble, gracious tone. Your questions can expose weaknesses, flaws, or inconsistencies in other people's arguments. You can learn a lot by asking questions like "How do you get to that conclusion?" or "How do you account for _____?" or even "What do you see as the biggest weaknesses to your perspective?" You can learn a lot this way—and open the door for private dialogue with others, even your professor, in which you can winsomely convey your Christian perspective.

- "We can be good people without God."
- "Organized religion causes divisions and wars."
- "There can't be a good God because there is so much evil in this world."
- "Evolution has proved that 'God' had nothing to do with the origin of the universe."
- "To be a tolerant person, you can't believe in moral absolutes."*

Many of your professors will be overtly anti-Christian. That may seem hard to believe, but it's true. In the United States, 4 percent of the overall population is either atheist or agnostic. That percentage, *among college professors*, varies from 24 to 37 percent. It increases the more elite the university.[1] My wife, Marni, attended Stanford University and was told within the first two weeks of her biology class, "Some of you may believe that God created the world. That's nice. But your faith is personal, and it has no place in this classroom." You see, the professor wanted to *privatize* Marni's faith—as if Christianity were a nice, warm fairy tale that made her feel good, but of course could not possibly be true.

What should you do if this happens to you? First, recognize that you are not alone. Other Christians have been and *are* right there with you, and even at your school, you can find them if you look in the right places. You are not alone in another sense, either. The struggle with these questions

---

* A helpful, contemporary book for dealing with a lot of these common criticisms is *The Reason for God: Belief in an Age of Skepticism* (New York: Penguin Group, 2008) by Tim Keller.

is not new. Whole libraries are devoted to books by intelligent, scholarly, godly Christians that respond effectively and in detail to each of the criticisms I listed. I'll mention a few in this chapter, and your pastor or parents may know of others.

Let's lay out some of the nuts and bolts of how Christians can not only stand firm, but be emboldened to live their Christian faith in every facet of their lives, including the classroom setting. With regard to intellectual challenges, we can more or less put them into two categories. The first has to do with the *evidence* or *believability* of Christianity. Can the Bible, written thousands of years ago by various men over many years, really have ongoing validity today? And could Jesus Christ really have risen from the dead? I mean, don't we now know that miracles are impossible?

THE BIBLE IS RELIABLE AND ACCURATE

If you test the Old and New Testaments the way a historian would test any old book, you'll find more supporting evidence for the sixty-six books of the Bible than for any other ancient book. No other book even comes close.† That means we can be very certain that the Bible we have today is the same Bible that early Christians had.

But does that mean our Bible is *accurate*? Well, no other

---

† There are over twelve thousand ancient copies of the Old Testament and more than fifteen thousand manuscripts of the New Testament available. These manuscripts overwhelmingly agree with one another, confirming that the Bible we have today has been passed down to us with no substantial changes. See, for example, F. F. Bruce, *The New Testament Documents: Are They Reliable?*, 6th ed. (Downers Grove, IL: InterVarsity Press, 1981) or Walter C. Kaiser Jr., *The Old Testament Documents: Are They Reliable & Relevant?* (Downers Grove, IL: InterVarsity Press, 2001). Also, Greg Koukl of Stand to Reason has several helpful shorter articles on this topic.

historical book, written by Christians or non-Christians, has ever successfully contradicted it on a matter of history. It has never been disproven. In fact, archaeological findings over the last fifty years have *strengthened*, not weakened, the case for the Bible's historical reliability.

But what about Jesus? Consider the alternative of accepting the Bible's message. Could a group of monotheistic Jewish men really have concocted the story of a man claiming to be God—and not just *a* god, but the *one* God who made the entire universe? And then this man is horrifically killed, after which he rises from the dead? And the guys making up this stuff are so certain of it that they are willing to get themselves killed for it? It takes more faith to think that such a wild story could be made up than to accept it at face value!

Jesus was the most amazing person who ever lived. Most regard him as a profoundly wise moral teacher. But what they neglect is that he also claimed, repeatedly, and to his own demise, that he was the Incarnation of the one God who made the entire universe. That sort of claim is either lunacy, the most sophisticated lie, or the utter truth.‡ Again, which explanation takes more faith?

Now, of course, *if there is no God*, believing Jesus was deluded or a liar is easier than believing in the Resurrection. The disciples could have evaded the Roman guards, stolen Jesus' body, and then convinced the world that he rose from the dead. They could have been experiencing a series of mass

---

‡ These three possibilities—Lord, liar, and lunatic—are discussed in C. S. Lewis's classic book *Mere Christianity*.

hallucinations (some form of wishful thinking) when they thought they saw him after his death. Or they could have made up the whole story, and Jesus of Nazareth never lived. Many bizarre things are more possible than a man rising from the dead, because a man rising from the dead is *impossible* if there is *no God*.

But that's just the point. The person seeking to discredit Christianity has generally *assumed* that the miraculous is impossible. Just as your non-Christian friends may be questioning your assumptions, feel free to examine theirs. We need to compare which perspective or assumptions make better sense of reality. What's more "open minded," to believe that miracles are possible or to believe they are impossible?

CHRISTIANITY MAKES GOOD SENSE

That brings me to the second category of intellectual objections to Christianity: *coherence*. In other words, is Christianity self-consistent? Does it explain and make sense of what we see in the world? Let me show you what I mean.

The Christian view

Christianity teaches that men and women were created in the image of God, as moral, intelligent agents, capable of abstract thinking and possessing consciousness. The fact that the universe exists means that something or someone must have always existed—the created order screams that God is real (Psalm 19:1-6; Romans 1:19-20).§ As humans, we are all born into a fallen world and are, individually, fallen. What the Bible calls "sin" has infected every aspect of our lives. We often think bad thoughts and do bad things because, let's face it, our very nature is corrupt. There is evil in the world, and there is evil *in us*. (The world, after all, is just a bunch of "us" multiplied billions of times.)

But God remains infinitely good and pure. And since we're made in God's image, we have an innate sense of right and wrong embedded into our conscience. Because God is good, he must be opposed to that which is evil—which includes us. Part of goodness is *justice*, and it is *just* to punish wickedness. The punishment is death, both physical and spiritual (eternal). That may seem harsh, but if we consider that God is infinitely worthy of our obedience, then our disregard of him is an infinite offense. So the punishment fits the crime. To reject God's rightful rule in this life is to invite his rejection in the life to come.

But because God is also merciful, he has done something amazingly kind: He has chosen to become one of us and, as a man, succeed where we have failed. We (humanity) failed the test, disobeyed God, and became corrupt, while Jesus

---

§ Theologians and philosophers call this a basic form of the cosmological argument for the existence of God. As R. C. Sproul puts it, "If anything exists now, then something must have the power of being within itself, that is, something must have necessary being" (*The Consequences of Ideas*, Wheaton, IL: Crossway Books, 2000, 73). Very few scientists would argue that the world is just an illusion or that it has always existed in its current form. Some atheists have taken the position that matter has always existed, but that essentially deifies matter and simply pushes out the problem of existence: How does matter as matter have the power of being within itself? Is matter alive? Where do life and personality come from? The most rational conclusion is that everything both living and nonliving was originally created by something which itself is self-existent (namely, an intelligent being, God). See, for example, *Classical Apologetics* by R. C. Sproul, John Gerstner, and Arthur Lindsley (Grand Rapids, MI: Zondervan, 1984).

aced the test, obeyed God, and was exalted (Philippians 2:6-9). That obedience, for Jesus, included receiving God's punishment on behalf of every person who would ever trust in him, love him, and obey him. For every Christian, there is a "double exchange." Jesus takes all our corruption (our sin) upon himself, paying for it in full, and his perfect record of obeying God is transferred to our account. After that, God begins the work of remaking us in his image, the image that was corrupted by our rebellion against him. In fact, he puts us into a community (the church), which corporately is meant to be a reflection of the glory of God's grace in redeeming (or buying back) people who had rebelled against him.

All evil in the world will eventually be punished by the just, merciful, and omnipotent God.

The atheist view

The atheist view claims there is no God who created the world. The world is an accident that came together as a result of time and chance.[¶] Human beings are just complex collections of molecules. Our brains are not the product of any sort of intelligent design—there was no Designer. Consequently, life cannot possibly have any transcendent meaning whatsoever—there is no Person who stands outside of history and gives purpose to the events of our lives or lends validation to our instincts about right and wrong. That said, each

---

¶ Have you ever asked yourself, What is "chance"? Chance is a nonentity. It has no ontological being. Chance is merely a way we describe probabilities. It cannot accomplish something, like the creation of the world. If I flip a coin, I have a 50 percent chance of getting tails, but chance doesn't cause the coin to flip. I do.

of us can create "meaning" for ourselves through living in a way that gives us satisfaction, by choosing our own values and pursuing them. We can and should pursue what is in the universal interest of mankind, since we ourselves make up mankind. And precisely *because* there is no God to enforce or eternally reward the right behavior, or punish the wrong behavior, doing what's right is all the more virtuous than if we were to do good merely to be rewarded by some deity.**

The "spiritual but not religious" view

This view is an eclectic tossed salad in which people pick and choose what they want to believe from various religions—Christianity, Buddhism, Hinduism, Judaism, Islam, New Age, you name it. Or they make up their own principles from popular self-help or psychology books. There isn't one clear set of beliefs for these people, but there are a couple of common threads. They tend to believe that truth is relative, not absolute, and that all the religions of the world have something valuable to offer because they all teach us to be basically "good" people, whatever that means. They think God won't particularly care about their religious beliefs when they die. The true higher power is much bigger than the tribal "gods" of Christianity, Islam, Judaism, and all the other "-isms" we foolishly divide over and fight about. Even internally, organized religions cause conflict because they inevitably degrade into battles over power, ego, and money.

** Atheist writer Christopher Hitchens, for example, has advanced this argument.

This is the religion of *Star Wars*, *Avatar*, and John Lennon's "Imagine," a song played for mandatory meditation in a psychology class I once took. Being sincere and trying to do good is what counts. Peace out.

LET'S COMPARE

Okay, so which of these three views makes the most sense of reality? Notice that the Christian view is the only one that gives any meaning to morality—or to humans themselves. In the atheist scheme, you and I are just accidental blobs of molecules. Telling us it is wrong to kill each other is meaningless. The funny thing is that many atheists today (like Christopher Hitchens) are intensely interested in justice in the world, but if they are consistent, they'd know that there cannot possibly be any true justice, since morality is just a human construct. From their perspective, there can be no "objective good" because there is no true, universal standard of good that comes from outside us. Only God can supply that.

The old atheists like Nietzsche, who influenced Adolf Hitler, at least were more consistent. Unlike Hitchens, they didn't display moral outrage over atrocities like ethnic genocide. They realized that, from their perspective, there simply was no fixed moral standard from which to critique such actions, even if many find them to be heinous. Neither was there any basis for transcendent beauty or meaning (only a subjective beauty or meaning that each defined for himself).

As a result, the writings of men like Jean Paul Sartre and Albert Camus are basically depressing.††

Our moral core—our conscience—makes the most sense within the Christian worldview, where it is understood to be a reflection of God's nature that we, as God's image bearers, have hardwired into us, no matter how much our corruption may have warped it.‡‡

Plenty more could be said on this topic, but the bottom line is that the story of Christianity is *intellectually credible.* But more than that, it is *deeply satisfying.* C. S. Lewis once said, "I believe in Christianity as I believe that the sun has risen: not only because I see it, but because by it I see everything else."[2] Life (even the academic pursuits of biology or physics) makes more sense from the framework of Christianity than from any alternative framework.

Particularly at secular colleges, face the fact that you'll be swimming upstream. Your beliefs will be questioned if not overtly attacked in most academic disciplines.§§ Your Christianity won't relieve you from conflict; it will guarantee that you have it. But *your* belief is the one that consistently

---

†† Dinesh D'Souza, in his thoughtful book *What's So Great about Christianity*, has a chapter where he documents the millions of people who have been killed throughout human history under the direct influence of atheism. You may have heard that many have been killed "in the name of the Christian God." There have been some sad cases (e.g., the Salem witch trials), but they pale in comparison to the atrocities wrought as the overflow of atheistic thinking. Hitler had no reason to believe the Jews had any dignity. Stalin and Mao could murder their tens of millions, since of what value were these lives, anyway? Christianity teaches that every human being has enormous value as an image bearer of a holy and righteous God. In fact, God instituted capital punishment in the Bible because of the high value he places on his image, which marks every member of humanity (Genesis 9:6).

‡‡ For more on this line of reasoning, see the classic book by C. S. Lewis, *Mere Christianity*, or Francis Schaeffer's Trilogy, composed of three great works on a common theme: *The God Who Is There, Escape from Reason*, and *He Is There and He Is Not Silent.*

§§ With the possible exception of applied, professional courses. Engineering professors are apparently less likely to be atheists or agnostics than biology, chemistry, physics, or geology professors. It can also be pretty tough on the liberal arts side.

coheres with reality. Your non-Christian friends—trying to make sense of the world and develop a moral framework—are the ones who are truly conflicted. Be sustained by a deepened faith in Christ, and speak words of truth and life to them.

At Christian colleges, you'll want to be aware that there may be a measure of theological diversity among the faculty. Some may subtly undermine the authority of the Scripture or the exclusivity of Jesus Christ. It is wise to stay connected to your parents, youth pastors, or other mentors who can help you work through new ideas. College is a great time to really examine what you believe and why you believe it. But remember what G. K. Chesterton once said: "The object of opening the mind, as of opening the mouth, is to shut it again on something solid."[3] *Perpetual* uncertainty is not a virtue. Yet precisely such uncertainty is promoted in our day under the guise of "tolerance."

THE "TOLERANCE" ISSUE

Before we go on to talk about moral challenges, let's hit on an intellectual challenge that is particularly big in our day, especially on the college scene: the issue of "tolerance."

In a 2007 Associated Press (AP) poll among thirteen- to twenty-four-year-olds,[4] about 68 percent agreed with the statement "I follow my own religious and spiritual beliefs, but I think that other religious beliefs could be true as well." Only 31 percent agreed with the statement "I strongly believe that my religious beliefs are true and universal, and that other religious beliefs are not right." And generally speaking, these were religious people. Of those surveyed, 44 percent said that religion was "very important" to them, and only 14 percent said that religion played "no role" for them. The others were somewhere in between.

So here we have a group of mainly religious people—people with specific religious beliefs—most of whom think that other religious beliefs could also be true. You've probably heard the phrase "What's true for you is true for you, but what's true for me is true for me."

And as a society, isn't agreement with that concept considered a necessary ingredient for being "tolerant"? But is that really how we should understand the concept of tolerance? *Merriam-Webster's Collegiate Dictionary* defines *toleration* as "the act or practice of allowing something" and *tolerance* as "sympathy or indulgence for beliefs or practices differing from or conflicting with one's own." To be tolerant is to allow people to believe or do things that you don't agree with. But the very lack of agreement means that *you think they are wrong*. So to tolerate someone, you need to think they are wrong, but be willing to accept them or allow them to be that way. Perhaps an example will help.

My agnostic friend Josh and I used to discuss religion and science all the time. We got along well and treated each other respectfully, though, of course, he thought I was wrong, and I thought he was wrong. We respected each other without ignoring the ocean between our perspectives. Josh knew that I thought he was going to hell unless he repented and followed Jesus. In fact, he respected my willingness to express my convictions to him because he recognized that, given my perspective, that was the most loving thing to do. And I was committed to treating him with kindness and respect. I had no desire to force him to conform to my beliefs and practices.⁋⁋ He treated me in the same manner. That's real tolerance: vigorous disagreement combined with a gracious demeanor, respect, and kindness.

The sentimental "tolerance" of our day suggests that relational harmony requires that truth be relative: what's true for me need not be true for you. Only then can we get along. But real tolerance involves treating others with kindness and respect while *at the same time* believing them to be in serious error. After all, don't many so-called tolerant atheists and agnostics think we Christ followers are in error for embracing religious absolutes, like the view that Jesus Christ is the only way to God? In fact, the one thing they are absolutely sure of is that there are no absolutes. They don't realize that such a statement is itself a claim to absolute truth. By the same token there is nothing unloving about believing that someone else is wrong. In fact, if Christianity is true, telling others they need Jesus is the most loving thing to do. Even Josh agreed on that one.

So practice true tolerance with your non-Christian friends. Like you, they are made in the image of God and have many

---

⁋⁋ In fact, I told him that it was essential that he not be compelled to change his mind except voluntarily through the use of reason. I would oppose any reduction on the rights of Muslims, Hindus, and atheists to continue to believe what they believe if that's what they wish to do. It's a whole other topic, but there are some people who think that Christians are trying to take over America (if not the world) and forcibly impose their beliefs on everyone else. It's pure nonsense. By definition, true Christianity cannot be spread by force because it requires individuals voluntarily declaring their allegiance to Jesus Christ.

wonderful attributes as a result of God's common grace. Share meals, play sports, and study with them. As opportunities present themselves, show them the inconsistencies in their worldviews. Winsomely present arguments for the Christian faith (2 Corinthians 5:11; see Paul's example in Acts 26), maintaining an awareness that, though you must appeal to their minds with reason and logic, God must open their eyes to see what you've seen (2 Corinthians 4:3-6).

MORAL CHALLENGES TO CHRISTIANITY

Particularly at secular colleges, be prepared for an enormous opportunity to absolutely destroy your life through careless living. I say that with all seriousness. The biggies are generally sex and alcohol, and they increasingly go together on the college campus—sometimes even at Christian colleges.

The Christian faith is strong enough to build your life on. In God's Word, we've been given "everything we need for a godly life" (2 Peter 1:3, NIV). God's teaching about sexual purity before marriage is for our own good and for our long-term happiness (1 Thessalonians 4:3-5). God's teaching about the dangers of drunkenness is for our own good and for our long-term happiness (Proverbs 23:31-35). God isn't some cosmic killjoy looking to rob you of all the fun in this world. He wants to maximize your deepest happiness in this life and in the one to come. Many of the deepest joys require saying no to lesser pleasures that would only kill your ability to enjoy the real deal.

Imagine a delicious meal at your favorite restaurant. What

Q: *I struggle with how to live out my faith when I'm surrounded by nonbelievers. When should I say something, and when should I let it go? When should I bring my faith up, or when should I let my light shine in my actions?* —GRACE, FRESHMAN, Finance

A: Those are tough calls to make. Some of us are too pushy and aggressive with our non-Christian friends, needlessly driving them to be less interested in Jesus. Others are so careful to avoid stepping on anyone's toes that their non-Christian friends never hear about Jesus.

How much the other person is ready to hear generally depends on where they're at in life, the depth of our relationship with them, and the context of a particular conversation. We need to be good listeners as well as clear presenters of the gospel. We also need to fight the fear of rejection. If other people are really our friends, they'll care to know what we believe, if for no other reason than that they care about us. We can present our faith in a manner that doesn't convey that they're just a conversion project (2 Timothy 2:24-26). We're just sharing our perspective, and we can respectfully explore areas of disagreement. We can communicate that we care about them even though we disagree. In fact, it's because we care that we want them to know about Jesus.

if I told you that I was going to take you there tomorrow night? Six thirty sharp, I'm driving, and (most important) I'm buying. Let's say your sister comes home at five and says, "Hey, I was hungry and went to Burger King on the way home. Picked up some extra French fries for you. You want some?" Hmmm, yummy. You want them. They *would* taste good. But . . . if your brain is on, you would say no. Why? Because *something better is waiting at six thirty.* You can delay an immediate pleasure if you really believe that a greater pleasure awaits you. *The key is to remember (and believe in) that greater pleasure.*

That's how God's commandments work. Every one of them was meant to help us avoid destroying our capacity to enjoy the greatest pleasures. The pleasures of sin are immediate, but afterward come negative consequences such as relational distance, disharmony, loneliness, emptiness, or even physical sickness. You do it, you enjoy it, but then physical and/or emotional pain and guilt follow. From that pain eventually comes the temptation to escape by doing it again, and the cycle repeats itself. That's what the hookup scene is all about. In fact, it often comes with binge drinking to numb the pain and the loneliness. But those behaviors create an addictive pattern that can make it more difficult for you to develop trust and intimacy in an exclusive, lifelong, monogamous commitment.

Resolve *now* not to go there. But don't just say no; say yes to something better. Decide now to form strong friendships with like-minded peers who share your ideas of a good time.

There are so many healthy, exciting ways for recreation in college that don't involve experiencing the chemical, mind-altering, and addictive behavior brought on by alcohol and casual sex (with their associated headaches and heartaches). We'll talk more about the importance of choosing good friends in part 2.

THE SAD CASE OF (CURIOUS) GEORGE

We've talked about the intellectual challenges that Christian students often face in college, particularly at state universities or other secular campuses. And we've also talked about the moral dangers, particularly the Greek or party scenes, which can be incredibly overrated, depending on the college.

Now let's hit on an interaction between the two that might take you by surprise: Sometimes, intellectual "problems" with the Christian faith are nothing more than a smoke screen for serious moral problems. People come up with objections to the faith in an attempt to rationalize behavior they know runs counter to God's moral law. In these cases, the problem is located in the head *and* heart, but mostly in the heart.

I remember my old friend George (not his real name). George went to Rice University and was a couple of years behind me. He seemed like a solid guy, identified himself as a Christian, had a good Christian background, etc. George had a hometown girlfriend who arrived at Rice the same year he did. It took a few months for us to realize that, especially for a pair of freshmen, they seemed . . . well, a bit too into each other. They chose the same major, took all the same classes, always studied together, came and left the cafeteria together, went to church together. They were seemingly inseparable. They even lived in the same dorm building.

Over time, George and his girlfriend became less interested in developing their relationship with Christ or attending church or any other corporate expression of their faith. Their hearts drifted away from Jesus Christ and exclusively toward each other. Unfortunately, nobody felt comfortable asking the obvious question until it was too late. As you might have guessed, they had been spending so much time alone that their sexual purity was being sacrificed. And though neither one would have overtly admitted it, they knew what they were doing was contrary to biblical teaching. So—and here's the subtle part—they began to question the moral "narrowness" of Christianity. How could something that felt so right actually be wrong? After all, they loved each other and planned to get married someday. And why bother trying to figure out what God would say about it or asking others, like their pastor, what they thought? They figured people at church just wouldn't understand.

I graduated and ran into George a couple of years later. His spiritual condition had deteriorated. In addition to questioning the Bible's teaching on sexuality and marriage, George could no longer accept the Bible as a reliable standard, and he bristled at the idea of Jesus being the only way to God. His arguments against the Christian faith were little more than an attempt to justify what he wanted to do until

eventually Christianity no longer had any meaning or interest for him.

Factoid

Did you know that 70 percent of young adults who
attended a Protestant church regularly for at least a year
in high school will stop attending church regularly between
the ages of eighteen and twenty-two?[5]

APATHY INDICATES IDOLATRY

You'll also meet plenty of folks whose morality is contrary
to the Bible, and they can't be bothered to come up with
intellectual objections to Christianity. They simply don't
care. In my experience at a secular university, the majority of
my non-Christian acquaintances didn't have detailed, philo-
sophically sophisticated arguments against Christianity. They
just had no interest in Christianity being true because they
simply wanted to live life their own ways. This is exactly what
Romans 1 warns us of:

> *The wrath of God is revealed from heaven against all
> ungodliness and unrighteousness of men, who by their
> unrighteousness suppress the truth. For what can be
> known about God is plain to them, because God has
> shown it to them. For his invisible attributes, namely,
> his eternal power and divine nature, have been clearly*

*perceived, ever since the creation of the world, in the
things that have been made. So they are without excuse.
For although they knew God, they did not honor him
as God or give thanks to him, but they became futile in
their thinking, and their foolish hearts were darkened.
(Romans 1:18-21)*

Like George, they've pushed out God "by their unrighteous-
ness," suppressing the truth. That's why it is especially important that you keep your conscience clean if you do go through
phases of intellectual doubt at college, as many of us do. That
way you can allow the honest questions to drive you deeper
into your relationship with Christ, increasing your assurance
(like the Bereans in Acts 17:11). And you won't be allowing
any particular sin to attach itself to you, pushing you away
from Christ.

MAKE JESUS YOUR TREASURE

Christianity doesn't just make sense; it provides a firm basis
to build your college years and your entire adult life upon.
Here's what Jesus said:

*Everyone then who hears these words of mine and does
them will be like a wise man who built his house on the
rock. And the rain fell, and the floods came, and the
winds blew and beat on that house, but it did not fall,
because it had been founded on the rock. And everyone
who hears these words of mine and does not do them*

will be like a foolish man who built his house on the sand. And the rain fell, and the floods came, and the winds blew and beat against that house, and it fell, and great was the fall of it. (Matthew 7:24-27)

To build your life around God's Word (Jesus' teaching + the rest of the Bible) is to build your life on a *firm foundation.* Christianity is a worldview; its Truth has applications for every area of your life. Putting Jesus in a compartment is not really an option. Going beyond how to avoid getting derailed by intellectual doubts or sinful choices, let's talk about how to practically build your life on the truth of Jesus Christ and what he has done for you.

In Matthew 13, Jesus taught a pair of two-sentence, back-to-back parables that are fascinating: "The kingdom of heaven is like treasure hidden in a field, which a man found and covered up. Then in his joy he goes and sells all that he has and buys that field. Again, the kingdom of heaven is like a merchant in search of fine pearls, who, on finding one pearl of great value, went and sold all that he had and bought it" (Matthew 13:44-46). Jesus is comparing the Kingdom of Heaven to a treasure worth more than every other treasure, a treasure worth letting go of everything else to get.

> To build your lives around God's Word (Jesus' teaching + the rest of the Bible) is to build your life on a firm foundation.

The treasure and the pearl were of greater value than anything else the man and the merchant possessed. We see the opposite value system in the story of the rich young ruler. Jesus told him, "One thing you still lack" (Luke 18:22)—the treasure, the pearl, Jesus. The ruler needed to open his hand, let go of his money, and take hold of Jesus. And he wouldn't do it! Why? Because he didn't realize how great a treasure Jesus was.

The question we all have to ask ourselves is this: Is God going to occupy a compartment of my life, or will he be *central*? It can be nice to have God in a neat, safe place where he can comfort us when we're lonely or confused, but not really interfere with us when things are going our way. But then he's more our copilot (as the bumper sticker says) than our Lord and Treasure. And that kind of faith is a facade; it's not the real thing. Jesus said, "Not everyone who says to me, 'Lord, Lord,' will enter the kingdom of heaven, but the one who does the will of my Father who is in heaven" (Matthew 7:21). Obeying Jesus is not an option for the Christian; there is no such thing as a nonpracticing Christian.

God doesn't just want a *place* in your life; he wants your *entire* life. If he's not Lord of all, then he's not Lord at all. Don't squeeze God into your plans; find your place in his plan.

Keep college in perspective. It's not just a place to be intellectually challenged or to have the most fun you'll ever have in your life. It's not just a place to hear cool speakers or to have amazing, famous professors. It's not only a place to find a spouse or build a professional network. *College is a temporary season of academic preparation and growth so that you can serve God more effectively with the rest of your adult life.* If you've chosen to go to college, then *God's plan is that college be a springboard into all that goes with responsible Christian adulthood.* Consider every commitment you make, every activity you sign up for, every class you choose, in light of the greater purpose of why you are at college: to develop the gifts he's given you so as to live a life of maximum Kingdom impact.

Knowing that college is a launching pad—a season of preparation—gives you perspective and shapes your priorities. Godly priorities will help you say no to things that take you off the track of where God is leading you. And I'm not just talking about saying no to immoral things, but about saying no to some *good* things that just aren't for you. You only have so much time in the day, the week, and the semester. Discernment will flow from a sense of who God made you to be, as a Christian with unique interests, talents, skills, and long-term desires. These will guide you as to what classes to take, what major to pursue, what clubs to be a part of, what friends to spend time with, and more. God already has good works prepared for you to do (Ephesians 2:10); you need to prepare for them.

> *College is a temporary season of academic preparation and growth so that you can serve God more effectively with the rest of your adult life. . . . Consider every commitment you make, every activity you sign up for, every class you choose, in light of the greater purpose of why you are at college.*

But how should we practically go about balancing our

priorities? We'll tackle that question in the next chapter, where we unpack the mistake of assuming college is just like high school.

CONCLUSIONS

Many find college to be a season in which their Christian faith is put to the test like never before. You may be under the influence of professors with secular agendas and classmates who make immoral decisions. But don't chuck your faith at this critical time. Instead, grow closer to God by pursuing a greater understanding of your faith and wrestling honestly with any doubts. The Christian faith is grounded in historical events and has been faithfully passed down to us through reliable Scripture, both the Old and New Testaments. Christianity also makes good sense of the world; it satisfyingly gives meaning to our innate longing for truth, beauty, and goodness. Don't buy into the wishy-washy concept of "what's true for you is true for you." Recognize God's commandments were made to increase and intensify your long-term happiness—to help you see through the lies of deceptive pleasures that would rob you of greater, deeper, more satisfying joys (Psalm 16:11). Make Christ your treasure, and build your life around the truths found in God's Word.

DISCUSSION STARTERS

1. What intellectual doubts have you had (or still have) about the Christian faith? What have you done (or what are you doing) to address them?

2. Have you ever talked to a non-Christian friend who said you were "intolerant"? How did you handle that? Have you ever met people who speak of "tolerance" but who aren't very tolerant themselves?

3. Do you agree with the phrase "a Christianity not practiced today becomes a Christianity that is absent tomorrow"? Why or why not?

4. Are there any areas in your life where you are making moral compromises?

5. How are you seeking to live from the foundation of your Christian faith?

COMMON MISTAKE #2:
Treating College as if It Were High School

> *Thrive Principle: Maintain Healthy Habits and Boundaries*

LAST CHAPTER WE looked at the first mistake you don't want to make: abandoning your Christian faith. Instead, you'll want to grow closer to God and live in light of his infinite value. The second mistake you don't want to make is to assume that college is just like high school. If you want to thrive at college, you'll probably need to make adjustments, particularly if you're living on campus, which is what I'll mainly assume in this chapter. Even if you're already into your college years, keep reading because there may be some "tweaking" you can do to improve your experience.

YOU MUST BALANCE YOUR PRIORITIES

As a college student, you need to manage the various arenas of your life. Maybe you're thinking, *Well, yeah. How is that any different from what I did in high school?* I'm assuming that most of you lived with at least one parent before going to college—a parent who cared enough to set guidelines and boundaries for you (a curfew, rules about having to finish certain tasks before being allowed to visit friends, etc.). Maybe your family was strict; maybe they weren't so strict. But unless you are at an unusually strict private college, your parents were almost certainly stricter than your resident assistants. There was a day when colleges considered themselves *in loco parentis* ("in the place of parents"). Except in a few rare cases, that concept is no longer practiced. That means you'll have enough freedom to strengthen your decision-making abilities through regularly making responsible, wise choices. You'll also have enough freedom to throw tens of thousands of dollars down the toilet. I've seen both, and you probably will too.

The students you'll meet on campus will each weigh his or her priorities differently. You've got the athletes who are there on scholarships, and sports are more important to some of them than academics. In my view, this makes sense only if you have a reasonable chance of earning a living in a particular sport. But even at non–Division I schools you'll find students who put sports before studies. You'll also find students who are all about relationships and growing spiritually and don't place enough emphasis on their class work.* Others will study so hard they'll be pasty white, sick, exhausted, and lonely. And the list goes on.

Here's the thing to keep in mind: Because you aren't living with your family, *you* are the one who needs to establish your boundaries based on a God-given sense of what God's calling you to do and the role that college plays in preparing you for that. Like I said in chapter 1, college is a temporary season of preparation and growth so that you can serve God more effectively with the rest of your adult life. It should be a springboard into all that goes with responsible Christian adulthood. Remembering that will give you the freedom and the discipline to say no to many *good* things that simply aren't the *best* for you. Later we'll talk about discerning your strengths, choosing an academic major, and recognizing your calling.

In this chapter, I'll first list the areas of college life that need to be balanced, and then I'll unpack four unique challenges of college as compared to high school. They aren't the only ones, but in my experience they're the biggies that can make or break your experience: consistently getting sleep, working when it's time to work, keeping pre-college life in check, and choosing close friends wisely.

ELEMENTS OF COLLEGE LIFE

Let's divide college life into the following categories: work (classes, labs, homework, studying, projects, writing papers,

---

* This often comes from a truncated, mistaken view of spiritual life, which insufficiently values secular or academic work. We'll get to that later.

part- or full-time job, etc.), relationships (dorm life, hanging out, social activities, intramural sports, clubs, etc.), significant extracurricular commitments (a sports team, a musical group, a theatrical group, etc.), and what I'll call "personal maintenance" (taking care of your body and your soul through sleep, a balanced diet, exercise, reading your Bible, going to church, Christian accountability and support). There often will be overlap: You'll hopefully enjoy nutritious meals with friends (combining eating with socializing/relaxing). Going to church should both feed your soul and nurture relationships, etc.

You'll notice I distinguished between intramural sports and clubs on one hand and official team sports, choirs, musicals, and plays on the other. At California Baptist University (where I teach), intramural flag football is popular. There's a guys' league and a girls' league. Students might be on an intramural football team but only attend half the games due to classes or labs. But if a student is on a university sports team, that student misses classes and is excused for away games. The team activity is considered essential. In fact, they'd probably receive discipline if they did *not* join their team for the game.

I put intramural sports and clubs in the relationships category because the motivating factor or benefit is generally social. Conversely, being on an official college sports team or regularly participating in theater is a significant *commitment* that can sometimes take priority over attending class. In fact, at both small and large colleges and universities, a student's participation in sports, music, or theater can be a means of receiving a partial or full-ride scholarship.

So these are the categories to balance: *work, relationships, significant extracurricular commitments, and personal mainte-nance.* With these in mind, let's tackle the four unique chal-lenges of college: consistently getting sleep, working when it's time to work, keeping precollege life in check, and choosing close friends wisely.

GETTING ENOUGH SLEEP

Our first challenge, getting enough sleep, falls under the category of *personal maintenance.* Your dorm life may not promote what doctors call good sleep hygiene. If you think about it, when is the last time you lived with a bunch of other guys or girls your age? Maybe a summer camp setting, a high-school youth group retreat, or some kind of short-term educational program. Perhaps they *made* you sleep with a firm lights-out, no-talking policy. Or perhaps you powered through the weekend with four to five hours of sleep a night, then crashed hard when you got home.

Factoid

Did you know that stress about school and life keeps 68 percent of students awake at night—20 percent of them at least once a week?[1] In fact, a study of 1,125 students conducted by the *Journal of Adolescent Health* found that only 30 percent of students sleep at least eight hours a night—the average requirement for young adults.

A typical college semester is about fourteen weeks, a lot longer than a three-day weekend. It is not a nonstop vacation like a youth group event, where continuous recreational and social activity keeps everyone going. And it is highly doubtful that someone will force you to turn off the lights, unless you have a domineering, well-disciplined roommate. So if you *are* in constant slumber-party mode, you will *never* make it. Your body is resilient, but it won't keep up forever. It's crucial that you establish some guidelines for yourself.

We live in a culture in which sleep deprivation has become the norm. I sometimes hear my students almost bragging about how busy they are and how little sleep they get by on. But unless you're highly unusual, research indicates that you need, on average, at least eight hours of sleep each night on a regular basis. If you don't get adequate sleep, you'll be less able to concentrate on your classes and homework. In fact, if you sleep even seven hours a night, you'll probably be more productive in the long haul than if you try to make it on six hours a night.

You'll get the most out of your sleep if you keep a regular sleep schedule, but you don't need to be super-rigid about it. Try to sleep and get up at about the same time (within sixty to ninety minutes) every day, seven days a week. This habit trains your body on when to go to sleep and when to wake up.

My college friend David was the classic violator of this principle. He'd sleep for about four hours a night from Sunday to Thursday, staying up late either talking to friends or

Q: *What suggestions do you have for eating habits in college? I think nutritional health is a very important aspect of maintaining overall health in college. How do you recommend we go about that?*
—KATE, FRESHMAN, Creative Writing

A: There is a saying out there that freshmen tend to gain fifteen pounds over the nine or so months they live and eat on campus. Dining halls provide all-you-can-eat meals and a variety of choices. Most cafeterias have pizzas and burgers, as well as a variety of rich desserts and soft-serve ice cream—at *every* meal. Not only is it easy to overeat, but you have the option of living on pizzas, burgers, and desserts without anyone telling you to eat fruits and vegetables. Then there's late-night snacking while studying or talking to friends, or pizza ordering and eating out. It's easy to be undisciplined, gain weight, and deprive yourself of the healthy food you need to avoid illness, have energy, and think clearly.

Guidelines help. For example, you might make it your goal to have a piece of fresh fruit with every meal, a salad with lunch, vegetables with dinner, and a limited amount of sweets. Give yourself small portions and wait a few minutes before taking a second helping. You may not be as hungry as you think. Set limits to what you snack on and how much, especially late at night when it's easy to lose track. And don't forget to make time for exercise. It will help you burn calories and relax.

studying. Then on Friday and Saturday nights he'd sleep eleven to twelve hours a night, wandering into the cafeteria at one in the afternoon in his pajamas. Come Monday morning, you'd think he'd be well rested, caught up on sleep, right? Wrong. He'd be worn-out and irritable and could barely get himself going. He had trained his body all weekend that it didn't need to get up. Come Monday morning, he had to *retrain* his body for the new, grueling regimen of four to five hours of sleep for the next four nights. He did well in his classes, but he probably could have been more productive and efficient (freeing up more time for non-academic activities) had he taken better regular care of his need for sleep.

Other issues to consider include environmental factors such as noise and light, or psychological factors like anxiety. I find it helpful at night to turn off the computer or television at least two hours before I plan to sleep—bright lights and exciting plots seem to keep my brain active. Also, if you sleep near where you work, which is probably inevitable in college, try to clean up your work area before going to sleep. Seeing piles of homework and notes might make it harder for your brain to relax and shut down.

I used to get up and work if I couldn't fall asleep right away. *I don't have time to be unproductive.* So I'd work an extra couple of hours, which trained me to be a semi-productive insomniac. The next day I'd be tired, more irritable, slower, less productive, and more likely to repeat the experience, since my work wasn't done come bedtime. Now if I can't fall asleep right away, I try to focus my thoughts on God's protection until I naturally drift away (Psalm 3:5-6, 4:8; 121:4). By sending your mind to something restful, stimuli to the brain is reduced and you naturally fall asleep. The more you get in a routine, the easier it is to keep it, since your body gets used to it. If possible, pick a roommate who will help you keep your commitment to sleep.

Being busy is not the same as being diligent, faithful, or fruitful.

Before we get into discussing the academic work of college, I want to draw a distinction between being busy and being productive. This may seem weird, but did you know it is possible to be both busy and lazy? What I'm about to share with you has literally transformed the way I view my own time management.

I used to think being busy and being productive were the same. *As long as I'm doing "stuff," I'm good.* But I realized that some of my busyness was procrastination and laziness in disguise. I was doing a bunch of easy things, like responding to e-mail, rather than the one major task that needed to get done. As a result, I'd put off the big task until the only way I could get it done was to work until 2:00 a.m. the night before it was due. For weeks prior, I should have been chipping away at it, but I didn't. Why? Because I was busy. That is, because I chose to fill my time doing things that were easier and less important. Yet that Big Task would just hang over my head, reminding me that *It Was Not Done.*

Now I start my days asking myself, *What do I need to get*

done today? From this list of tasks, I prioritize not just the urgent (whatever's due tomorrow) but also the important, because assignments due ten days from now won't be overwhelming if I spend an hour a day on them. I start with the most important task whenever possible. By doing so, I actually have *fewer* things that eventually become urgent because I chip away at them long before they're due.

There's also a bunch of things I don't do because they're just not sufficiently important given my sense of the priorities God has placed on my life. By knowing my roles (person, Christian, husband, father, professor, writer), I'm able to ignore tasks that aren't relevant. As a person, I need to sleep, eat, and exercise. As a Christian, I need to take care of my soul by praying, reading the Bible, and being active at church. As a husband, I need to spend time talking with my wife and making sure our relationship is strong. As a father, I need to spend time with my kids. As a professor, I need to prepare for class, teach, help students, grade, go to meetings, and a bunch of other stuff. As a writer, I need to read, think, click away at the keyboard, reflect, edit, and rewrite.

I encourage you to go through this exercise so that you're scheduling your priorities rather than allowing a million unimportant but seemingly urgent things to keep you busy. Remember that college is a temporary season of preparation and growth so that you can serve God more effectively the rest of your adult life. God's plan is that college be a launching pad into all that goes along with responsible Christian adulthood.

Now we're ready to discuss the second unique challenge: working when it's time to work.

WHEN IT'S TIME TO WORK, WORK

When you got your first schedule your freshman year, your initial thoughts may have been similar to mine: *Woo-hoo! In high school I got to school at 7:45 and stayed in class until 3:20, except for lunch. Now, you mean to tell me that on Tuesdays and Thursdays I've got class from 9:00 to noon and then nothing? So after lunch I can just play tennis, Foosball, Ping-Pong, and video games all afternoon? And my parents can't even tell me what to do because they're miles away? This is going to be way too much fun.*

That would be the *wrong* way to start the semester. It's true that you'll spend less time in class during college than you did in high school. But they'll expect more from you between classes than they did in high school—a lot more. (Remember, this book is as close as I can come to taking you out to coffee and telling you what I wish someone had told me.)

Our second unique challenge falls under the category of *work.* The principle is this: When it's time to work, you work, and you *only* work. We'll talk about how many hours you'll need to work on your classes later this chapter.

I probably don't have to tell you that we live in an age of endless distraction. Facebook, Twitter, and text messages crowd our day, helping us stay connected with our friends and families, but hurting our ability to concentrate for extended periods of time. For example, I've seen studies that have correlated Facebook use to a decrease in GPA by as much as 0.50 to 1.00 (on a 4.00 scale).[2] Ouch!

Factoid

Did you know that some researchers have found that Facebook use can go hand in hand with a lower GPA?[3]

Likewise, the huge number of text messages that some (most!) of you are sending is beginning to worry doctors and psychologists, who say it's leading to anxiety, distraction in school, falling grades, repetitive stress injury, and sleep deprivation.[4] I've even seen students texting while crossing a busy street! And though I don't personally use texting because I'm too cheap to pay the extra few bucks each month, I definitely include myself in this discussion. I've had to put strict rules on my Facebook and e-mail use to be productive, even before I had the deadline of finishing this book.

Let's talk frankly about the concept of *multitasking*, because that is a common reason many of us give for catching up on e-mail while having several simultaneous IM conversations, or texting while watching a TV program, or surfing the Web while plowing through homework assignments. Most of us think that's being efficient. But a group of researchers at Stanford University investigating multitasking discovered something surprising: People who are regularly bombarded with several streams of electronic information do not pay attention, control their memory, or switch from one job to another as well as those who prefer to complete one task at a time.[5]

But you are used to this bombardment from high school. What makes college different? Just the fact that you are more on your own in terms of setting your schedule—Mom and Dad aren't around to watch or nag you into doing your homework, chores, etc. Whether you even *go* to class is entirely up to you. Since I've both been a student and observed students for more than six years as a professor, how about a few pointers?

1. Attend class with your cell phone off.

Be fully present, and fully participate during class times. Some classes are lecture based, meaning you'll listen as the professor explains concepts and spits out vital information, writing furiously on the whiteboard. Other classes are more discussion driven and will require you to interact with others. In either environment, receiving or sending texts is distracting to the professor and to other students, and you will fall behind. Even if your professor doesn't notice right away, it's disrespectful. Love your classmate as yourself (Matthew 22:39).

Watch those laptops, too. The rapid clickety-click sounds can be distracting for others, and if you're bored or tired, you may easily be tempted to check Facebook or play video games. You're probably better off taking notes with an old-fashioned pen or pencil.

2. Start your homework as soon as possible, and do it somewhere quiet and away from distractions.

You'll want to start your homework right away: Your brain's retention of the material is sharpest the moment class ends. After that, you start forgetting a certain percentage of what you just heard. By starting your homework soon after you've learned the material, your brain takes the concepts and pushes them from short-term memory into long-term memory. This principle holds whether it's a math or science course or an English or history course. It's universal: we remember most what we just learned.

The other benefit of starting your homework right away is that you'll have plenty of time to pursue the professor with questions that may come up along the way. You won't have that opportunity if you wait until the last minute. In addition, challenging concepts may require multiple exposures and "an incubation period" to fully sink in and make sense to you. It is common to not fully understand complicated concepts until the third or fourth time you go over them.[†] Give yourself that opportunity by starting early.

Find a quiet place on campus for a regular study nook. Don't try doing homework in the dorms, where there will always be way too many distractions. (Remember, multitasking won't work!) The library is usually a good place,

---

† In his best-selling book *Outliers* (New York: Little, Brown and Company, 2008), Malcolm Gladwell gives a fascinating illustration of a woman spending twenty-two minutes learning a fundamental concept of algebra. According to math professor Alan Schoenfeld from the University of California at Berkeley, who videotaped her, she was persistent and determined, making progress only by going over it repeatedly, making mistakes, and correcting herself. In contrast, Schoenfeld discovered that the average high school student gives up on a math problem in two minutes.

especially if they have private study rooms, like my college did. I could go in there with a friend and study (it had a chalkboard, too—I'm old), or I could go in alone. Either way, that became my regular study spot. If I had an hour between classes, I'd go there rather than go back to my dorm.

3. Make a good schedule, and then discipline yourself to keep it.

Speaking of wisely using those extra hours, there is arguably no productivity aid as powerful as a schedule. Use Excel or a personal planner to make something like this:

SCHEDULE FOR 16 CREDIT HOURS							
TIME	M	Tu	W	Th	Fri	Sat	Sun
7:00 - 7:50	Bible/Breakfast	Exercise	Bible/Breakfast	Exercise	Bible/Breakfast	SLEEP IN	Bible/Breakfast, Church
8:00 - 8:50	ENG113	Bible/Breakfast	ENG113	Bible/Breakfast	ENG113		
9:00 - 9:50	HIS135	PHI200	HIS135	PHI200	HIS135	Bible/Breakfast	
10:00 - 10:50	Study in Library		Chapel		Chapel		
11:00 - 11:50	HIS185	Study in Library	HIS185	Study in Library	HIS185	Study in Library	
12:00 - 12:50	LUNCH	LUNCH	LUNCH	LUNCH	LUNCH		Lunch with Friends, Families/ Maybe a Nap
1:00 - 1:50	Study in Library	Study in Library	Study in Library	Study in Library	Study in Library	LUNCH	
2:00 - 2:50	MAT145		MAT145		MAT145	Free Time	
3:00 - 3:50	Free Time		FLAG FOOTBALL		Study in Library		Sports/Friends/ Hang Out
4:00 - 4:50	Choir Practice	Choir Practice		Choir Practice	Free Time		
5:00 - 5:50	Dinner with Friends	Dinner with Friends	Dinner with Friends	Dinner with Friends	Dinner with Friends	Dinner with Friends	Dinner with Friends
6:00 - 6:50							
7:00 - 10:50	Study in Library	Dorm Bible Study	Study in Library	Study in Library	Free Time	Group Study Session	Free Time
11:00 PM	BEDTIME	BEDTIME	BEDTIME	BEDTIME		BEDTIME	BEDTIME
12:00 Midnight					BEDTIME		

This schedule has sixteen hours per week of classes, three hours per week of choir practice, two hours per week of chapel (a standard feature at a Christian college), a couple of time slots for exercise, and time for a weekly flag football commitment.[‡] It also has a firm bedtime (allowing for about eight hours of sleep per night and a little catch-up on Saturday morning) and thirty-two hours per week for studying.

You heard me right: thirty-two hours per week. Why so many? Well, the general rule is two hours of work outside class for every one hour of work in class—and that's on average. You'll have some challenging classes that will demand more than that. So if you add up the "academic" hours, in class and out of class, including chapel, they come to fifty hours per week. If you're a full-time student, school is a full-time job. Given how much you're spending to be there, you might as well do it right.

The general rule is two hours of work outside class for every hour of work in class. . . . If you're a full-time student, school is a full-time job.

Likewise, if you have over fifty-five to sixty *committed* hours per week in a semester, you are probably overcommitted. By committed, I'm referring to activities you absolutely must do (classes, homework, a job, and any official commitments like a college sport team, orchestra, band, or theatrical group). If you can make it financially, I generally encourage students to earn money exclusively on academic breaks (like Christmas, spring

---

‡ I'll talk about part-time or full-time jobs in chapter 10.

break, and summers), because the actual academic portion of the year is usually only about eight months (four months per semester). Building a solid GPA is an investment in your future, as it will make you more marketable upon graduation. When I've seen students take a full load of classes (seventeen to eighteen units) and juggle a fifteen- to twenty-hour-per-week off-campus job, they've often struggled academically because their brains could only handle so much.[§]

I left the open boxes to signify free time. You'll notice that there's still quite a bit of downtime for hanging out with friends, playing sports, or just reading a good book. Friday night and almost the entire weekend are open, besides church on Sunday morning. And the dorm Bible study probably doesn't last four hours. The key is to *keep* to the schedule, which means limiting interruptions. For example, you might send a quick text message in the ten minutes between classes, or use some of your lunch or dinner break to catch up on e-mail. But don't take forty minutes of your study time to respond to all your Facebook posts. When I was a student, five o'clock was exercise or unwind time every day. I'd work until five, then meet a friend for tennis or

> Whatever you're doing, be fully present in it.

go for a run before heading to the shower, cafeteria, then on to an evening activity by about seven. There really is a lot of time if you plan and use it well.

[§] That said, there are some unique paid academic opportunities that are exceptionally worthwhile. We'll discuss these in chapter 10.

Work when it's time to work. Play when it's time to play. *Whatever you're doing, be fully present in it.* Avoid the temptation to try to mix studying with texting or Facebook. It may seem efficient, but it's not.

4. During work times, do one thing at a time, the most important thing first.

We've already mentioned the danger of multitasking: It gives a feeling of efficiency, but it's only an illusion. It's *productive* to do one thing at a time. But here's another key: Start with the most important thing. Let's say you have a two-hour time block; your energy and focus are often greatest at the beginning. Plus, you don't know for sure how long the most important thing may take you. So get after it first. Depending on how that goes, you might need to restructure your schedule a bit for the remainder of the week. Whatever's next most important can wait for its turn. After all, it's *less* important.

What's most important sometimes changes. Working on an English paper may be most important on a Wednesday afternoon, but Thursday's when your math study group gets together, so math comes first on that day. That's fine. It even gives your brain a break and prevents dullness. One thing I did a lot in college was work on one subject for a couple of hours until I made decent progress; then I'd take a break by shifting to another subject. Maybe I'd work on a paper from one to three in the afternoon, then meet with my math study group. The shift gave my brain a change of pace, but

Q: *Do you have any advice for the workaholic, over-achiever college types on how to feel okay (not anxious or stressed) about making time for the relationship and personal maintenance areas of college life?*

—KELVIN, JUNIOR, Physics/Engineering

A: I err on that side myself, so I hear your concern. I think there's a role for godly ambition—for a desire to excel and develop the talents and interests God gives us. To help keep us in balance, we need to remember that unless the Lord builds the house, we labor in vain (Psalm 127:1). We're ultimately dependent on the strength that God supplies (1 Peter 4:11). Even our basic, daily needs for things like sleep and food point to that dependence.

It also helps to step back and recognize that, in addition to getting good grades and experiencing academic success, it's also important to have significant life-sustaining relationships—the kind that spur us on to do the good, hard things that God calls us to do. "Two are better than one, because they have a good reward for their toil. For if they fall, one will lift up his fellow. But woe to him who is alone when he falls and has not another to lift him up!" (Ecclesiastes 4:9-10). While it's wise to be discerning in your choice of companions, *all* quality friendships take time and energy to cultivate. These relationships are investments you won't regret.

One thing at a time. Most important thing first. Start now.

I was still productive because I was doing one thing at a time. In this case, both the paper and the math were about equally important.

A friend of mine who's an executive in a Christian organization reads a lot on productivity. He summarized their message for me in eleven words: *One thing at a time. Most important thing first. Start now.* That's good advice.

KEEP PRE-COLLEGE LIFE IN ITS PLACE

Our third unique challenge falls under the category of relationships. There are various relationships from pre-college life that you inevitably leave behind when you go to college: friends still in high school, friends who have gone on to other colleges, siblings, parents, etc. Now by "leave behind" I'm not suggesting that you are forever cut off from them. But there is an extent to which your relationships, as you've known them, become permanently altered.

There's simply no way around it. Geographically, you are now in a new place (I'm assuming you're living in the dorms or some other college housing). You can't have the same kind of contact with Mom and Dad, your siblings, and your high-school friends that you used to. If you try, you will diminish your college experience. To thrive in college, you need to keep pre-college life in its place.

One of the huge benefits of social media, of course, is that it keeps you connected with the people you love, your family and hometown friends. Yet that very ability to connect whenever you (or they) want can hinder your personal growth.[¶] A good check on how you are doing away from home is to think about how many hours you spend on Facebook versus meeting new people.

I'm not suggesting you try to live outside community. On the contrary, you'll grow more by forming and joining new communities at college. It is part of embracing adulthood.

Draw some lines. Others may disagree, but depending on your situation, it may be healthy to limit phone calls and texts back home. Let yourself transition. If you don't, the principle we just unpacked—working when you're supposed to be working—will be far more difficult. In fact, playing when you're supposed to be playing will also be more challenging because your new social connections at college will be weaker if you're spending a big chunk of your free time preserving a super-high level of connectedness with those back home.

Let me ease any anxiety you may sense: The relationships will still be there for you. In fact, they can gloriously become stronger, not in spite of but precisely *because of* the geographical distance and time gap between visits. As you fully adjust to college and grow as your own person, you will be maturing into the type of adult who can be even more of a blessing to your old friends in the future. Hopefully they will be going through a similar process.

[¶] The same researchers who are warning that too much texting may be taking a toll (Katie Hafner, "Texting May Be Taking a Toll," *New York Times*, May 25, 2009) are also expressing concern that the natural progression into adulthood, meant to occur during the teen years, is inhibited by the constant chatter of instant messages. If you can constantly get input from others (naturally, your parents and pre-college associations), it is more difficult for you to develop the "muscle" of thinking for yourself, let alone foster new relationships (face-to-face, with other young adults also stepping out of the cocoon).

With your parents, transitioning away from the nest should be even more natural. That was hopefully the goal of their raising you all along. The child-parent relationship is meant to migrate from control to influence. When you started life, your parents had 100 percent control of what you ate, of where you played, and of whom you played with. You were absolutely powerless, and they were seemingly omnipotent in comparison. As years went on, you grew in your abilities, and your parents allowed you more of a say, but they still (if they loved you) sought to be positive influences, to inform your choices, to encourage you, and to rein you in if you lost your way. Now, at college, their control is arguably at an all-time low—but not zero. After all, if they're footing the bill, you couldn't be there without them!

But if your relationship with them is strong, their influence is at an all-time high. They're your biggest cheerleaders and supporters. And they are hopefully among those you first turn to for advice and guidance. But it's okay to start letting go a bit, and Mom and Dad may need help with that, which we'll look at in a later chapter. It might feel natural to text Mom, "I'm so overwhelmed this week. Should I start looking for summer internships at the career center or read every page of every book assigned in my lit class?" Mom might be happy to weigh in on that dilemma, but this is the time of your life to start managing your priorities and moment-to-moment decisions for yourself. Adulthood is your destination. Like arrows, you've almost been released into the world (Psalm 127:4). By taking steps toward responsible independence, you honor all their labors. They will rejoice in your triumphs. And if your relationship is good now, it can only get stronger in the years to come.

CHOOSE CLOSE FRIENDS WISELY

Our fourth unique challenge also falls under the category of *relationships*. To thrive in college, you'll need to be really plugged in to a good group of friends. And these bosom buddies—these close confidants—must share your Christian values. If they don't, faith will always be a source of tension.

I'm not saying that you cannot be friends with non-Christians. No, we are to be the light of the world (Matthew 5:14); we'd have to leave the world altogether to stop associating with nonbelievers (1 Corinthians 5:10). We're to be in the world, but not of the world (John 17:11, 16). What I'm saying is that your *closest friends* should be those who can support you, who share your values, and who will help you become what you aspire to become. I'm talking about the kinds of people who will help you put away childishness, do hard things, and attempt great things for God—people who help you live your college years full throttle for God's glory, with no retreat and no regrets.

I've known young adults over the years, people raised in Christian homes, who for whatever reason found non-Christians to be better friends for them than Christians. Within a few years, many of them no longer identified themselves as Christians. It used to puzzle me, but it doesn't anymore. If you think about it, the more like-minded you are with someone, the closer you can naturally be. If the people with whom you feel the greatest synergy and deepest connection don't share what's supposedly the most important thing in your life, then . . . well, maybe it's really not that important to you after all.

The Bible says it this way: "They went out from us, but they did not really belong to us. For if they had belonged to us, they would have remained with us; but their going showed that none of them belonged to us" (1 John 2:19, NIV). In other words, not everyone who says they're a Christian really is one.

> If the people with whom you feel the greatest synergy and deepest connection don't share what's supposedly the most important thing in your life, then . . . well, maybe it's really not that important to you after all.

Some "Christians" abandon Christianity and by doing so reveal that they never really were Christians. They may have *professed* faith, but they didn't *possess* faith.

So even before you go to college, pray that God will give you a good group of friends. Be patient—you may not find these kinds of friends right away. Be true to who you are, and don't compromise your values as you seek them. If you're at a secular college, look for them in the Christian organizations and in a nearby, solid church. If you're at a Christian college, don't just assume that every student is a Christian. Observe the way they talk, the way they handle situations, and what they admire and enjoy. If you're naturally a follower, be on guard in this phase and don't be easily swayed by those whose standards seem questionable.

You'll also want a good church in the area where you can find even more like-minded friends, as well as good Bible teaching and authentic worship to keep you growing spiritually. Find someone (preferably with you at school, but he or she could also be from home) who will hold you accountable by asking you hard questions about your sexuality, your relationships, drinking, illicit drugs (including popular "brain enhancers" like Adderall and Ritalin, which many students take to stay awake and alert on major assignments and upcoming tests), how you're spending your time, etc.

Not all your dorm mates, teammates, and study partners need to become your best friends. Be careful about who you make your closest confidants, because you will inevitably become like them. Proverbs 13:20 tells us, "Whoever walks with the wise becomes wise, but the companion of fools will suffer harm." It is inescapable; you will not prove to be an exception. Choose close friends whose character you admire, who give you courage and strength to do what's right, and who don't drag you down.

Proverbs 27:17 compares this kind of synergy to "iron sharpen[ing] iron"; each person sharpens the other. There's a principle here: How do you best *find* these kinds of people? In part by *being* this kind of person. That way you attract each other.

They don't have to be your same major. You don't necessarily have to enjoy all the same hobbies—they can expand your horizons, and you can expand theirs. You don't need to be equally good at math, or writing, or academics in general.

But you do need to have the same God and the desire to go hard after him. These are the friends that can tangibly and regularly impart to you measures of the grace of God in Jesus Christ (Romans 1:12).

CONCLUSIONS

College requires you to take ownership of your own life: your work, your relationships, your extracurricular activities, and your health. This responsibility comes with four unique challenges: getting enough sleep, working when it's time to work, keeping pre-college life in check, and choosing close friends wisely. A schedule is a helpful tool for encouraging discipline with regard to work and sleep. It's helpful to get into a rhythm so that your body and brain know when it's time to rest and when it's time to get into high gear. Aim for productivity and faithfulness in commitments. Almost everyone is busy; not everyone is diligent or fruitful. Prioritize what's most important, or you'll get caught up with a hundred distractions that will only slow you down and leave you with less downtime to enjoy. In relationships, walk with the wise, and you'll become wise. Identify and invest in friends you not only enjoy but who also reinforce your value system. This requires intentionality—the topic of our next chapter.

DISCUSSION STARTERS

1. Rank your top five priorities.

2. Now consider how much time you allotted to these priorities over the last two weeks. Are you living consistently with your priorities? If not, how might you be letting others (or the spur of the moment) determine your *actual* priorities? Resolve with God's help to be a faithful steward of the time God has allotted to you.

3. What kinds of things prevent you from getting enough sleep?

4. What are the biggest time wasters you are tempted with when it's time to do your schoolwork? Take some time to consider a strategy for fighting them.

5. Have you considered making a schedule for yourself, like the sample schedule shown in this chapter? If not, what do you use to manage your time? How is it working for you?

6. Facebook has forever changed the way we view "friendship." Yet having one thousand Facebook friends can sometimes be a distraction from having a few really true friends. In a speech to college students, William Deresiewicz made this observation: "Instead of having one or two true friends that we can sit and talk to for three hours at a time, we have 968 'friends' that we never actually talk to; instead we just bounce one-line messages off them a hundred times a day. This is not friendship, this is distraction."[6] Have you ever replaced friendship with distraction?

PART 2
RELATIONSHIPS MATTER

COMMON MISTAKE #3:
Not Being Intentional

> *Thrive Principle: Find Great Friends and Mentors*

RELATIONSHIPS ARE CRUCIAL throughout our lives—they shape us in profound ways. Though before God we each bear individual responsibility for our actions, it would not be an exaggeration to say that no person succeeds in life on his or her own. Those who triumph in ways great and small do so by standing on the shoulders of others. That is why every award speech begins with someone thanking parents, coaches, friends, mentors, etc.—the people whose sacrifice, support, instruction, and example have made success possible. The flip side is that when people *lack* strong, positive relationships, not only do they miss out on the happiness that comes from high-quality, like-minded, iron-sharpening-iron friendships, but they also have less support to help them live fruitful, productive Christian lives to the glory of God and use their skills and God-given talents most effectively.

In this chapter we'll focus on two categories of people with whom we should seek connections: peers and mentors. Peers are those who are roughly the same age as we are or in approximately the same life stage. They live in our dorms, play on our teams, perform with us in our choirs and theatrical groups. Mentors are those who are older or more accomplished than we are in at least one area in which we hope to grow. A mentoring relationship can be comprehensive, covering every part of your life, or it can be particular, covering just one aspect. For example, when I was a student, there were professors I sought out for advice on academic and professional development matters but not on spiritual or personal issues.

In both kinds of relationships, it's important to be intentional. In other words, you'll need to act with purpose both in how you pursue others and who you pursue. It's also your responsibility to be discerning in how you respond to those who initiate relationships with you. The opposite of being intentional is being passive, which means merely doing what's easy or convenient without much thought about the consequences.

RELATIONSHIPS WITH PEERS

Upon arriving at college, you immediately acquire a large number of acquaintances. An acquaintance is someone you're connected to but not because of a choice either of you has made. They include your roommate (assuming you didn't pick him or her), those who live down the hall, classmates, teammates, students in the same campus organizations, etc. Acquaintances often turn into friendships over time—not all to the same degree, of course. Even as some of your acquaintances are becoming friends, the number of your acquaintances tends to multiply as people you know introduce you to people they know. Some of those new acquaintances also become your friends, and so on.

You naturally find yourself drawn to some people more than others. You click with Matt and Joe, but not so much with Justin and Anthony. Why? Lots of reasons. We have "chemistry" with some friends more than others; certain people are easier to talk to, some have the same temperament or sense of humor, or others may come from a similar background. We tend to develop friendships with people who like doing the same activities we do.

But sometimes those who are easiest to be friends with are not the best people to invest in. Jessica might be super funny and a blast to go out with on the weekends, but she's a total slacker and complainer when it comes to her classes and doesn't share any of your values or your commitment to Jesus Christ.

Now, here's where intentionality is important. Intentionality involves taking the time to examine our values so that our relational lives more accurately mirror our deepest priorities, so that we're making relational *decisions* rather than *reactions.* Many of us live relatively unexamined lives. In other words, we go with the flow and connect with whoever is most available. Someone knocks on your door and asks you to play Ping-Pong, so you say sure. If you're not intentional, your circle of friends can easily become the result of reactions rather than conscious, proactive decisions.

Intentionality involves taking the time to examine our values so that our relational lives more accurately mirror our deepest priorities, so that we're making relational decisions rather than reactions.

And then you get to graduation and look around and wonder how your relationships shaped you. Sure, you had some great times. But did they motivate you to "lay aside every weight, and sin which clings so closely" and to "run with endurance the race that is set before us" (Hebrews 12:1)? Did they help you to put away childishness and embrace the responsibilities of adulthood, like the biblical examples of Daniel in Babylon (Daniel 1:8, 18-20), Joseph in Egypt (Genesis 39), and David at Socoh (1 Samuel 17), whose adult-size faith in God emboldened him to take on Goliath, though stronger, older, and more experienced Israelite men lacked the courage? Did they help you live wisely (Proverbs 13:20), endure sacrifices and learn self-discipline (Lamentations 3:27), and delay gratification for the sake of future rewards (Hebrews 12:2)? Did they help you expect great things from God and attempt great things for God?

It is my prayer that you form these kinds of friendships at

college—and that you have a great time doing so. It's not an either-or: have friends with strong Christian values or forge great memories while having a blast. It can be both. But it will take more intentionality to make it happen. So expanding on what we said in the last chapter, what qualities should we be seeking in close, personal friendships? I would suggest a few.

A Similar Worldview

James Sire defines a worldview as a set of presuppositions we hold about the basic makeup of our world.[1] What is ultimate reality, and who (if anyone) is behind it? What is a human being? What (if anything) gives humans intrinsic value? What happens to us when we die? Is it possible for us to truly know anything about reality, including matters of right and wrong?

If someone shares our Christian worldview (see chapter 1), he or she is more likely to share the values and priorities that flow from that worldview. That doesn't mean you won't occasionally have differences of opinions or convictions on smaller matters. Maybe you come from slightly different denominational backgrounds or your families have different traditions. I'm talking about agreement on the big, overarching issues, like that Jesus Christ is the only way to God and worthy of absolute allegiance. That the Bible is the inspired, infallible guide for Christian living and maximum joy (2 Peter 1:3-4; Psalm 16:11; 2 Timothy 3:16). That, consequently, there is nothing more wonderful than a God-mastered life, from childhood to death. That one should remember his Creator in the days of his or her youth (Ecclesiastes 12:1). This is the kind of person who will be able to relate to us at a deeper level than someone with whom we don't share these common values.

Responsible

Personal responsibility tends to flow out of someone's worldview. If we believe that God will ultimately hold us accountable (Ecclesiastes 11:9) and that we're to avoid grumbling and complaining so that we can be lights in the world (Philippians 2:14-15) and that we're to do even mundane tasks such as eating and drinking to the glory of God (1 Corinthians 10:31), those beliefs will shape our attitudes toward our employers, our professors, and our schoolwork. Someone who's responsible will also encourage us to respect our roommates and apartment mates by keeping our part of the living space relatively clean and joyfully participating in our share of any communal cleaning duties.

Loyal

You need to know that you can count on your friends. It's important to trust that if you share with them something important, it will not be inappropriately repeated. A true friend won't just be with you in good times; he or she will also stick with you when things are tough. "A friend loves at all times" (Proverbs 17:17). Look for faithfulness. Watch how a person talks about his or her other friends when those friends are not around. If that person is sharing secrets or making negative remarks about others, don't feel special, as if you're on some kind of inside track with him or her. The sad truth is that your friend is probably saying similar things about you when you're not there.

Perhaps one of the greatest examples of loyalty in the Bible is found in the friendship between Jonathan and David. David arrives at Socoh, where Goliath is mocking the Israelite army. David is on an assignment from his dad (1 Samuel 17:17-18) to bring food to his brothers, only to be greeted not with thankfulness but by the questioning of his motives and the belittling of his duties (1 Samuel 17:28). David, by contrast, sees the connection between faithfulness in small things and faithfulness in big things, even though King Saul questions what a "youth" can do (1 Samuel 17:33-36). When the battle is over, Jonathan, Saul's son and the heir apparent to the throne, amazingly responds not with jealousy and hostility but with admiration and love (1 Samuel 18:1-5). His father, Saul, is later incredulous, unable to understand why his son won't share Dad's self-serving, power-trip agenda (1 Samuel 20:30-31). But Jonathan recognizes what God is doing in David's life and is happy to come alongside him as a true friend, even if it puts his own life at risk. That's a true friend.

Loving and Truthful

The Bible commands us to speak the truth in love (Ephesians 4:15) and tells us that the wounds of a friend are better than the kisses of an enemy (Proverbs 27:6). Don't just make friends with people who always tell you what you want to hear. You need people who can not only track with what you're thinking and saying but also challenge you to be godlier and wiser in your attitudes, priorities, and actions, like iron sharpening iron (Proverbs 27:17; Hebrews 10:24). Again, it's so important to have friends whose characters you admire because, like it or not, as they go, you will go.

> *It's so important to have friends whose characters you admire because, like it or not, as they go, you will go.*

Encouraging

Quality friends have a life-giving effect. Even if you're having a tough day or they've disagreed with you on something, their effect should be positive because it is grounded in the grace of God, whose mercies are new every morning (Lamentations 3:22-23). God accepts us in Christ and calls us to do good works. But those works are never the reason he accepts us. So when we fail and stumble, we can boldly come to him, repent, and get right back in the saddle. You want friends who have this effect on you so that they regularly encourage and refresh your faith (Romans 1:12).

Self-Sacrificing

Not that you should abuse it, but this quality of self-sacrificing goes hand in hand with loyalty. You want friends who don't just care about you when it's convenient but are willing to help you in a pinch. I lost track of how many times my friend Matt helped me move when I was in school. Whenever I hear or think of him now, I remember how generous he was, and it makes me want to be the same way.

Spiritually Challenging

You want friends who push you to go hard after God. Friends who challenge your thinking with insights they find in the Scriptures and who challenge your living by the example they set. I find that this quality is foundational for the others mentioned above. It is so important that when I find this quality in a friend, I work particularly hard to maintain that relationship because I want his or her impact on my life.

Respectful

I had a friend named Zach for a couple of years. We both enjoyed tennis, basketball, skiing, Ping-Pong, and pool, so we had plenty of choices for when we got together. Zach had a very challenging personality—he liked to push people to do the right thing, the best thing. The only problem was that his intensity wasn't tempered with empathy, warmth, or good listening skills. I found myself increasingly on edge around him, as if I was always on the defensive, being pressured to do or say things a certain way, lest he jump all over me.

Good friends are respectful, especially when they challenge or disagree with you. They listen to the flow of your perspective and can accurately represent it. They're not dismissive or demeaning. Instead, they sharpen you and make you stronger, even if you occasionally agree to disagree on relatively minor issues. They are also understanding and supportive of your other commitments, wanting you to be fruitful and happy in all areas of your life.

BACK TO INTENTIONALITY

If you want these kinds of friends, then *be* this kind of friend. Don't wait for others to initiate. Get the ball rolling. Those who share your values and priorities will be drawn to you like a magnet. In addition, periodically take stock of your relationships. Which ones are promoting godliness and excellence in your life? Are there certain people you need to move away from because they're having a bad influence on you? Are there people you'd like to spend more time with and go deeper with? What do you plan to do about it? It may sound uncomfortably forced and fake to analyze your friendships like this. But whenever we say yes to developing one relationship or set of relationships, there's a bunch of other relationships we're not developing. All choices represent limitations: When we choose X, we don't choose Y. If you spend all your time hanging out with your teammates just because it's easiest, there are other people you won't really get to know. Sometimes the good is the enemy of the best. We miss out

Be the kind of friend you want to have, and go after those friends who spur you on to live full throttle for Christ. Ten years from now you'll be happy you did.

on the best opportunities because we're doing things that are merely good. It's true of activities, and it's true of relationships. Be intentional with your friendships. Be the kind of friend you want to have, and go after those friends who spur you on to live full throttle for Christ. Ten years from now you'll be happy you did.

FRIENDSHIPS CAN NEVER BE FORCED

Having stressed the importance of intentionality, it's important to also recognize that friendships can never be forced. We live in an amazingly interconnected world. If you know someone's name, chances are you can contact them somehow (e.g., Facebook). And we attempt to maintain so many more relationships than we did even ten years ago. Social media makes this possible, and by and large it can be very helpful and a lot of fun. A friend of mine just got laid off from his job. He'll probably find his next job not through randomly responding to an employment ad but through the expansive network of relationships that technology has enabled him to maintain. We live in a world where our connections to people often translate into a greater amount of social or professional opportunities.

And that reality presents a unique challenge. With more relational connections occurring in and around our lives, the chances for overload increase. We can only relate so much. Our relationships work when both participants mutually accept these constraints and the amount of access they have to each other. The problem arises when Megan wants

Amanda as a close friend, but Amanda is too busy or uninterested to have anything more than a casual connection. The more Megan presses, the more Amanda is repelled. The principle here is that we can never force ourselves on others. All we can do is seek to serve them, to present a part of ourselves that would encourage or help or attract them. If they feel that we constantly need them, they will probably be repelled. Proverbs 25:17 says, "Let your foot be seldom in your neighbor's house, lest he have his fill of you and hate you."*

All we can do is seek to serve [our friends], to present a part of ourselves that would encourage or help or attract them.

When someone we want to connect with fails to reciprocate, it's always disappointing. But that's a chance worth taking. We need to be understanding if he or she simply doesn't have the bandwidth. Better to keep the connection at the casual or acquaintance level than burn the bridge by pushing too hard.

DIFFERING CAPACITIES FOR FRIENDSHIP

Speaking of limitations, how many "BFFs" can we have? That may depend on our temperament. There are various personality assessments out there (StrengthsFinder, Myers-Briggs Type Indicator, etc.). Some are quite detailed, but a category that's helpful here is the extrovert-introvert continuum. In

---

* The other rarer but also more unhealthy possibility is that they'll develop a need for you to need them—a "savior" mentality, which makes them want you to keep coming back to them. That, too, will poison the relationship.

short, an extrovert tends to find energy in the company of others, processes a high volume of information externally (thinking out loud), and actively maintains a wide variety of interests. Introverts, by contrast, tend to restore their energy through solitude, process information internally (thinking or perhaps writing it out before attempting to speak with others about it), and prefer depth in a few interests to breadth in a large variety of areas.

These differences extend to the way we manage relationships. Adam McHugh explains in his book *Introverts in the Church: Finding Our Place in an Extroverted Culture*:

> *Introverts tend toward high degrees of intimacy in our relationships, which we usually have fewer of than extroverts. Introverts are rarely content with surface-level relationships and do not generally consider our acquaintances to be friends. We may find small talk to be disagreeable and tiring. Because we prefer to spend time in one-on-one interactions, rather than group socializing, our relationships can run deeper.[2]*

Some of you will thrive in the college dorm environment, where there always seems to be something going on. Others may find the constant barrage of people to be overwhelming at times. As you develop your relationship network, it's good to know yourself and the effect that the stresses of life and people have on you. Those of you who are more bent toward needing solitude and contemplation will want to take steps to make sure you get it, as it is not always easy to come by in communal living situations. When you have a say in the matter, select your roommates and apartment mates with care. Make sure that you can be honest with them and that they will respect how you manage your soul and body, just as you'd want to give them both the space and the interaction that would most bless them.

RELATIONSHIPS WITH FACULTY

Before addressing the idea of faculty as mentors, I want to give some general thoughts on how to best interact with professors. These tips also apply to employment supervisors and other people who have seniority over you.

One of Jesus' parables reads this way:

> *When you are invited by someone to a wedding feast, do not sit down in a place of honor, lest someone more distinguished than you be invited by him, and he who invited you both will come and say to you, "Give your place to this person," and then you will begin with shame to take the lowest place. But when you are invited, go and sit in the lowest place, so that when your host comes he may say to you, "Friend, move up higher." Then you will be honored in the presence of all who sit at table with you. For everyone who exalts himself will be humbled, and he who humbles himself will be exalted. (Luke 14:8-11)*

Q: *Do you see a correlation between the time students spend visiting with a professor and their academic performance?* —JOSHUA, RECENT GRADUATE, English/Philosophy

A: To a degree, yes. The more time a student spends discussing course content with me, the better he or she generally does over time. I think other professors also find that to be true.

In more cynical moments, professors sometimes commiserate that if they hold a review session for a test, it seems that the students who most need to be there are absent. The sad truth is that the absolute lowest performing students who fail courses sometimes don't do the work or seek help until it's far too late.

There are a couple of other interesting effects I've observed: Asking and answering questions in class, even if the answers are incorrect, correlates with higher academic performance. I think there's something in the act of expressing your ideas out loud and having verbal back and forth that strengthens learning. It's also true that a great way to learn something is to teach it to someone else. Sometimes in class I call on a student to answer another student's question. Those afraid to risk failure seldom have to face success.

Chain of command is important in the academic world: undergraduate student, graduate student, postdoctoral fellow, adjunct, lecturer, assistant professor, associate professor, full professor. Taking the lowest seat makes sense because, quite frankly, that's where you are right now. It's also the principle of Romans 13:7: "Pay to all what is owed to them: taxes to whom taxes are owed, revenue to whom revenue is owed, *respect to whom respect is owed, honor to whom honor is owed*" (emphasis added).

Do not presume a place of status in your relationships with professors or with anyone in a position of authority or seniority over you. Give the respect and honor that is due them, even if you disagree with them and even if you don't like them. Don't act like you're "entitled." Let your work speak for itself, and be very reticent to toot your own horn.

That doesn't mean that you can't ask for help—for a letter of recommendation or leads on jobs—or that you can't express disagreement with their opinions. But always do so from the "lowest place" at the table. That is, with an attitude that says, "I know you've studied longer than I have, and you've received academic recognition I have not yet earned. But I still think that when you said X, you may not have been accounting for Y. I'd love to understand this better." Most professors love to talk and debate, so they'll eat up that sort of thing. But don't assume they owe you something extra. That's a sure way to get on their bad sides.

SIGNS OF A BAD PROFESSOR

Most professors are fairly decent at what they do, but there really are some bad apples out there. It's good to ask around about professors before you sign up for classes with them, especially if you have a choice on which professor to take for a course.

Never ask another professor, "Is Dr. Seymour a good teacher?" We'll never answer that question except by saying yes. To do otherwise would be unprofessional and would jeopardize our relationships, because we know it would spread like wildfire and potentially on public forums.

So who else can you ask? You could ask your friends, but take what they say with discernment. Prioritize the feedback of those who have actually taken a class from the professor in question; the others are just going off hearsay. Second, listen carefully to how your friends formed their judgments. What didn't they like? Just because he was tough doesn't mean he was bad, and just because he was easy doesn't mean he was good. Here are some of the key, early warning signs of a bad teacher. Catch on to them fast enough to drop the class:

A vague syllabus

If it's very short, unspecific, and says something like "We'll figure it out as we go along," then you *know* the prof is clueless. He should know which sections of the textbook he'll be covering, how you'll be graded, and roughly how the class times will be structured.

Poor communication skills

If your friends tell you the professor could not give clear explanations about the course content, that's bad. She should know how to communicate her stuff. Former students may not have fully understood the material, but the professor should not only know it, but be able to sound like she knows it. If she's confused, you'll really be confused.

Boring classes

Being boring is not the worst trait a professor can have, but it's definitely not good. We're not all stand-up comedians, but professors should be personable and warm, and you should sense that we care. The more we hold your attention, the more you'll be engaged, and the better you'll do in the course. You will probably have a sense of a prof's personality within the first two weeks.

Bad relationships with their student researchers

Graduate students are like indentured servants. They work for a professor who advises them as they pursue a master's or PhD degree. Some of them have wonderful experiences; for others it's an absolute nightmare. Some professors assume they can push around their graduate students to the nth degree because the students generally are stuck. Complaining only makes things worse, and switching advisers and projects is a major hassle over which they lose a lot of time—time during which they could have graduated and actually started making some real money. I have friends who literally took one to two years longer to graduate just because of adviser problems. If a professor has a bad reputation from most of his students, he may be a great lecturer, but you're advised to stay away from him as a person.

As I noted earlier, there's a chain of command even among faculty; there are adjuncts, lecturers, assistant professors, associate professors, and full professors. The last three are all equal in the sense that they have their own offices and generally the same level of availability to students. On the other hand, lecturers and adjuncts tend to share offices and have less availability for students. Quite honestly, they are paid way too little and often have two or three jobs (possibly teaching at several different schools) just to make ends meet. So don't be too hard on them. They are sometimes very good teachers, but I typically suggest taking classes from "regular" professors if you have a choice. Professors simply have more time than adjuncts to put into their courses. Oh, and if you need a reference letter from an adjunct, get it right away because adjuncts often don't stick around for long. On the other extreme, if you take a class from a really famous professor, you might be inspired and have fun listening in class, but you'll probably have a hard time getting a hold of your professor outside class as he or she will often be out of town.†

---

† For other advice along these lines, a helpful book is *Lecture Notes: A Professor's Inside Guide to College Success* by Philip Freeman (New York: Ten Speed Press, 2010).

RELATING TO PROFESSORS

Christian universities tend to require that their faculty be Christians. Some Christian institutions are more doctrinally or denominationally narrow than others, so your faculty may or may not come from your particular faith tradition. Either way, Christian faculty are often willing to bring students into their personal lives and their walks with God, but you will likely need to initiate. If you do, professors may not be as available as you would like, given how many demands we have upon our time, but most of us would be honored to connect with you on a deeper level and be there for you if you ever want our advice.

Christian students in secular universities sometimes wonder to what extent they can learn from the advice of secular professors. I know I did. In fact, my first instinct was to not seek guidance from them. But others helped me reflect on the examples of Joseph and Daniel in the Old Testament. Both were in environments that were hostile to their faith in God. Like Christians at many secular universities, they were in the minority, yet through their diligence each earned the favor of those outside their faith tradition. This favor led to their promotions (Genesis 39:2; Daniel 1:20).

We need to remember that even though Christians are the recipients of God's saving grace, everyone benefits from what we call God's *common grace* (Psalm 145:9, 15-16; Matthew 5:44-45; Acts 14:16-17). The blessings of life, talents, skills, and employment all come from God, whether

Q: *No one likes a suck-up or brownnoser, so how can I invest in my professors and try to get advice from them without kissing up or looking like a teacher's pet?*

—LUKE, FRESHMAN, Worship Arts

A: Don't overestimate this danger. Like anyone, professors genuinely appreciate students taking interest in us or our work.

Be attentive in class. Approach the professor afterward about something from the lecture that sincerely interested you. Ask about things you got wrong on a recent test—but not to get points back, just to understand it better. Ask about his or her experiences. Invite your professor to an event your academic club is organizing. My classmates and I used to invite our professor, Dr. Geische, to play volleyball with us in the gym. He often came—and he was a terrific player. At smaller colleges, professors are generally more open and have more time for these kinds of interactions. At larger schools, you'll probably need to rely more on seminar courses and professional organizations.

If you do these things with honorable intentions, don't worry if some of your classmates think you're brownnosing. They think that because they can't imagine any other reason to invest in a professor, and in doing so, they're (inaccurately) projecting their immaturity onto you.

people recognize and thank him for them or not. Your non-Christian professors are in all likelihood extremely intelligent, gifted individuals from whom you can learn a great deal.

But there's more. Because we all bear God's image, common grace includes an innate desire to cultivate and help others, just as God, at his core, is a life giver and sustainer (1 Timothy 4:10). Nonreligious parents (usually) care about their kids and are willing to make sacrifices for them. Likewise, secular professors (usually) care about their students and are willing to advise them and write letters of recommendation for them, even though they've got a thousand other things on their plates.

What's the point? Most professors out there have chosen to pursue academic careers because they want to propagate knowledge and help the rising generation become skilled in a particular branch of learning for which they have a passion. In most cases, your history professors, Christian or otherwise, truly want to help you excel in history. Now, they may also mock the God of the Bible, and they may, out of prejudice or ignorance, regard the biblical record as unhistorical and unreliable. So you do have to be on your guard. But if you're discerning, you can pick the flowers of truth and beauty that fall from their lips, while pulling the weeds of their God-belittling worldview.

In my freshman year, my writing improved tremendously due to the influence of my philosophy professor and the director of my college's honors programs, both of whom were not Christians. But each was passionate about his discipline.

I learned not to complain about their feedback, but to learn from it. And to this day I am grateful for their kindness to me.

Some Christian students assume that any serious criticism of their work is purely a result of religious discrimination. In fact, they may simply be doing low-quality work.‡ Especially if you're a Christian at a non-Christian school, be very hesitant to claim ill-treatment as a result of your faith. Let's say you get a bad grade on an essay in which you quote a Bible verse and explain how it influenced your decision making, or a philosophy paper in which you explain why you believe in God. That happened to me a couple of times. You start to wonder, *Would I have gotten a higher grade if I hadn't mentioned the Bible, God, or Christianity? I know my professor is either an atheist or agnostic based on what's he's shared in class, so does he just think I'm an idiot?*

Please don't *assume* a bad motive on the part of the professor. Go humbly to him or her and ask for help on how to do better. Give the benefit of the doubt. A professor is generally willing to spend time strengthening your skills if you have a respectful, gracious demeanor that acknowledges his or her abilities and experience rather than an arrogant disposition that is simply looking to trap him or her into giving you a higher grade. If you're at a large university, keep in mind that

‡ Other Christians overreact in a similar way. Not wanting to be conformed to the pattern of this world (Romans 12:2), they minimize the value of academics, giving larger priority to Christian relationships and campus fellowship organizations. When I was in college, some friends and I went through a phase when we would have long, far-reaching discussions on spirituality and the Bible instead of doing our homework. It somehow felt more God honoring. But in reality we were being poor stewards of our academic responsibilities.

a teaching assistant (a graduate student in many cases) may have read your essay, not your professor.

Although Christians are sometimes unjustly treated in academia, we should never conclude this is happening without clear evidence. And when we *do* explicitly present our faith, we should always do so with humility and gentleness, not arrogance and hostility (2 Timothy 2:24-26). Both a lack of respect for academic excellence and arrogant, caustic presentations of our faith set a bad example for others and make a poor witness to Christianity. Moreover, they create bad memories that stick firmly in the minds and hearts of non-Christian professors and students, often inoculating them from developing an interest in Jesus Christ.

> When we do explicitly present our faith, we should always do so with humility and gentleness, not arrogance and hostility.

There is nothing un-Christian about loving God with all your mind and pursuing academic excellence. On the contrary, Christianity should make us diligent students, and down the road, faithful employees, good neighbors, and exemplary citizens in any religiously diverse community (Titus 2:11-12; 3:1-2; Romans 13:1-2). It's good to remember passages like Colossians 3:23 (NLT), which instruct us to "work willingly at whatever [we] do, as though [we] were working for the Lord rather than for people."

Lastly, take advantage of chances to get to know good professors. Some large universities have special seminar courses that have small class sizes. If you're part of a professional organization, invite faculty to some of your events, like dinners. At smaller schools some faculty invite their classes to their homes for a meal at the end of the semester. And use office hours. Don't be shy. Ask professors what interests them and how they chose their field. Or ask them what they're working on. Professors tend to be on the introvert side of the spectrum, but once you get us talking, we can be hard to stop.

CONCLUSIONS

Relationships matter. A lot. Who you choose as your friends and mentors will permanently shape who you become. If you walk with the wise, you'll become wise. Long after you've forgotten much of the content of your courses, who you've rubbed shoulders with will continue to profoundly impact you. Be thoughtful and intentional about your relationships, especially about who you draw in to your circle of close, personal friends.

In giving of ourselves to others, we gain empathy, maturity, emotional strength, and a wider capacity to love and connect, to enter the sorrows and joys of others.

Great relationships have a way of pushing us out of ourselves and allowing us to experience, on perhaps a small scale, what it means to find our lives by losing them: In giving of ourselves to others, we gain empathy, maturity, emotional strength, and a wider capacity to love and connect, to enter the sorrows and joys of others. These qualities will not only enable you to experience greater levels of happiness throughout your life, they'll make you emotionally intelligent—able to deeply impact others for their eternal good. Emotional and relational skills are crucial to your fruitfulness in God's Kingdom.

DISCUSSION STARTERS

1. How intentional have you been in seeking out quality close friends at college?

2. Are you in any relationships now that bring you down or pull you away from God? What do you plan to do about it?

3. List the names of two close friends and the character qualities you most admire about them. How do they help you love God more?

4. Can you identify some people you'd like to get to know more? Write down a few low-key action steps to get the ball rolling.

5. Some students never speak to their professors except to complain or to ask for letters of recommendation. How would you characterize your relationships with professors? Can you identify one or two you'd like to know more or from whom you'd like to receive some form of professional or personal advice?

COMMON MISTAKE #4:
Distorting Dating and Romance

> *Thrive Principle: Attract the Right Kind of Person*

Guy-girl relationships in college can be wonderful or confusing, representing amazing opportunities or huge dangers. They can be the crucible in which you discover a lifelong bond that brings you love, joy, and rock-solid stability, or an arena marked with heartbreak, regret, and gut-wrenching loneliness. Do I have your attention?

Perhaps more than any other area we've discussed in this book, the stakes are high when we're talking about dating and sexuality. You're playing for keeps here. You can change your major. You can find new friends. But the patterns you develop in the way you think and interact with the opposite sex can cause you lifelong problems. You will reap what you sow (Galatians 6:7). While God's grace, forgiveness, and power to change are clearly available, it's better to avoid the painful discipline of God and the consequences of sin and to experience instead the sweet blessings of living in a way that glorifies him.

But you don't just want to avoid overtly sinful activity with regard to the opposite sex (like sleeping together). You also want to stay clear of attitudes and actions that just aren't wise or helpful. You want to *thrive* in your guy-girl relationships by charting a course that most honors God and others while bringing you deep joy and happiness.

> It's better to avoid the painful discipline of God and the consequences of sin and to experience instead the sweet blessings of living in a way that glorifies him.

Think of your future for a moment. It may not be something you'd comfortably admit in public, but *most* if not all of you want to experience a high level of emotional and/or physical intimacy with a member of the opposite sex. *That* desire can lead you into trouble, or it can lead you toward the altar (as in the marriage altar). Why's that? Because God made all three to go together: emotional intimacy, physical intimacy, and marriage (Hebrews 13:4; Proverbs 5:15-23).

THE DESIRE FOR INTIMACY IS MEANT TO DRIVE US TO MARRIAGE

Your desire for intimacy, sexual and emotional, was designed by God to drive you to marriage. For the majority of men and women throughout most of human history, entrance into adulthood and getting married went more or less hand in hand. But single adulthood is much more common in our day than it was even for our parents. To some extent, this trend is a by-product of an increasingly knowledge-based economy in which more people spend more time getting more education before they can land a well-paying job.

But the rise in single adulthood in our day is also a direct result of the delayed adolescence I touched on in the introduction and which I'll discuss more in chapter 5: Recent college grads often aren't ready or willing to take on adult commitments, one of which is making a lifelong promise to a particular man or woman. More so than previous generations, we've seen our parents' marriages fail and want to be careful before taking the plunge.

Other aspects of our society are similarly less stable; you probably know recent college grads who seem to switch jobs and sometimes even cities every few years. In fact, that's the norm: Each year, one out of every three Americans in their twenties moves. They experience more job changes than in any other period of life.[1] No wonder we don't settle down and marry: We're used to living with less permanence, and therefore we naturally prefer independence and flexibility, which includes staying unattached.

Yet that hasn't stopped us from seeking most of the benefits of marriage without the associated costs. Over nine out of ten American adults are sexually active before marriage,[2] and six out of every ten women under the age of twenty-four have *already* cohabited with a boyfriend, while two in every three will do so sometime in their twenties.[3]

Factoid

Over nine out of ten American adults are sexually active before marriage, and six out of every ten women under the age of twenty-four have already cohabited with a boyfriend, while two in every three will do so sometime in their twenties.

What about the desire to have children? In 2007, four out of every ten American children were born out of wedlock. Are these mostly careless teenage pregnancies? Nope—that only accounts for about half of them.[4]

But not Christians, right? Think again. We're not doing that much better. Just fewer than four out of every five *church-going, born-again* Christians who are currently dating someone are sexually involved in some way.[5] And one in every five abortions is committed by a woman who professes evangelical Christian faith.[6] So as Christians, we are not immune from seeking to separate sex and reproduction from marriage.

But marriage is more than just a chance to have sex and not feel guilty, or to have cute babies and raise them. It's an environment in which God molds us into his image by forcing us to address our selfishness and pride, which inevitably get revealed in an intimate, lifelong relationship. Marriage is a picture to the world of Jesus Christ's relationship with his bride, his church, his people (Ephesians 5:23-32). Of course, some people are particularly intended to live a life of singleness so that they can serve Christ with undistracted devotion (1 Corinthians 7:32-34). But those who believe God has called them to get married someday should make marriage a goal, just as we set other long-term goals, like earning degrees and achieving financial independence. To pursue the opposite sex apart from the consideration of marriage exposes us to sexual temptation and increases the odds that we'll fail to stay pure.*

Therefore, the objective—the goal—of your dating should be to see if the two of you should marry in the not-too-distant future.† In your dating, don't be *marriage averse*. If the person won't make a good mate, then they don't need to be your date.

In mentioning the danger of being marriage averse, I want to be careful. Some of you have (or will have) the opposite inclination: Your parents drop you off, and you're on the hunt from day one. You haven't known the person for two months, and you're mentally shopping for a wedding dress or thinking

> *If the person won't make a good mate, then they don't need to be your date.*

---

* I deal with these themes in more detail in a book I wrote called *With One Voice: Singleness, Dating and Marriage for the Glory of God* (Christian Focus, 2006) as well as an article I published called "A Balanced View of Singleness." The article is available here: http://www.boundless.org/2005/articles/a0002123.cfm.
† Of course, you might want to graduate before marrying; there are plenty of good reasons to do that. That said, some folks tie the knot before graduation, and it works out just fine for them. This is a wisdom issue that each prospective couple needs to consider.

about how you've met the woman of your dreams (yes, I've seen your Facebook status and pictures). Many of you, particularly freshmen, get too romantically involved too quickly. Though this tendency sometimes leads to happy marriages, it more commonly leads to inappropriate intimacy and burnout. So let's deal with this danger first.

DANGER ONE: LIVING FOR ROMANCE AND MARRIAGE

1. Getting romantically involved too quickly

Being suddenly joined at the hip to a "significant other" makes it harder for either of you to enjoy the college experience—being free to study, meet new people, and try out new experiences—because you're each tied to the other, even though you've hardly known each other.

This kind of relationship is emotionally consuming and can lead to sexual impurity, given how much one-on-one time you spend together and how little accountability you have, either because you haven't developed strong same-sex friendships, or because you've stopped investing in those friendships in order to spend virtually every waking hour with Mr. or Miss Wonderful. Compromises in personal purity standards often lead to guilt and regret hanging like a black cloud over the relationship, which then dies for lack of air.

It's easier to avoid being too intimate if you commit to getting to know men and women through natural avenues and in group settings like classes, church, student organizations, campus ministries, group outings, choir, intramural sports, mutual friends, or residence life activities. You can better evaluate character in these contexts than in one-on-one settings because you see not only how they treat you, but how they treat others whom they are perhaps less motivated to impress. You can naturally get a feel for how you two hit it off. Keep in mind that a romantic relationship is best pursued on the foundation of a strong friendship that develops naturally and in an unforced, unrushed context.

One of the problems with jumping too quickly into a romantic relationship is that you barely know the other person. The thrill is intense, so you end up spending gobs of time together because you *want* to know him or her. But the other problem is that you may not even yet know *yourself* that well. Where do you see yourself going in life? Is your relationship with God on firm ground? Have you transitioned to the academic demands of college? Why are you in this relationship? Do you want a boyfriend just for the status or the security you think it brings? Do you want a girlfriend just to stroke your ego?

2. Knight-in-shining-armor dating

Before you jump into a dating relationship, you need to take responsibility for your own Christian life so that you aren't looking for someone else to be for you what only God can be, or to provide the spiritual motivation that you haven't quite been able to muster. In other words, you need to *already* be growing in Christlikeness and pursuing your spiritual life with vigor. It's tempting to think that a godly boyfriend or girlfriend might be a sure ticket to spiritual growth, but the truth is that nobody can fight your temptations or develop spiritual muscles on your behalf (Proverbs 9:12; Galatians 6:3-5). Yes, a quality guy or girl will push you to be a stronger Christian. But there's a big difference between being challenged by your boyfriend's Christian commitment and living off it. Check yourself with this question: He may challenge me, but do I challenge him in return?

> Before you jump into a dating relationship, you need to take responsibility for your own Christian life so that you aren't looking for someone else to be for you what only God can be.

A godly man should only want to be in a relationship with a somewhat equally godly woman, and vice versa.‡ That said, there is a knight-in-shining-armor effect that's very real: A guy can easily fall for a "damsel in distress" because he "can really help her grow." Bad idea. She will probably pull you down or slow you down before you pull her up. By the same token, girls sometimes reason, "Oh, he's not a strong Christian yet, but I told him he had to come to church with me if he wants

---

‡ Note: I'm not saying that they must necessarily be Christians for an equal length of time. Let's say Tyler was raised in a Christian home and came to faith early in life. Ashley was saved through a campus ministry and two years later has become a vibrant, growing, stable, godly Christian. Tyler should not slight her because she's only been a Christian for two years. It's very possible that her experience of the transforming effects of the gospel could be equal to if not greater than his. (Think of the sinful woman who loved much because she was forgiven much—Luke 7:36-50.) Likewise, it matters less where someone has *been* than where they are *going*. That said, an issue that could come up for Tyler and Ashley down the road is how their expectations regarding marriage and family were shaped by perhaps markedly different families of origin. But that's no reason things couldn't work out for them.

to see me. He's really sweet. I know he'll come around." By God's grace, he might. But don't presume upon God's grace. The result is often just the opposite.

Guys, an overly dependent girl may make you feel like a knight in shining armor, but that's a bad foundation for a marriage and an unhealthy feeding of your ego—you start needing her to need you.

Girls, a weak boyfriend may feel better than having no boyfriend, but in the end it will be worse. Even if he doesn't divert you from your Christian faith, he won't strengthen you in it. And he'll be filling a gap in your life that a stronger guy can't be filling. One of the biggest problems with dating someone who's not marriage material is that it wastes time that could be spent with someone who truly might work out.

Never date someone who doesn't share your desire to live for God's glory. To do so will set up a competition between your love for Christ and your interest in your significant other, and something will inevitably give. The only person worth dating is someone who pushes you to be stronger in every area of your life—your relationship with Christ, your academics, and your other relationships and commitments. Likewise, an overly possessive girl or guy is a red flag, as it demonstrates insecurity or a lack of appreciation for other important aspects of your life.

3. Shopping for an MRS. degree

This one is less prevalent in our day, but it happens from time to time, especially at Christian and Bible colleges. The woman shopping for an MRS. degree may care more about that pursuit than about her classes, her major, and the development of her intellectual abilities. Happily, she looks forward to marrying as soon as possible. She wants to have plenty of time for children and figures her husband will provide for her. So why bother being a good student? She's better off biding her time and staying on the lookout for eligible men.

Before critiquing this mentality, we need to acknowledge that there is nothing wrong with a female college student wanting to be a wife and mother whose husband provides for her. These are God-given, biologically rooted desires, and it's foolish to ignore them. But be warned: For a woman to admit to such aspirations at secular universities will generally result in mockery and scorn. I wish it wasn't that way, but it really is.

Professors will think such a student is naive, selling out, and failing to reach her professional potential (especially if she is a strong student). Even at Christian colleges, there are lots of people who will counsel her to "get established in her career before settling down and starting a family." The problem with this advice is that, statistically speaking, marital options tend to decrease after graduation.[§]

[§] A great book on this issue is *What Our Mothers Didn't Tell Us: Why Happiness Eludes the Modern Woman* by Danielle Crittenden (New York: Simon & Schuster, 1999). Crittenden winsomely critiques the tendency of some feminist leaders to promote career over marriage to the detriment of the marital goals and aspirations of many women.

So if being a wife and mom are noble aspirations, what's the point of college? Well, as we'll discuss later, there is much more to college academics than getting skills for a particular job. If you study math, literature, speech, biology, philosophy, history, etc., you'll see more of God and the truth and beauty that pervade his created world.

If you're in college, one of the things God is calling you to do is develop your brain for *whatever* he has in store for you. Written and oral communication skills, analytical skills, math skills—all come in handy in a variety of environments, including home management and raising kids. Working hard in classes is also good for *character* development (not just for your brain), as those who are disciplined in one area tend to be disciplined in others. And it's presumptuous to *assume* that you'll get married, have children, and never need to earn income. Even in the best scenario, your husband could lose his job or become injured for a while, requiring you to enter the workforce. Things happen.

Last, there is nothing unfeminine about being intelligent and academically excellent in any or every discipline. In some conservative Christian circles, women are fearful that, if they're too competent, guys will be intimidated and won't pursue them. But if you're living for the glory of God, your overriding concern will be to develop and maximize the skills and gifts God gave you. Sure, some wimpy guys may be too chicken to pursue you, but that's no big loss. The more talented men will pursue you precisely because of your diligence, faithfulness, and capability. So shoot for the moon.

DANGER TWO: BEING MARRIAGE AVERSE

We've just looked at three ways that some college students overvalue romance and pursue relationships foolishly. The opposite danger is being needlessly marriage averse, and it also shows up in a variety of ways.

Some students pursue physical intimacy through the mutually abusive practice of "hooking up" or having "friends with benefits" (whose "benefits" aren't worth the costs); but they detach it from emotional intimacy or the prospect of marriage. Other students seem to do the opposite: They have emotionally intimate guy-girl friendships but claim the relationships are platonic and that there's nothing going on between them. A third group of students sabotage relationships with good potential by the mistaken idea that they need to find a "soul mate."

Let's look at each of these.

1. "Hooking up" and "friends with benefits"

The myth at the heart of the "hookup" and "friends with benefits" culture is that there is such a thing as "just sex."[¶] But you can't have "just sex" with someone else. Granted, many people find casual sex to provide an immediate thrill, but the heartache comes in the morning.[**] The more physical

---

[¶] This myth is closely related to the common secular university admonition to practice "safe" sex. "Safe" here means "safe from pregnancy or getting a sexually transmitted disease." There is no consideration of the emotional implications of giving your body to someone who has no permanent commitment to you.

[**] One research study indicated that 70 percent of college students report having engaged in intercourse with partners they did not consider romantic (S. S. Feldman, R. A. Turner, and K. Araujo, "Interpersonal context as an influence on sexual timetables of youths: Gender and ethnic effects," *Journal of Research on Adolescence* 9 (1999): 25–52). However, even according to secular researchers, "Depressive symptoms were also associated with engaging in casual sex" (C. M. Grello and D. P. Welsh, "No Strings Attached: The Nature of Casual Sex in College Students," *The Journal of Sex Research*, 43 (3) (August 2006): 255–267).

intimacy you have with another person, the more your heart becomes bonded to him or her. It feels awkward afterward because you *are* bonded to them, yet you either don't see that person again or he or she shows up for another session of mutual abuse, with no depth of emotional connection ever developing.

Women generally feel this disconnect more acutely than men, and they rightly feel cheated.[††] But neither derives a lasting benefit from this so-called friendship: Women feel degraded over time, and men increasingly learn to detach their libido from their soul, becoming less capable of experiencing true intimacy with a woman, let alone sacrificing their own interests to best honor and cherish her. Either way, it's not the best preparation for experiencing pure, selfless, open, and generous intimacy someday with someone you truly want to love for a lifetime. When the Bible teaches that we shouldn't have sex outside marriage (1 Thessalonians 4:3-8; Hebrews 13:4), it isn't just an arbitrary, thrill-killing prohibition designed to rob Christ followers of legitimate enjoyment. It's an important and practical guideline meant to secure our greatest happiness.

[††] For those of you interested in this subject, there is a wealth of research that has been done on it. For example, the Institute for American Values did a study in 2001 called *Hooking Up, Hanging Out, and Hoping for Mr. Right: College Women on Dating and Mating Today*. It shows that women suffer more obvious and immediate emotional scarring from the mutually abusive practice of casual sex. Another good resource is the book *Unprotected* by Miriam Grossman (Penguin, 2007). Grossman, a psychologist, draws connections between the practice of sexual promiscuity on college campuses and the rising number of mental health issues (like depression and anxiety) reported on those campuses, particularly by women. The negative effects for men are, in my view, equally real, though perhaps less immediately apparent.

2. "Platonic" relationships

Can a guy and girl enjoy a strong, strictly platonic relationship? You know, do things one-on-one, be really good friends, bare their hearts to one another, but not have the slightest romantic interest in each other? The term *platonic relationship* comes from Plato, the philosopher. Plato believed that we humans are preexisting souls encapsulated in physical bodies upon birth. So our bodies are not a part of our essence in the way that our souls are. The soul of Mike can be best friends with the soul of Amanda, but their bodies be completely absent from the friendship. So Mike and Amanda will remain "just friends." Neither will ever develop a romantic or sexual interest in the other.

Does that happen in real life? From our own experiences, and from the romantic comedies that play on this theme, we know things normally go another way. Why? Because our souls are not compartmentalized from our bodies; we are emotional-physical-spiritual beings. Emotional intimacy is a prelude to physical intimacy, and in marriage these go together, each promoting the other.

So can a girl be friends with a guy? Certainly. Just don't pretend that you're compartmentalized. If you aren't interested in pursuing the possibility of marriage with him, keep the emotional intimacy at bay. A good way to avoid getting too emotionally entangled with a guy is, in my view, to cut down or cut out one-on-one time with him. You might not think of it as a "date," but he might, even if he tells you

Q: *Do you have any advice on how to simply be friends with the opposite sex without sending the message that there inherently needs to be something more to it than that?* —KELVIN, JUNIOR, Physics/Engineering

A: I'd recommend spending time in groups rather than one-on-one. If you ask someone of the opposite sex to do an activity just with you, it raises suspicions about your intentions. And let's face it: Such suspicions are often reasonable. After all, you've singled that person out. If you only want to be friends, you're best off getting to know the person through group meals in the cafeteria, intramural sports, dorm activities, church events, etc.

On occasions when you do find yourself alone with the person, avoid suggesting through your words, tone, or gestures that he or she is somehow special to you or that you are expecting a certain level of relational constancy or emotional connection from that person. For example, "You haven't called me this week" could suggest that he or she *should* have called you.

Avoid highly personal, sensitive topics that tend to uniquely bond a man and a woman. Avoid or minimize physical expressions of affection like hugging, which could be innocent to you but highly meaningful to him or her. Be respectful to the fact that he or she might be more sensitive than you. Avoid physical intimacy or any sort of "friends with benefits" mind-set.

otherwise. And if you *are* interested in pursuing the possibility of marriage with him, let him know that your feelings for him have grown and that at this point he needs to either "man up" and declare his intentions and set a marriage-oriented direction for the relationship, or free your heart and ultimately your time for another guy.

3. The myth of the "soul mate"

You only need to find one quality person, but is there just *one right person* out there? Should you be looking for a "soul mate"? Wikipedia defines the term *soul mate* as a "person with whom one has a feeling of deep and natural affinity, love, intimacy, sexuality, spirituality, and/or compatibility." The idea is that a man meets a woman and the feeling is so intense that they just *know* that each is "*the one.*" Nobody else will suffice. Our job is to scour the globe until we have this sort of lightning-bolt experience of connection.

There are several problems with this concept:

a. It places too much emphasis on the emotions.
Emotions are great when we feel good, and they stink when we feel bad. But in neither case are they reliable, inerrant indicators of what's objectively true or best. I may walk out of a math test and feel terrible, but I may have gotten a high grade. Believing that there is just one individual in the whole world for me and that I'll "feel it" when I connect with him or her lends huge credibility to an aspect of my being that

is prone to overpower and mislead me. In fact, it's the same faulty reasoning used by many adults, Christians included, who abandon their spouses for some new flame who "makes them feel so alive." They just "know" a relationship change is "right" for them. Yet feelings deceive, both before and after marriage.

b. The initial emotional thrill eventually wanes.
When Samantha met David over the summer, she felt a huge burst of energy. They had great conversations at work. Since they were both interning with the same accounting firm, they got to see each other all the time. Samantha remembers when she first discovered that David was a Christian. It all just clicked; he was attractive, sweet, *and* a good Christian. Was this God or what? She hadn't even been looking for something to happen. As the fall approached, David made plans to go back to his college about two hundred miles away from Samantha. He promised to call and text her often, and at first he did. But when mid-term exams rolled around, both Samantha and David found themselves immersed in their respective campuses. It took more discipline and intentionality for them to connect, and they did so less often. Samantha's initial excitement began to die. David seemed so far away. Maybe he really wasn't *the one* for her?

Samantha is thinking about breaking up with David, for no other reason than a decrease in the initial thrill. But it's very common for that first rush of excitement to fade: The relationship now takes work, whereas before it was almost effortless. Does that mean David is wrong for her? Not necessarily. Placing too much emphasis on an emotional high is a double-edged sword: *It can lead you into a bad relationship and out of a good relationship.* Better to use both your heart and your head.

c. It is overly idealistic.

The more you get to know a special guy or girl, the more you will encounter their flaws. It should not surprise you that your boyfriend or girlfriend isn't perfect and that some shortcomings (and occasional bad breath) may take a few months to reveal themselves. What you'll need to decide is if these flaws are so great that they disqualify him or her as a life partner for you. It's a wisdom issue.

Beware that just as some people are so eager to get hitched that they lower their standards, others are so scared of a permanent commitment that they raise them to unreasonable levels. They fear not only commitment, but the possibility of missing out on someone better. An overly idealistic notion that there is just one right person out there leads to break-ups over nothing and later wondering why all the "good ones" are taken.

Who we marry, provided he or she is a growing Christian, is a matter of Christian liberty. We don't need to scour the globe. God works through many means, and college gives us a chance to meet

Just as some people are so eager to get hitched that they lower their standards, others are so scared of a permanent commitment that they raise them to unreasonable levels.

lots of eligible Christians. If you like the person, and the relationship promotes godliness and excellence in your life and your potential mate's, then that individual is a perfectly viable catch.

BECOMING AND ATTRACTING THE RIGHT KIND OF PERSON

Okay, so I've warned you about a few ways people pursue romance too quickly, too thoughtlessly, and with insufficient time spent developing personal maturity or laying the foundation of a solid friendship. I've likewise warned you about a few ways people needlessly avoid the pursuit of marriage.

So what's the right way? While I believe that there is no one prescribed, biblical method for pursuing a spouse, there are a few solid, timeless principles. The key is to *become* the right kind of person so that you *attract* the right kind of person.

1. Use male/female friendships to grow in character and relational maturity.

Make an effort to be in community with godly members of the opposite sex, even if you have to go out of your way. You'll make great lifelong friendships. One of them may later become your wife or husband.

I mentioned the dangers of "platonic" relationships, but there is plenty of room for healthy interaction with the opposite sex, particularly in group settings. Use these opportunities to hone your relationship skills. Ask good questions,

Q: *You mention that college is a convenient place to find a spouse. From my experience, however, being in a relationship takes so much focus and attention that I find myself paying less attention to things like my schoolwork and my relationship with God. It's for this reason that I am explicitly seeking to remain single for a while in college. What are your thoughts on this?* —KATE, FRESHMAN, Creative Writing

A: You're right—a significant other can be a major time commitment and distraction, especially in the early years of school. College is a unique season for discovering your vocation and preparing academically for that work. It's also a time to establish functional independence. And it's often easier to develop healthy habits of work and life management without someone else in the picture.

That said, there are many ways to have healthy friendship-level relationships in college—to keep the relational intimacy at bay and just enjoy getting to know people through your everyday activities. In this process, should a particular guy or girl appeal to you as a potential spouse, I would caution against two dangers: going too fast (risking burnout) and overlooking the relationship because life is too busy. Life will always be too busy, especially for ambitious, capable students. Ask yourself if this person helps you promote godliness and excellence in your life. If so, that person doesn't have to be a distraction; he or she can be a vital and meaningful part of your college life and perhaps the rest of your life.

and listen empathetically. Be observant. Look for ways to graciously express care and concern without being invasive. Show respect and give praise. Part-time jobs, campus ministry activities, and study groups give you lots of chances to practice being sensitive and showing friendly, non-romantic affection for fellow students of the opposite sex.

2. Embrace the biblical paradigm (Genesis 1–2; Ephesians 5:22-32).

God's plan is for husbands to love their wives as Christ loved the church—in an intentional, sacrificial, initiating fashion. God's plan is for wives to nurture and affirm the loving leadership of their husbands, complementing and completing them, so that together they stand far stronger than either of them could separately.

Don't just date someone who is physically attractive but morally or spiritually questionable. And don't just date someone to pass the time. Be intentional. Think about what you'd want in a husband and father or wife and mother. Guys, cultivate a mix of toughness and tenderness, self-restraint and boldness, quiet confidence and humility. Don't wait for women to take all the initiative. Even in your circle of friends, look for ways to cultivate servant leadership, taking the lead for the sake of blessing those around you, not merely getting your own way. Be aware of how your signals are picked up by women; they are usually attuned to such things. Be intentional and consistent. Don't tell her you're not interested but then act like you are. And don't "fish" to see if she's interested in you before you state your interest in her—that's passive and cowardly, and the smarter girls will see right through it.

Girls, cultivate a disposition of secure, friendly disinterest. Meaning, keep your emotions in check and don't show all your cards. If you want him to take the initiative, give him a chance to do so. Guys value what is more difficult to attain, that which represents a challenge. Let him work to earn your trust and ultimately your heart. If you dress merely to attract guys to your body, don't be surprised if you lure a string of shallow, weak, and overly sexualized males. They're not there for your conversational skills. By contrast, a combination of internal and external beauty, combined with modesty and discretion, attracts higher-quality guys. Think about the kind of man whose character you'd want your children to emulate. Then become the kind of woman who would attract that kind of man.

3. There's no rush, but don't unnecessarily delay.

It's generally a good idea to take your first year to make a smooth transition to college, to form a variety of friendships, and to focus on your academics. You're a few years away from functional independence (which we'll discuss more in chapter 5), and there's no rush to get into a boyfriend-girlfriend situation, particularly if you're still discovering who you are and what you want to do academically. Let friendships develop naturally in the context of your regular activities and responsibilities.

Don't let the other person pressure you into moving too fast, spending too much time alone, discussing your future, or getting too intimate. You can get to know each other without having detailed, personally revealing conversations. Just say you're enjoying his or her company, but you'd like to slow things down a bit. Spending more time in groups or in public places will help. Steer your conversations toward less sensitive topics. If he or she seems uncomfortable with a more leisurely tempo or pressures or manipulates you, that's a red flag.

Having a "significant other" can be a time-consuming commitment (some compare it to taking an extra course!), but it doesn't *need* to be, especially in the earlier stages. Pace yourself with a realistic view of your life situation and personal maturity. It's reasonable that two seniors who come from towns five hundred miles apart might be trying to figure out whether they're right for each other more quickly than a pair of freshmen.

Young men sometimes ask me how quickly they should bring up the big conversational topics that keep the relationship moving toward engagement. I admire their question, since the broader culture in our day leans toward passivity among men, characterized by an unwillingness to commit and the desire to get as much "female benefit" for the least cost. But I usually respond by asking, "When would you like to propose, if all goes well?" If they say, "Oh, two years from now," my response is "Okay, then what's the hurry? Just enjoy getting to know each other and keep the pace reasonable. You're running a 10K, not a 50-yard dash."

Meet each other's families as opportunities present themselves, and just take things one day at a time. Look for how you influence her and how she influences you. Does she push you to love and serve Jesus more in all you do? Do you have that effect on her? Look for broad trends. When conflict or friction arises, be humble and seek to work through hurdles together. All marriages have their bumps in the road. Do you demonstrate humility, apologizing when you're wrong, or is your relationship characterized by trying to hide your mistakes and shortcomings while criticizing hers? Sure, you want to win her (or his) affection, but don't pretend to be someone you're not. At the same time, strive by God's grace to become who you should be.

About six to nine months before you would like to pop the question is a good time to work through significant issues such as marital expectations and roles, work/life balance, finances, children, church, in-laws, etc. To have cold feet in the last stages is not terribly uncommon. Seek input from older Christians you trust. Sure, there are legitimate reasons to break off the relationship at this stage, but discovering that your fiancé-to-be falls short of perfection is probably not a good one.

What are good reasons to break up? If you're determined to be a missionary in Afghanistan, and she wants nothing to do with that. If his idea of the family's church life means you would go to one church with the kids, and he would go to another church whose theology or style is more to his liking. Of course, some of this can be evaluated earlier in the relationship, depending on how much you both know about yourselves when you meet.

If the input of mature Christians you both trust confirms the character qualities you admire in each other; if you like spending time together and have a record of resolving conflict well; if you've discussed work/life role expectations and what marriage would look like; if you're ready to embrace functional independence and a new, permanent roommate, then don't wait for a voice from heaven to tell you she's the one. And if he puts a ring on your finger, you probably don't have to put out a fleece three times before you get back to him (Judges 6). What was the point of dating?

CONCLUSIONS

God made us male and female, and it'd be boring if he hadn't. Our physical and emotional desire for each other was meant to point us toward marriage. Don't try to grab the blessings without accepting the responsibilities: They were meant to go together, so things work best that way. We need to say no to the selfish, joy-defeating ways of the world and yes to God's plan for honoring one another as brothers and sisters in Christ. A godly wife or husband is a gift from God (Proverbs 18:22). May the God who withholds no good thing from those who walk uprightly bless you in his perfect time (Psalm 84:11).

DISCUSSION STARTERS

1. Which is a greater danger for you: living for romance and marriage or being too marriage averse?

2. How have your previous dating relationships (if any) gone? How did they start? How did they end? Looking back, what can you learn from these experiences?

3. How are you doing at becoming the sort of person that the kind of person you'd like to marry would want to marry? What are some areas in which you'd like to grow?

4. How are you doing at honoring members of the opposite sex?

5. Has this chapter challenged your attitude or motivation about dating or the opposite sex? If so, how?

COMMON MISTAKE #5:
Refusing to Grow Up

> *Thrive Principle: Become Independent of Mom and Dad*

MATT, ROB, BRITTANY, AND LAURA all graduated from college in the last few years. They each grew up in the Chicago area, and now they're all back living at home with their parents.

Matt's degree was in biology, but he's been painting houses for the last year as he considers a variety of graduate-school programs. He turned down a couple of full-time job offers in Wisconsin and Ohio because he was shocked at how little they were offering for entry-level positions. He figures a master's degree will get him more money.

Rob has a degree in accounting and was happy to get an internship when he graduated. The internship doesn't pay very well, so he's living at home as he saves up. He doesn't know what he'll do if he can't find a job when the internship ends in a couple of months, but at least his parents aren't bugging him about it.

Brittany studied English literature but isn't sure what she wants to do. She's always loved animals and is thinking about going to veterinary school. She's been working as a server at Applebee's for the last six months, her third job since graduating two years ago.

Laura, a business major, moved back home after graduating last year so that she could be closer to Matt. They've dated off and on, and she's hoping something serious might develop, but so far Matt seems ambivalent at best. In the meantime, she's been doing a bunch of odd jobs for her dad's business, but that's definitely not where her heart is. She wonders if she should move out, perhaps take a job as a flight attendant and see the world while she has a chance. But she's also nervous. She's not sure she's ready for independence.

You probably know friends or relatives like Matt, Rob, Brittany, and Laura. Truth is, none of them seem quite ready for independence. And they're not alone: A CollegeGrad.com survey of 2009 graduates found that nearly 70 percent of recent grads did not have jobs lined up when they graduated, and about four out of five moved back home.[1*] Depressed yet? Even before the recent economic slump, more college

---

* The trend may have since gotten worse. According to Twentysomething, Inc., a marketing and research firm based in Philadelphia, 85 percent of college seniors planned to move back home after graduation in May 2010. This percentage has risen steadily from 67 percent in 2006.

students have been taking longer to graduate, and longer to really find their niche and achieve financial independence. So after taking off their caps and gowns, they often move back in with Mom and Dad. Even if they get the jobs they want, they might not be able to afford to live on their own after all the debt they've accumulated in college or graduate school, or they're just not ready to take on the responsibility.

Many of us are close to our parents; we get along well and communicate frequently. So what's the problem? The problem is that some are so close to their parents that it may be harder to achieve what I'll call functional independence: the ability to "function" (balance a checkbook, pay bills, juggle social life with responsibilities, resolve conflict with bosses and coworkers) without the direct involvement of Mom and Dad.

THE CELL PHONE—WONDERFUL GADGET OR UMBILICAL CORD?

I didn't have a cell phone in college, so it took more effort to consult with my parents on classes, friends, conflict, or how to clean a ketchup stain off my shirt. Even though I used e-mail a lot, my parents didn't yet have a broadband Internet connection. To magnify the separation, my college in western New York was 650 miles away from my hometown Chicago suburb.

The result? After eighteen years of hardly ever being away from my dad and stay-at-home mom, it seemed as if I barely communicated with them for three months before going home for the first time at Thanksgiving of my freshman year. The four years of college would fly by, and only one summer found me living at home (internships took me elsewhere). I had to learn how to do laundry, clean (sort of), cook (barely), shop, balance my checkbook, handle a credit card, take care of my car, and pay bills. It wasn't always easy or smooth, and I definitely sought advice from my parents from time to time, but I developed functional independence if for no other reason than because I had to.

But today, cell phones allow you to call your parents at any moment. You can ask Dad for advice about dropping a class while walking to the class. You can call Mom in the cafeteria line to get her thoughts on the lunch menu. A lot of advice ends up getting dispensed through daily conversations about the mundane.

Factoid

How often do first-semester freshmen talk to their parents on cell phones? According to a study conducted by Barbara Hofer of Middlebury College, freshmen spoke with their parents an average of 10.4 times a week during the first semester—three times more often than they had expected to.[2]

It turns out that one in every three first-year students even receives *academic* assistance from their parents to the degree that observers wonder if the students or the parents are doing the learning. The evidence suggests that moms and dads today often blur the lines between helping with homework and doing it themselves. I've had good first-year students who turn in work with many careless math or spelling errors. I generally find this puzzling, since I know they're intelligent and capable. When I ask them why they don't look over their work more carefully before submitting it, they sometimes privately confess that it's harder to avoid such mistakes without Mom around to check their work for them.

Perhaps your parents call you—at both convenient and inconvenient times. I know a student who attends a Bible study near his college that is led by a friend of his family. If he has a major test and misses a week, his mom calls him to express her concern that he's abandoning his faith. I'm sure that sort of thing happened fifteen years ago, too, but it's more common today. Technology keeps us connected to our city, friends, and family of origin, which probably contributes to the high value we place on relationships, particularly with Mom and Dad.

Many are suspecting, however, that this same technology is delaying development in the college years by making it more difficult to establish personal identity and to take ownership of decisions.

Hara Estroff Marano writes,

Think of the cell phone as the eternal umbilical cord. One of the ways we grow up is by internalizing an image of Mom and Dad and the values and advice

they've imparted over the early years. Then, whenever
we find ourselves faced with uncertainty or difficulty,
we call on that internalized image. We become, in a
way, all the wise adults we've had the privilege to know.[3]

Think of it this way: Whereas one generation grew up leaving for the afternoon with a plan for doing X, Y, and Z, and having to adjust on the fly for unexpected mishaps or delays, another generation has grown up only needing to remember one thought: *If something happens, call.* And the very fact that you *can* immediately call may prevent you from developing critical-thinking and problem-solving skills. It's easier to make a phone call than to engage in deep reflection and critical thinking for yourself. Yet these are absolutely necessary steps for making hard decisions with incomplete information—a crucial real-world skill.

It's easier to make a phone call than to engage in deep reflection and critical thinking for yourself. Yet these are absolutely necessary steps for making hard decisions with incomplete information—a crucial real-world skill.

My wife remembers driving home from an evening event in high school, taking a wrong turn, and ending up on a long bridge that sent her in the wrong direction and to a bad place for a sixteen-year-old girl to be, especially alone. There was no cell phone, so she had to figure something out. Scary, yes, but formative. I had a similar experience as a college student when I was in a nasty car accident.

Interestingly, I had a similar car accident two years ago with a college student. She was about the same age I was when I had my first accident. (This time it wasn't my fault.) From inside her badly damaged car, blocking two lanes of traffic on a crowded freeway, her first call was not to AAA or the police or her insurance company. It was to her mom. They stayed on the phone for ten to fifteen minutes discussing in detail what happened in the accident and the resulting situation. She remained *on the phone with Mom* as a police officer helped her out of her car and as a pair of tow trucks began to clear the freeway.

I don't mean to rip on cell phones—they're useful in so many ways. Being close to parents is a wonderful thing. And who can argue with the principle of getting advice? But it's worth considering: Can being close to Mom and Dad be overdone? Can it delay personal development? And might some parents—with the best and most loving of intentions— exacerbate the situation by "checking up" on their kids too often, afraid to let go of their authority and control?

DELAYED ADOLESCENCE AND HELICOPTER PARENTS

In the Bible we see that children are commanded to obey their parents, but that all should honor their parents (Ephesians 6:1-3). We also see the pattern in Scripture of "leaving and cleaving" (Genesis 2:24). The natural order is to grow up, cease being a child, and create your own union whereby new children are produced and the race is propagated. Children are "a heritage from the LORD . . . like arrows in the hand of a warrior" (Psalm 127:3-4) to be released into the world to themselves live lives of impact. We belong to our parents for a season, though our friendship with them can last for a lifetime. The move toward graduation should involve transitioning from viewing parents as authority figures to be obeyed to colleagues and friends to be honored.

> *The move toward graduation involves transitioning from viewing parents as authority figures to be obeyed to colleagues and friends to be honored.*

Unfortunately, many college and post-college young adults in our culture remain in a state of delayed adolescence. They'd like to be relieved of the obligation to *obey* their parents, but they're not exactly willing to embrace adult responsibilities. So they graduate, move back home, and spend twenty to thirty hours a week on Facebook or going out with friends. They hope to remain in no-man's-land as long as possible, putting off any major commitments or responsibilities. At the same time, many parents, out of a sense—justified or unjustified—that their seventeen- to twenty-two-year-olds are not very mature, keep a grip on the reins and remain overprotective of their children during college and sometimes afterward. They cannot bear the possibility—or *probability*—of their children making occasional bad decisions, so they hover like helicopters.

In this manner, delayed adolescence and helicopter parents are problems that can feed one another. Some students have parents who want to see their course syllabi so they can

Q: *When would be a good time to call my parents for advice about a problem? How am I supposed to know if I should figure out a solution by myself or if I should consult my parents?* —GRACE, FRESHMAN, Finance

A: First, try to solve the problem on your own as best you can. Then, if the issue is significant, call to get your parents' perspective and see if you might be missing something. But don't ask them to make the decision for you. Ask them to help you think through the relevant issues so you can make a good decision for yourself. (This is assuming we're talking about an amoral decision here—a decision for which there is no clear biblical mandate.) Recognize that if you call your parents for everything, it will stunt your growth.

tell them which tests to study for and when. Others have parents who come to the rescue when they make bad decisions, like my friend Daniel, who racked up $15,000 in credit-card debt during his junior year. Rather than have him develop and implement a serious plan to pay it all back, his parents simply sighed, shook their heads, slapped him on the wrist, and paid the bill in full.

So whether it's delayed adolescence or helicopter parents, these phenomena really happen. Both lead to a "failure to launch" that has become common in our culture.

Let's be honest: Being totally responsible for oneself *can* seem scary. Perpetual play and endless entertainment, especially on your parents' dime but even on yours, can be very appealing. But it's ultimately dishonoring to both our parents and God. It distorts and strains the child-parent relationship by needlessly extending it. It prevents young adults from reaching their potential and making a difference in the world for God's glory.

The Bible doesn't have a category for "teenager." It only uses the terms *child* and *adult*. Actually, the term *adolescence* was invented in 1904 and comes from the Latin *adolescere*, meaning "to grow up."[4] It's a word we use for the stage between childhood and adulthood. For most of us, it includes the college years. But we were made to embrace adulthood. It's what needs to happen over time. You honor your parents most when you move toward it intentionally and without delay.

We read in Numbers 14:28-31 that, other than Caleb and

Joshua, none of the men over the age of twenty who came up from Egypt would enter the Promised Land. These men were wrong to share in their parents' lack of faith, and God judged them as adults (Numbers 13:1–14:38).[†] Meanwhile, those under twenty were apparently off the hook, as they were considered children. In our culture, eighteen is the age of legal adulthood. Though I know very few eighteen-year-olds who are totally ready for adulthood, given the importance of college or vocational training for financial independence, it seems that every eighteen-year-old should be demonstrating some independence and be on a clear path for totally embracing the responsibilities of adulthood as soon as is reasonably possible.

FUNCTIONAL INDEPENDENCE: AIM TO ACQUIRE IT OVER FOUR YEARS

A lot happens during the college experience. It would be wrong to expect a freshman to be as independent as a senior about to graduate. At the same time, there are steps that even freshmen should be taking. In fact, the shock is probably greatest the first year, because of the jump to living in a new environment. The change from high-school senior to college freshman is much bigger than the change from college freshman to college sophomore.

So what should the transition look like, practically? What things should you take ownership of immediately, and what things should you more gradually start to own? Especially if

---

† I'm indebted to Jim Newheiser and Elyse Fitzpatrick for this insight. They wrote to parents on this theme in a helpful book they coauthored, *You Never Stop Being a Parent: Thriving in Relationship with Your Adult Children* (P&R, 2010).

you're living away from home, I think you should immediately do the following:

Take responsibility for your time management.

For starters, your parents shouldn't remind you when to study, sleep, wake up, read your Bible, exercise, or eat. You'd be insulted if they did! They can encourage you in these areas if necessary, but the actual implementation and balance is something young adults must own from day one of college. Remember, whatever you don't rule will rule you. This is equally true for those still living at home, though in that case adult children need to be respectful of any household rules their parents deem appropriate (such as a curfew or a requirement to eat dinner with the family on occasion). Parents' house, parents' rules.

Among Christian colleges, dorms usually have rules regarding quiet hours, visitation hours (guys in girl buildings and vice versa), and curfews. Some or all of these limits are nonexistent at many secular campuses. Whatever the rules of your environment, the best government is self-government. The fruit of the Spirit is self-control (Galatians 5:22-24). Refer back to chapter 2 for some practical suggestions.

Take responsibility for your class schedule and choice of major.

You are responsible for what you do with the talents, interests, and skills that God gives you. Some parents have the philosophy that "every firstborn son in this family stud-ies medicine" or goes into the ministry or takes over the family business or must pursue an especially high-paying, lucrative career. Though more prominent in some cultures than others, that kind of thinking does not find biblical sup-port. God gifts people in different ways both in the church and in the society at large. You may need to humbly help your parents realize that you are not wired for whatever it is they think you should do. If that means forfeiting their financial support, so be it. Hopefully it won't come to that, but in extreme cases it might.

As I will discuss in the chapters on academics, you should strongly consider your parents' input. We aren't always the best judges of our talents and skills. We may think we're good at something that we're really not good at, or be better at something than we think we are: "In an abundance of counselors there is safety" (Proverbs 11:14). Your parents may be considering the full gamut of your desires in life; an academic path leading to $150,000 in debt could create strain on your wanting to be a stay-at-home mom a few years after graduation. Even in disagreement, it's important to

Some parents have the philosophy that "every firstborn son in this family studies medicine" or goes into the ministry or takes over the family business or must pursue an especially high-paying, lucrative career. Though more prominent in some cultures than others, that kind of thinking does not find biblical support.

maintain kindness and graciousness toward them.‡ But what you pursue must ultimately be your choice, as you alone will live with the consequences.

Take responsibility for your choice of friends.

In high school your parents may have set restrictions over which people you could spend time with. They may have seen you going in a bad direction and questioned (or outright limited) your choice of companions. It's inescapable that a companion of fools will suffer harm and that bad company ruins good morals (Proverbs 13:20; 1 Corinthians 15:33). Ideally, your parents worked with you in these matters, but perhaps they were more heavy handed, imposing rules without your buy-in. Either way, now is the time to start owning these decisions. Your parents can advise you, but you must ultimately decide whom you spend time with, how much time, and in what contexts. Especially if you're living away from home, your parents will have little ability to control this aspect of your life. You need to be led by internalized, godly priorities.

---

‡ If your parents aren't Christ followers, you may be wondering how to best honor them while maintaining ultimate allegiance to Christ. It's worth remembering that being Christians should make us more respectful, grateful, and considerate sons and daughters. We shouldn't act like snobs toward our parents, as if their lack of faith renders everything they say as worthless. Chances are, they still love you and want you to be happy. And chances are, they've known you long enough to identify possible blind spots and to be able to offer insightful feedback, though perhaps not on every topic. Hear them with discernment. On small matters, make concessions as expressions of honor and respect. But don't feel obligated to sacrifice scriptural imperatives on their behalf. Ultimately, your accountability is to God.

Take responsibility for your professional relationships.

Friends of ours employ a nineteen-year-old "handyman" (Brandon) from time to time. He attends a local college while living at home. Brandon does various odd jobs around their yard and minor things, such as oil changes, with their cars. A few times he's agreed to do a particular task only to have his mother send his employers (our friends) a last-minute message apologetically urging them not to require this task of Brandon. His mom gives various reasons, some of which are quite valid: The task is beyond his ability, or he has a big test coming up in school and just needs an extra week, or he's actually sick but embarrassed to tell them. Had our friends been aware of these concerns, they would have happily negotiated the work item with Brandon and come up with a mutually agreeable solution, even if that meant hiring someone else for a particular task.

But here's the problem: Brandon, *as an adult*, took on the responsibility. *He* gave his word. So *he* now has an obligation to keep his word or call his employer *himself*, explaining why he must be released of a duty he took upon himself (Proverbs 6:2, 5). Brandon's mother, by coming to our friends directly and privately, is actually circumventing the budding maturity and adult development of her son, who needs to learn to make wise choices, to keep his commitments, and to take responsibility for any shortcomings along the way.

Your parents should never insert themselves in your communication with your boss or coworkers. They should never negotiate the terms of your job or your salary. If you get a job offer and you don't like something in the job description, you need to respectfully raise the issue yourself. If you think a salary you are offered is low, you need to (yourself) respectfully ask for more.[§]

By extension, you should never have your parents call your professors to complain about your semester grades or exam scores. Now is the time to start learning to fight your own battles. And by the way, unlike high school, your professors are not legally able to discuss your grades with your parents unless you specifically signed a waiver granting them access to this information.

If each of the above is a responsibility to assume from day one, what areas of responsibility should you assume more gradually? While progressing through college, aim to do the following:

Grow in your ability to make wise decisions.

Good decision making requires critical thinking, recognizing complexity and nuance, considering your options in terms of their pros and cons, and assessing risk and uncertainty. Not all of these skills are required in every decision, but each of them is important.

In his excellent book *Age of Opportunity*, Paul David Tripp describes a situation in which his son Chad, while working

---

[§] It helps if you have data to back up your concern: "My friend Amanda has a similar job, and she makes three dollars more an hour than what you are offering. Here's her job description. It looks pretty similar to what you're asking me to do. Do you think you could please raise your salary offer to match what Amanda is earning? I'd really appreciate it. Thanks for considering my request."

a part-time job, was asked to do something he felt was both dangerous and outside his job description. The task would not have been explicitly sinful, but he felt uncomfortable doing it. He called his dad and asked if he could fax him the job description so they could discuss it. Mr. Tripp agreed. Over the phone it seemed Chad wanted his dad to decide for him. Dad resisted doing so, though there is nothing easier and more ego boosting than to show off one's wisdom by dissecting a situation and making a decision for someone else. Fathers, in particular, are wired to glory in their sons' respect, and therefore are especially vulnerable to spoiling a situation sent by God to develop their young adult sons' maturity.

But instead of telling him what to do, Mr. Tripp wisely reserved his remarks to asking questions and examining how his son was thinking. In the end, Chad was able to make his own decision and own the consequences.

This is the type of thoughtful decision-making skill that you should be moving toward. Most of the tough calls we end up facing are *amoral*—there is not a clear right answer, but instead a host of competing principles to be weighed, pros and cons to be evaluated, and a variety of possible outcomes to be considered. You'll need to learn critical thinking skills and to accept responsibility for whatever happens. You don't need your parents to make these decisions for you, but to ask good questions with you and to help you think of considerations you may be neglecting.

Grow in financial responsibility and independence.

Start off college using a debit card instead of a credit card. That way you can only spend money that you actually have in the bank. Value frugality and living within your means. Look for deals and be a smart, savvy shopper—it's a great life skill. Don't presume upon your parents just because you know they will give you money. It's one thing to accept an occasional gift (such as money to come home for Thanksgiving and Christmas); it's another thing to bask in an unearned lifestyle. Learning to manage a small amount of money is a wonderful skill. If you can't manage a small budget, you won't be able to manage a large budget either. The problem isn't the size of your budget but the size of your appetite for material things and the degree to which you get seduced by *wants* that masquerade as *needs*.

Check out this real-life case.

DANIEL'S STORY, IN HIS WORDS

My journey into debt began about twenty years ago when I started college and was old enough to get my first credit card with the help of my dad cosigning. I think the limit was $500 or maybe $1,000. After a few months of making payments on time, the offers started flooding in and didn't require a cosigner or income verification. At first I told the truth about my income level, but I soon began to lie, telling the credit card

Q: *Overall my parents and I have worked out a good system of dividing the various financial responsibilities of college. I never assume that I will get help with things like buying supplies or paying for gas when I am home, but often my parents feel like they want to buy things for me as a reward for my work at school and at home. Now that I'm entering my junior year of college, is it okay to accept these gifts from my parents? Or should I start transitioning away from their help and paying more of my own way?* —KELVIN, JUNIOR, Physics/Engineering

A: It sounds like you're successfully managing your own expenses and budget for much of the year. If you're living within your own means and not carrying a balance on a credit card, that's a great display of maturity for someone entering his junior year. And if you're working around the house during your breaks, there's a sense in which you're already offsetting your living costs when you're at home.

My gut feeling is that you're doing just fine. I would suggest transitioning to paying more of your own way as you move into your last semester, but there's nothing wrong with an occasional gift, particularly if you're going on to graduate school or getting married. What's most crucial, I think, is your willingness to progressively handle more of your own costs and not assume ongoing dependence on Mom and Dad. The details of your transition to functional independence are up to you and your parents. And I bet they appreciate your wanting to take the lead in this regard.

companies I made more money than I really did so that I could get more cards and higher credit limits.

Going deep into debt wasn't an overnight event, but a lifestyle I adopted little by little. The external problem was that I was spending more than my income, but the deeper problem was my attitude toward money, debt, and material things.

First, I started going into debt by spending more than I could pay back. I got used to carrying a balance but felt responsible by making payments on time. I justified having a balance by thinking, I'll pay it off in a few months. As that balance grew, I thought, I'll pay it off when I figure out how to make more money. When the balance got so big that I had to admit I couldn't possibly pay it off by graduation, I reasoned, I'll pay it off after I graduate and start making real money. When the balance got out of control, I figured, If I'm already $10,000 in debt, what's another $____ (fill in the blank)?

I thought I was still in control because I was making the minimum monthly payments. When the minimum payment was the most I could afford, I began to realize that the debt was controlling me. It got really out of control when I started taking out cash advances on credit cards to make minimum payments on other cards.

I hid all this from my parents. They would regularly ask me about my credit cards, and I would say that everything was fine, and either be vague about my finances or outright lie. I didn't want to be exposed, and I justified it in part by telling myself, They'd be very troubled if I told them the truth, because they're so sacrificial they might even try to help me or pay it off. I don't want to disappoint or burden them with my problems.

Well, they found out before I graduated. One day when they visited me, I came home to find all my credit-card folders opened with my statements laid out on my bed. They confronted me and asked me what happened. To my surprise, they responded with mercy and grace instead of in anger. They said in a loving tone that I should have told them about my problems because they're my parents who love me and are the only ones who could help me in times like this when I couldn't handle it myself. They said they would pay it off and that I would have to change my ways and be honest with them from that point on. I was surprised by their response, shocked by their grace, grateful for their generosity, and I vowed to change.

The problem with being bailed out of over $10,000 was that I never fully experienced the consequences, learned my lesson, and changed my thinking about

*money and debt. It wasn't until later in my adult life,
after I got further in debt several times that amount
and had to pay it off with my own hard-earned money,
that I learned how to think about and deal correctly
with money, debt, and material things. I actually
wished that my parents wouldn't have bailed me out
the first time, because then I probably would have
learned my lesson earlier and at a smaller cost. Change
for me happened very slowly. It wasn't one book,
one sermon, one talk with someone that marked the
turning point. It took me many years to learn through
mistakes, misery, self-induced suffering, wasted money,
impacted relationships, deliverances, books, discussions,
community, the example of others, etc.*

*In a nutshell, the external problem was that I bought
things I didn't need with money I didn't have to satisfy
needs that weren't real. But the internal problem was
deception. I believed false promises. I was motivated by
instant gratification instead of delayed rewards. I was
seduced and enslaved by my desires. I hoped in money
I could potentially make instead of living on money
I had already made.*

*With God's help, I now live on a budget within my
means and pay off my credit cards every month.*

SO NOW WHAT?

Daniel's story is all too common. A recent study showed that one in every four college students "rarely or never" pays his or her credit cards in full every month.[5] I suggest waiting at least until you've demonstrated that you can live within your budget before considering a credit card. Some Christian parents are categorically opposed to cosigning on a credit card for their children under any circumstances. Others are okay with it. If your parents won't go for it, you certainly won't miss much before you turn twenty-one, and they may be saving you from massive misery, like my friend Daniel experienced. Exercise and grow in financial responsibility, and when you're twenty-one you can make an informed decision for yourself. I'll discuss finances a bit more in chapter 10.

Another way you can grow in financial responsibility is to intentionally accept fewer material gifts or a lower allowance from your parents each successive year you remain in college. Circumstances differ widely—some of you are receiving significantly more financial assistance from your parents than others. The important thing is to be moving steadily toward total financial independence (ideally by the time you graduate—I'll say more about this later).

I know a recent college graduate who started turning down financial gifts from his parents as he approached graduation. He found that his mom wanted to keep on giving him things even though, as his independence was developing, he was less needful of (and less interested in) her generosity. He simply told his mom, "At some point, a man's gotta be a man." His determination to step up gave her confidence to back off.

Grow in your work ethic and financial stewardship.

Financial independence upon graduation is a good goal. Having said that, you'll probably be living at home during breaks. So how do you honor your parents in these situations?

Taking time to refresh yourself mentally and physically over holidays and spring break is no doubt wise. Those times can also be great for get-togethers and trips with friends. But the summer break is long, and as we'll discuss in chapter 10, you really should do something productive with it. Your work doesn't have to be for money, but you'll want it to be deeply significant and meaningful. If you're being paid and living at home, you may suddenly have a much stronger cash flow than you did during the academic year. Don't just spend money like crazy because you now have it. Live within the same sort of budget as you did during the school year.[1]

Chances are your parents wouldn't require it, but you could offer to pay a monthly contribution for your housing and food, now that your cash flow makes it possible for you to do so. It would help you learn the principle that work sustains living expenses. Or offer Mom and Dad this money as your contribution to next year's college tuition. Or start paying down any student loans you have (ahead of schedule). If you don't have any loans, ask your parents to help you set

---

[1] As much as possible—you might need to spend more gas money commuting to work, for example.

up a saving plan with a money market account and some quality mutual funds. Begin to learn basic principles of saving and investing.

LIVING AT HOME AFTER GRADUATION?

Although we covered the potential pitfalls of living at home for a season after graduation, I'm now going to focus on a few reasons why doing so can be strategic. If you don't secure a decent full-time job, going home may be all you can afford at first. Even if you *do* find a stable entry-level position upon graduation, living at home for a while can be a good way to build up your savings and enjoy the blessing of your parents' company.

Living alone in an apartment is generally the most expensive way to go post-graduation. In addition, the lack of moral accountability in that situation often leads to a period of spiritual dullness or wandering for many Christian singles.** At least get a quality roommate. If your entry-level job is near your parents' house, and it's a better option financially or socially than moving in with friends, go for it.

But whether you're in a permanent or temporary job, there need to be some clear guidelines to avoid the temptation to revert to the natural child/parent paradigm of dependence. Before you move back home with Mom and Dad, ask

---

** There are a variety of temptations that are exacerbated by living alone, particularly if you move to a new city for work. The structures and built-in community you enjoyed during college will be gone, leaving you to fend for yourself spiritually. If that's what you choose to do for the sake of establishing your career, be ready for a season of testing, and be purposeful about finding a strong network and Christian community, just like we talked about in the transition from high school to college. Good management of your time and money becomes even more important because with more income and freedom come more ways to get in trouble.

Q: *What's your advice to a student who goes home for the first time over Thanksgiving and hasn't had parental authority in three months? How do you prepare to go home and not be a slob or reject authority and be disrespectful? Some of my friends say that when you go back for break you notice all the little traits your parents have that bother you or annoy you that you didn't notice until you were away for a while. How do you deal with those things so you can make the most of your time when you go back?* —LUKE, FRESHMAN, Worship Arts

A: Well, anticipating that little things may bother you is a good start to preventing an irritation meltdown. In this case, knowing there will be a battle is half the battle.

As the day draws near, cultivate thankfulness for the work your parents did to help you get to where you are. Jot down a few things your parents will like and plan to do them as gestures of appreciation (such as making your bed, not leaving clothes on the floor, helping to clean up after dinner, taking out the trash, doing your own laundry, or filling the car's gas tank). If it doesn't seem too forced, talk to your parents about the fact that you've been living on your own for three months and that while you've been staying on top of your responsibilities, your daily habits may be a little different from what they were in high school. Thank them for having trained you to make responsible choices. Encourage them to talk to you if something you're doing during the break is bothering them.

them to work out a written contract with you. I'm serious. *Spell out* what will be required of you. It will save you hassle down the road.

Christians differ on whether adult children in this situation should pay for rent and food. One consideration should be the needs of your parents. If they're barely making ends meet, you should definitely step up to the plate and pay a reasonable amount, perhaps even a market rate.

My opinion is that you should pay them rent *whether they want it or not*. Why? Because *you* need to pay it even if *they* don't need to collect it. It's good for your soul to see how work pays for a living. The contract should have other specifications, like a late penalty if your rent isn't on time. Are there any household chores you'll need to regularly do, such as mowing the lawn each week or cleaning parts of the house? State financial penalties if you fail to complete them by a certain time each week. Have a move-in inspection so that you're accountable for any damages you cause, at least in your room.

If Dad or Mom puts in a fifty-hour work week to pay the bills, and they come home to find you goofing around on the computer with no strategy for finding a significant job, it is going to cause tension, even if you're able to pay your small rent through a part-time job as a waiter. If you're living as an adult with Mom and Dad, enjoying the blessings of food and shelter that they make possible, *you should be working at least as much as they are.*

By "work" I'm envisioning a combination of several

things, since you're in a season of transition. These things may include a part-time job; attending and studying for classes; volunteering (many fields require you to volunteer a certain number of hours); preparing for the MCAT, GRE, or LSAT; serving in specific ways in your church; babysitting; handling yardwork, cars, or household cleaning; or caring for aging relatives. In other words, productive activity that either provides an immediate service worthy of compensation (housework, hospice care for others, etc.) or that keeps you on a path toward greater functional independence.

> *If you're living as an adult with Mom and Dad, enjoying the blessings of food and shelter that they make possible, you should be working at least as much as they are.*

Add to your contract a minimum number of productive hours per week that you agree to maintain (fifty is a good number) so that your parents see you working as hard as they do. Identify some long-term goals for this season at home, and sit down with your parents every few months to see how you're progressing toward them. In other words, honor your parents as if they were both landlords and mentors.

You may be thinking, *But my parents and I get along so well. Imposing all this formality will only add stress to our relationship.* Two responses: First, in a sense, that's the point. Because you're so comfortable with your parents, you just might stay too long and delay full adulthood. Remember the phrase "failure to launch"?

And a second response: You may think the structure of

a contract will cause stress, but in fact the opposite is more likely to be the case. Think how much you hate being nagged by your parents. Imagine this scenario: You come home late on a regular basis because of your job. Your dad gets up early the next morning to find numerous lights left on and the front door unlocked. He barges into your room and chews you out for being irresponsible and inconsiderate. Good? No. This is better: Your dad calmly adds to your contract a fee (say forty dollars) if you ever leave the house door unlocked and an additional dollar for every light he finds left on in the morning. Now it's just business. You screw up, you pay. Nobody needs to yell at you or nag you. And I bet you'll learn quickly.

Or let's suppose you have trouble remembering to pay your rent on time. Your parents have to ask you five times before you get around to it. Knowing this, they start bugging you three days before the end of the month, twice a day until the first day of the next month. Annoying? You bet. This is better: Just include a late-payment penalty in the contract. That's what any landlord would do. Then it's not personal— again, nobody has to nag you. You'll start remembering because you have to.[6] That's the real world.

If you live with your parents after you graduate, it should generally be temporary and for the purpose of accomplishing specific goals. Unusual cases sometimes happen. If your parents became very ill, you may choose to care for them on an extended basis, even with your spouse if you have one. But generally, you should be "passing through," so to speak.

CONCLUSIONS

College is an amazing experience in which you start off in many ways an adolescent and graduate (hopefully) as an adult. The day your parents drop you off at the dorm their ability to control your life almost completely evaporates. But their influence remains in a healthy way if you've internalized the (hopefully godly) values they've painstakingly imparted to you and lived out before you. During and immediately following the college years, you honor your parents by gladly assuming the mantle of adulthood, growing in functional independence, and taking responsibility for your use of time, your academic pursuits, and your professional and social relationships. Embrace the opportunity to grow in maturity while honoring your parents and internalizing their wise counsel. "Train yourself for godliness. . . . Let no one despise you for your youth, but set the believers an example in speech, in conduct, in love, in faith, in purity" (1 Timothy 4:7, 12).

DISCUSSION STARTERS

1. Among your friends and classmates, do you see any signs of delayed adolescence? How about in yourself?

2. I mentioned the importance of taking responsibility for your time management, class schedule and choice of major, for choosing quality friends, and for your professional relationships. How are you doing in these areas? Are there any areas in which you need to take more ownership?

3. Are you growing in financial responsibility and independence? Are you living within your means? What have you decided to do with regard to credit cards and spending? How is that working for you?

4. What are some ways that you're grateful for what your parents have done to help you get to where you are? What are some steps you can take to honor them in your own embrace of adulthood?

5. What are your thoughts on post-graduation housing? Would you ever consider moving back in with Mom and Dad, and if so, under what conditions? What did you think about the concept of having a contract and paying rent to your parents?

PART 3
CHARACTER MATTERS

COMMON MISTAKE #6:
Being a Flake

> *Thrive Principle: Keep Your Commitments*

We needed to get a head count of how many were coming to the special event in two weeks. We were going to bring in a speaker to talk about summer job opportunities, so we sent out word to a couple hundred students. We asked them to RSVP so that we could order enough food. Out of 250 invites, we got 80 yes responses. So it was a big letdown when only 20 actually came.

I needed a ride to the airport. My friend Ryan graciously agreed to pick me up. The day and time comes, and I'm waiting outside for him. A few minutes go by. No problem, he's just running a bit late, may have caught traffic. I had built some slack into my schedule, so we're good. Ten minutes go by. I give him a call. No answer. I try him at work. No answer. At home. Nothing. It's too late at this point for me to walk to the train station. A couple more minutes go by; I make a few calls to mutual friends. "Has anyone seen Ryan?" Ten more minutes go by. Desperate at this point, I call a cab and barely catch my flight.

Our group was on the hook to give a presentation to the management team in a week. I'd already done all the work I could do without the input that I needed from Bill. If I didn't get his part of the project, I wasn't going to be able to finish my part on time. He'd told me that he'd have it for me by the end of the day yesterday. While he meant well, Chelsea and I knew that Bill just used words "differently." End of the day could just as easily mean end of the week. You simply couldn't count on the guy to keep verbal commitments. As nice as he was, and he always meant well, all of us in the office were starting to make excuses to avoid having him on our project teams.

What do these stories have in common? *Someone set expectations and then failed to deliver.* The students *said* they were coming to the special event with the speaker, but *didn't*. Ryan *said* he'd pick me up for the airport, but *didn't*. Bill *said* he'd get me his part of the report by the end of the day yesterday, but he *didn't*.

The essence of flaking out is giving an impression that you *will* do something and then not doing it. When we talked about the sluggard in the introduction, we saw this was one of his specialties: "Like vinegar to the teeth and smoke to the eyes, so is the sluggard to those who send him" (Proverbs

10:26). The sixth mistake you don't want to make at college is being a flake.

Stated positively, thriving in college means being a person who keeps his or her commitments. What you see is what you get—people who keep their commitments *are* what they say they *are* and *do* what they say they'll *do*.

CHARACTER, FAITHFULNESS, AND MATURITY

The formation of character is worth your attention in the college years as you launch into adulthood. Whether you're living at college or at home, you will develop habits in your thinking, speaking, and doing that will shape your *character*—morally upright or morally suspect: a courageous, firm backbone or wishy-washy spinelessness.

As the saying goes, character is who you are when nobody is looking. It's who you *really* are. So what's maturity? And what does it have to do with launching into adulthood? Put simply, to be mature is to be fully developed, to have reached one's developmental goal. A flower is mature when it's in full bloom. A person is mature when he's acting in a responsible, adultlike fashion and no longer as a child.

But maturity is not a black-or-white, yes-or-no, you-have-it-or-you-don't type of thing. There are degrees of maturity; it is something that you and I should

> *Your character is . . . who you really are.*

continuously pursue and be growing in. When I write in a recommendation letter, "John, a sophomore in college, is

Q: *My roommates are pretty inconsiderate when it comes to our shared space. They often play video games till two in the morning and don't respect the fact that I want to sleep or study and have nowhere else to go on campus at that time of night. What should I say or do to get them to understand that I take my education pretty seriously without seeming like a jerk?*
—LUKE, FRESHMAN, Worship Arts

A: That's a really tough—but common—concern. Have you tried to talk to them about it? Start there. Be honest and clear. Say something like, "Hey guys, if I was doing something that got on your nerves, I'd want you to tell me. Would you mind if I shared a concern?" Try to come up with some creative compromises. Can they wear headsets while playing and have the monitor facing away from your bed so you can sleep? I got my freshman-year roommate to drag the phone outside the room to talk with his hometown girlfriend (those were the pre–cell phone days).

The best way to avoid seeming like a jerk is to focus on the impact you're experiencing, not on what you regard as their poor judgment. The choice to stay up till 2 a.m. goofing around is unwise, but it's their life. They're adults; they need to make their own decisions and live with the consequences. It'd be great if they followed your example, but that's not really the point. The problem is that because they're pursuing their preference, you can't pursue yours. If the problem persists, you could try taking it up with the resident assistant or resident director. Part of their job is to help resolve such situations.

mature," I don't mean to suggest that John is as mature in every respect as a forty-year-old man who has been employed and self-supporting for fifteen years. No, what I mean is that John, *as a nineteen-year-old young man*, has a measure of maturity that is commendable *for his particular age and stage in life.* In fact, I'll expect more from him as a junior and even more as a senior. You should be continuously growing so that you can be prepared for the greater challenges that await you.

How can we measure maturity? One good way is *faithfulness.* Whereas children need constant reminders about what to do (or keep doing), adult behavior is characterized by the assumption of responsibility, which means decisively choosing a course of action and then faithfully sticking to it. Therefore, the extent to which a person naturally assumes responsibility, makes decisions (gives his or her word), and faithfully sticks with those decisions (keeps his or her word), is a measure of a person's maturity. *Not* keeping one's word, or failing to commit, on the other hand, reflects a lack of maturity (or integrity, in the case of bold-faced liars). And if we're inconsistent and unfaithful, our reputations will either immediately or eventually pay a price.

REPUTATIONS MATTER

As I said above, character is who you are when nobody is looking. But it is equally true that *character cannot remain hidden*: Who you truly are will come through and become evident to others as they get to know you. This will form your reputation, *what others think of you.*

While *character* is what we are in God's eyes, *reputation* is what we are in the eyes of others. At the end of Luke 2, where we read the only biblical account of Jesus' childhood, we learn that Jesus "increased in wisdom and in stature and *in favor with God and man*" (Luke 2:52, emphasis added). My guess is Jesus built some pretty awesome furniture in his day. As we grow up, we, too, should be growing in favor with others by doing high-quality work that reflects our best effort (homework, delivering newspapers, babysitting, raking leaves, mowing lawns, serving coffee) and by treating others with respect. This is important because a good name is more valuable than riches (Proverbs 22:1).

> *While character is what we are in God's eyes, reputation is what we are in the eyes of others.*

Our reputation is something that we accumulate over time, and it often goes before us. People we haven't even met may already have heard about us, in good or bad ways. So be aware that every relationship can have ripple effects. Every time you do a good job on a project, are punctual when you make an appointment (especially with professors), and come to class prepared, you're developing a good reputation. Every time you skip a personal appointment, are excessively late, or simply flake out on something, you're developing a bad reputation.

Words matter to God. A lot. On keeping promises, we're told, "When you vow a vow to God, do not delay paying it, for he has no pleasure in fools. Pay what you vow. It is better that you should not vow than that you should vow and not pay" (Ecclesiastes 5:4-5). Or in Psalm 15, as part of a description of what it means to walk blamelessly, we read of one "who swears to his own hurt and does not change" (verse 4). This means he keeps his word, even if it costs him. Likewise, Jesus tells us that our simple yes and no should be sufficient (Matthew 5:37); no "cross my heart" or "I swear" is required.

Before we go on, is there ever a time *not* to care about our reputations? Yes. The Bible warns us that the fear of man is a snare (Proverbs 29:25). It can make us into hypocrites, acting one way when people are watching and another way when they're not. Such hypocrisy is often rooted in pride, which leads us to put *reputation* above *character*. Likewise, it's wise to turn a deaf ear to unfounded criticism, which we, too, have been guilty of dispensing (Ecclesiastes 7:21-22). We should live well before God and let our reputations take care of themselves.

All that said, we should never needlessly disregard the opinions of others, particularly if they're the informed opinions of wise people. In fact, the wiser the person, the more you should care what he or she thinks of you. Just as it's arrogant to care too much what others think (being a hypocrite and a people pleaser), it's even more arrogant not to care at all.

EXCUSES, EXCUSES

So failing to meet the expectations we set is irresponsible. But what other bad habit often comes with it? You guessed it: making excuses.

We've all caught ourselves doing it. It generally comes in two forms. There are outright, bold-faced lies—overt misrepresentations of facts. These are obviously sinful (Exodus 20:16; Ephesians 4:25). Then there's the whole category of "spin"—where we "twist" or "spin" the facts of a situation to put ourselves in the most positive light possible, usually by distorting or failing to mention important details. Those most adept at this maneuver avoid actually making demonstrably false statements. We simply don't tell the whole truth, and in not doing so, we are being deceitful because we misrepresent facts, situations, or events. But half truth is a whole lie. And over time, people generally catch on. Even when they don't, God is dishonored.

Let's be honest: The temptation to make excuses when we fall short is incredibly strong. Why? Because we're embarrassed and disappointed with ourselves. We feel bad. Perhaps, we think to ourselves, there's a way to preserve our reputation. What does an excuse do? It deflects the cause to something outside us. And, voilà, we feel better!

Recently my wife asked me to help her declutter the living room before some guests came over. I agreed, but had to do one thing in my office first. When I got there, I noticed that I had a few new voicemails on my cell phone. While I was listening to them, I quickly forgot why I had gone to my office (and my agreement to help my wife in the living room *really* fell off the radar). After hearing my voicemails, I started hammering out a few e-mail responses. Meanwhile, the guests showed up. Oops.

Q: *What are your thoughts about group projects with people who simply don't want to put in the time? I know you speak against making excuses, so how would you suggest approaching a situation like this?*
—KATE, FRESHMAN, Creative Writing

A: The good news is, no matter how frustrating this can be, it is a very real taste of post-college life. You will frequently be evaluated for team efforts. Is there at least one other member on your team who does want to put in the time? Does he or she share your frustration? Join forces to come up with a strategy to motivate the others. Going about this as a twosome is much better than going it alone.

Another strategy is to assign roles—pick a leader and a secretary and any other positions that seem appropriate. When you meet, document action items and assign each one to a person on the team. You could even include a page with your project that shows who had what responsibilities, so if the bibliography is lame, the professor will know who owned it. Tell your partners you want to make sure everyone gets credit for their work. If lazy members see that their individual contributions are being monitored, that might give them the kick in the pants that they need.

As an absolute last resort, you could approach your professor. Don't complain or whine. Just tell him or her what you've already tried, and see if the prof has any additional suggestions.

Later that night, my wife said to me, "So what happened when you went to your office? I thought we were going to clean the living room together."

At that point, I could either absorb the blame and acknowledge my guilt or look for a "semilegitimate" explanation. Which felt better? I said, "Oh, I meant to, but I had a few really important voicemails and I needed to reply right away."

It's hard to take the blame, even when we know we deserve it. That's why we look for "explanations." (She didn't buy it.) Now, please don't get me wrong—sometimes there *are* very reasonable explanations for getting derailed. Suppose one of those voicemails was from my sister telling me our parents had been hurt in a car crash. Okay, that would be a huge deal. You drop everything. But a lot of our "explanations" are more of the "my dog ate my homework" type; they aren't really the reason why we fell short. Trust me, your professors, classmates, and friends will catch on to you if you make a habit of issuing these kinds of excuses for failing to meet commitments.

Making excuses yields a short-term payoff—we kid ourselves that we weren't guilty, and we end up feeling a little better. But taking full responsibility yields a long-term payoff. Here's what I mean. Let's say a baseball player drops a relatively easy fly ball.* As a direct result, the other team scores their winning run, and his team loses. Ouch. He could say, "The sun was in my eyes." The "I couldn't help it" feeling

---

* I've adapted this illustration from pastor and author Doug Wilson, whom I heard use a similar version in an audio message.

gives him a measure of comfort, and let's suppose it may even be true to an extent. Maybe the sun really was in his eyes.

But now let's suppose he responds this way: "The sun may have been in my eyes, but I had sunglasses and a hat, and I've been trained to catch that kind of ball. I *should* have caught it. I blew it. I let my team down. This was my fault, and I'm going to work hard to not let it happen again."

In the first scenario, he gains immediate *emotional* comfort, but his *competence* stays down. In other words, he *feels* better about his baseball-playing abilities, but he isn't *actually* better. His improved feelings are not rooted in reality. In fact, he's weakened the motivation to improve, since dropping the ball wasn't his fault, which makes it more likely that he will fail again in the future. In the second scenario, he embraces the pain of failure head on. He swallows the whole bitter pill. And in doing so, he picks himself up and is more likely to make the necessary improvements to avoid committing such mistakes in the future.

Here's the thing: *External circumstances alone rarely give a full account for a situation's outcome.* Our decisions—and shortcomings—are almost always a factor. And since we can't control the external circumstances, we should focus on what we *can* control: ourselves. I can tell my wife, "You know what, honey? I blew it. I went back to my office for one thing, but then I chose to check my voicemail, which led to my sending e-mails rather than helping you. I made poor decisions and acted selfishly. Please forgive me. Next time I'll try to be more careful."

Develop the habit of taking full responsibility, *even when* there are legitimate factors outside your control. You'll be picking yourself up, enhancing your ability to make better decisions in the future. Your character will become stronger, and you'll be developing a reputation for humility, sincerity, and responsibility. And you'll improve at whatever it is you're doing.

BE A STRAIGHT SHOOTER

A related danger, another form of dishonesty, can also damage your reputation: exaggeration.

My wife has a friend—let's call him Joe. If Joe attends a large dinner event with a significant speaker, he'll report to his friends, "I had dinner with so-and-so the other night," as if he personally enjoyed a private audience with some famous individual.

In the work force, I've seen folks give presentations that explain how great things are in their organization. They conveniently neglect to include any information that would weaken their case. We see this all the time in politics when candidates tell us how great their accomplishments are but dodge questions about anything that may tarnish their images.

Similarly, I've had students tell me that they knew "everything" we covered and that their test scores did not truly reflect their solid understanding. Occasionally, they are mostly right and just need to practice a few test-taking skills. But more often when the students and I discuss the exam, and I ask them other questions, they discover they didn't really know "everything" as well as they thought.

Long-winded explanations often accompany excuse making, but they also tend to accompany exaggeration. Be a straight shooter who accurately says what happened, not looking either to deflect responsibility or to exaggerate your accomplishments to impress others. Whenever possible, share credit and avoid praising yourself: "Let another praise you, and not your own mouth; a stranger, and not your own lips" (Proverbs 27:2). It is a good habit to get into and one that can diminish our natural inclination toward self-centeredness and pride.

For example, a job interview may require you to recount your role in a group project. Give the interviewer a brief description of the circumstances, what your team and you personally did, and what the outcome was. Communicate the significance of your contributions, but be sure to give credit to others when appropriate. "Staci and I noticed that student housing did not have any recycling bins. We saw that as an opportunity to grow in stewardship of our campus and the earth. We investigated the logistical challenges and developed possible solutions. Staci focused on the freshman dorms, and I focused on the student apartments and suites, which typically house sophomores, juniors, and seniors. Last month Staci and I

> *Long-winded explanations often accompany excuse making, but they also tend to accompany exaggeration. Be a straight shooter who accurately says what happened.*

were asked to deliver a presentation to the Student Senate, outlining how our proposed solutions could be implemented. The Senate approved our proposal, and recycling bins are now being placed throughout student housing."

PRIVATE FAILURE PRECEDES PUBLIC FAILURE

Let's suppose we blow it with regard to honoring our responsibilities, but others don't catch on; either they forget our initial commitment or they buy our silly excuses. We've preserved our reputation but not our integrity. We haven't exhibited maturity by keeping our word. There's an extent to which, if this situation goes on and we get good at hiding our mistakes, we migrate into the realm of hypocrisy, projecting a false image about ourselves. This is what I'll call private failure. Nobody knows it, but we've blown it big time.

Here's an important principle to remember: *Every public failure is preceded by private failure.* We sometimes hear on the news about a famous pastor who has a scandalous affair, apparently out of nowhere, or a politician who had put himself forward as the epitome of virtue, only to resign in scandal after being caught embezzling large sums of money. We think, *Wow! How could that have happened so suddenly?* It didn't.

What? *It didn't.* You see, before a major failure occurred, there were a thousand "minor" indiscretions, private failures, white lies the person told *perhaps only to himself.* These all contributed, like a series of dominoes, to a failure that could no longer be hidden. And in an instant the person's reputation collapsed like a house of sand.

It reminds me of Jesus' conclusion in his Sermon on the Mount:

> *"Therefore, everyone who hears these words of Mine*
> *and acts on them, may be compared to a wise man who*
> *built his house on the rock. And the rain fell, and the*
> *floods came, and the winds blew and slammed against*
> *that house; and yet it did not fall, for it had been*
> *founded on the rock. Everyone who hears these words*
> *of Mine and does not act on them, will be like a foolish*
> *man who built his house on the sand. The rain fell,*
> *and the floods came, and the winds blew and slammed*
> *against that house; and it fell—and great was its fall."*
> *(Matthew 7:24-27, NASB)*

This Scripture illustrates the principle of reaping what we sow (Galatians 6:7) or the Old Testament phrase "Your sin will find you out" (Numbers 32:23). In a moment, a pattern of private failure can result in public failure. So watch the habits you form. And "keep your heart with all vigilance, for from it flow the springs of life. . . . Let your eyes look directly forward, and your gaze be straight before you. Ponder the path of your feet; then all your ways will be sure" (Proverbs 4:23-26).

UNDERLYING CAUSES

Okay, let's dig deeper. What *causes* us to fall short—setting expectations, not keeping them, and then resorting either to excuse making or exaggeration as a form of self-protection (from the pain of failure) or self-preservation (from the loss of reputation)? From my own life, I've noticed a few common root causes:

1. Overcommitment (often for the sake of pleasing others)

Some of us are more naturally wired this way, but we all crave the approval of others, probably more than we care to admit. We want them to think highly of us—not just of our abilities, but of our sense of large-heartedness, our willingness to help, our well-roundedness as people. This desire explains precisely why overcommitment comes so naturally. Someone requests something of us, we want this person to like us, and the request sounds legitimate. They truly need our help; we're honored, and we don't want to be unfriendly. An uncomfortable few seconds of silence pass, and we hear ourselves saying yes.

Let's say you're explaining to a high-school teacher how you went about choosing your major. Your old teacher says, "Wow! That's so neat! Do you think you can come back and share that with my history class?"

At that point, your ego has been stroked. You're thinking, *Wow, she really likes what I have to say! That'd be cool to go back to give a presentation to my old high school.* But you haven't yet thought about the time involved and whether you can make it work with your current commitments.

In moments like this we often find ourselves *reacting*, not *choosing*. We think to ourselves, *If I say no, she may think I don't care, or that I'm not up to it.* This is particularly challenging when the person making the request of us is someone we admire or think we "need" to like us (like a professor or a friend of our parents).

Thinking we can do more than humanly possible can actually be a form of arrogance. The label *arrogance* can seem like overkill given our busy lives. After all, how is it *arrogant* to make a commitment—to say you are going to do something? It can be arrogant if the commitment doesn't acknowledge your need for God and the limitations that God has placed on you and the rest of humanity (including your need for sleep).[†]

Josh came to see me midway into the semester because he was failing the course. Bashfully, he acknowledged that he hadn't been putting in the time, but he was ready to change his ways. "Great," I said. "What are you planning to give up—to *not* do—so that you can spend a few more hours a week on the course work?"

"Nothing, Dr. Chediak. I can't afford to! I'm on the cross-country team (we have races every Saturday morning and

---

[†] A similar warning is found in the book of James: "Come now, you who say, 'Today or tomorrow we will go into such and such a town and spend a year there and trade and make a profit'— yet you do not know what tomorrow will bring. What is your life? For you are a mist that appears for a little time and then vanishes. Instead you ought to say, 'If the Lord wills, we will live and do this or that.' As it is, you boast in your arrogance. All such boasting is evil" (James 4:13-16).

practice almost every day), the university choir (we practice four hours a week, plus concerts on Sunday afternoons), and five other classes. But I promise to do my best!"

Josh meant well. He was a good guy. But I wasn't too surprised when he didn't make it. He was flat-out overcommitted. He simply couldn't balance all of those responsibilities; it was too much. Josh failed to account for natural limitations in his planning. He should have counted the cost earlier and not overloaded himself so much that semester. He was unrealistic, and he had more confidence in his capacities than was warranted.

The antidote for Josh, and for the rest of us, is to have a greater awareness that God is God and we're not. God is omnipotent, and he never needs to sleep (Psalm 121:4). Besides our natural limitations, we also need to build padding into our schedules for things to occasionally go wrong. We may need extra help for that math test or research paper. A continual awareness that God rules over a thousand details beyond our control makes us more guarded with how we speak about our abilities and plans (James 4:13-16). Humility of mind and a sense of our smallness and God's bigness are sure aids in battling overcommitment.

When God seems big to us, people (even our superiors) will seem smaller, and we won't be so scared to let them down. In fact, we'll often earn their respect by graciously saying no and explaining the priorities and commitments that we believe God has placed in our lives. Gracefully declining opportunities is a mark of maturity and humility. You'll find people generally take it pretty well, as long as you let them know in a reasonable amount of time (again, so we don't give them false expectations).

2. Lack of resolve; general flakiness

If overcommitment doesn't cause us to fall short, the other biggie is a general lack of resolve or focus. When things get tough or something more interesting comes up, we quit.

I'll have less to say on this one, because the way to fight it is very much like the way we have to fight overcommitment. *First, when we give our word, we need to count the cost.* "When you pay a vow to God, do not delay paying it, for he has no pleasure in fools. Pay what you vow. It is better that you should not vow than that you should vow and not pay" (Ecclesiastes 5:4-5). Though the verse is talking about making vows to God (a much more serious matter than agreeing to be dorm president), the general principle holds. Jesus made a similar point when he talked about counting the cost of discipleship (Luke 14:27-30). If you aren't sure you

> *Get in the habit of under-promising and over-delivering.*

want to do something, it is much better to say, "I'd love to be there on Saturday, but I've got a lot going on. Unfortunately, I probably won't make it." That's much better than setting expectations and then falling short. If you do have time on Saturday, you can still go, and they'll all be happy to see you. Get in the habit of underpromising and overdelivering.

KEEP COMMITMENTS, EVEN WHEN IT HURTS

Stick to a commitment whenever possible. Let's say you agreed to grade homework for a professor over the course of a semester. You did it for the money and the experience, but midway into the semester you've realized that your class work and student government position are taking up more time than you had anticipated. You're thinking of telling your professor that you won't be able to grade for her anymore. If you do that, chances are she'll say that's fine; she doesn't want someone working for her whose heart isn't in it. But she'll remember that you don't always finish what you start.[‡]

It's always much better to say no before making a commitment than to back out in the middle. At this point, it would be better for you to see it through, even if it means having a busier semester than you had wanted. Sacrifice your free time rather than require your professor to make other arrangements; keep your promise, even if it hurts (Psalm 15:4). Another benefit is that you'll probably learn more this way and won't be as likely to overcommit in the future.[§]

[‡] Proverbs 6:1-5 talks about being "snared in the words of [our] mouth" and having to humble ourselves by going to our neighbor (verse 3) and "sav[ing] [ourselves] like a gazelle." I take this to be an apologetic request to be released of a commitment we've made. Sometimes, this is necessary. Others are often understanding, since they, too, have fallen short on occasion. But we should be careful; such requests can impact our reputation.

[§] I took a chess class in college from Dr. Moritz, a grand master who was also on our math faculty. He'd simultaneously play the entire class every week and usually beat us all. He taught us that the moment we took our hand off the piece, our move was made and we could not take it back. What if we caught ourselves and saw the mistake a few seconds later? Too late. We'd need to play out the game and suffer any consequences. He said that was the only way we could learn from such mistakes—by having to play them out, unable to take them back. True in chess and in life.

OTHER SPEECH-RELATED ISSUES

So far we've been focusing on maturity in terms of how our actions need to match our words. But failing to meet commitments, excuse making, and exaggeration aren't the only speech-related ways to damage your reputation. Other ways include gossip, backstabbing, and being verbose at inappropriate times.

Take gossip and backstabbing, for example. Sarah approaches Carly and tells her that she has "issues" with Ashley. Carly could listen intently. Or, if she's wise, she'll find this to be a turnoff and refuse to participate in such a conversation. Whenever a friend gossips to me about a mutual friend, my first thought is, *What are they saying about me when I'm not around?*

Talking at inappropriate times tends to be a more subtle error. My student Tyler likes to approach me for private, personal conversations right when I'm trying to start class. He is always surprised when I tell him, "We can't have that conversation now. If you come to me right after class, or during my office hours, I'd be glad to talk to you then."

"Oh, when are your office hours?"

"Check the syllabus, Tyler. . . . They haven't changed since the last time you asked me."

Tyler has even tried to have extended one-on-one conversations with me from his desk in front of a thirty-person class. I don't think Tyler is a mean person, but he has earned a reputation of being a bit inconsiderate and impatient.

WATCH YOUR ONLINE PRESENCE

I needed to hire someone to help incoming students get ready for a year-long course. I wanted someone who wasn't just intelligent and capable but who also had a model work ethic and would be a solid role model for the students. Bethany and Keith applied. I remembered both of them as being good students. So before I even considered the pros and cons that each would bring to the position, I went to their Facebook pages to see what they'd been up to. We weren't "friends," but their wall, info, and photos were all public. Bethany had numerous, shall we say, questionable photos and quotes. That made my decision easy. Keith got the job.

You've grown up with the Internet, in an era when (as my students tell me) nobody uses e-mail anymore because there's Facebook, IM, and Skype. But remember that many professors know how to use Facebook, so you're broadcasting yourself to the world through whatever information you've made public—including photos your friends tagged you in. And just as your reputation can be damaged by a lack of maturity in word and deed, so your online reputation goes before you and can limit opportunities down the road.

CONCLUSIONS

The reputation you develop in the course of a semester impacts more than just the relationships you have that semester. Others hear about you, in good ways or bad, and future relationships can be impacted. So before you even take a class with a professor, he or she may have already heard things about you.

Be diligent to develop excellence in character. Be careful in making commitments, and go after those underlying causes like the fear of others and unrealistic expectations about your abilities. When you give your word, keep it. Remember to underpromise and overdeliver. Remain humble: Let your work and the mouths of others praise you. Embrace responsibility and avoid making excuses or exaggerating. And encourage your friends to do likewise.

Factoid

Have you ever caught yourself saying, "I'll get back to you later" just to get rid of someone? You already know you have no intention of getting back to him or her. In those situations, we're actually being deceitful in the name of tact. Be honest enough to respectfully say that you're simply not interested.

DISCUSSION STARTERS

1. Give an example of when someone flaked out on you. How did you feel? What do you wish the person had done instead?

2. Now give an example of when you disappointed someone else. What do you now wish you had done differently?

3. Ask your close friends to give you constructive criticism about your character with regard to any of these areas: finishing what you say you're going to do, taking responsibility for your actions, avoiding gossip, speaking truthfully, and keeping an honorable online presence.

COMMON MISTAKE #7:
Living out of Balance

> *Thrive Principle: Balance Work and Play*

WORK AND RECREATION MATTER TO GOD

One semester a couple of friends and I set aside Saturday mornings to study together for a big exam. The exam was divided into six sections, so we prepared for about three months, taking a chunk each Saturday. We'd work hard, and then to unwind I'd head to the Berkeley Marina for some windsurfing. This exhilarating hobby exhausted me physically, but it was just the refreshment I needed after all that time in the library.

Working hard and playing hard pretty much summed up school for me. The workload can be intense and exhausting. But the fun times provide much-needed refreshment and can lead to lifelong relationships and memories. Both are important. The refreshing escape of racing over the water while windsurfing was the perfect balance to the strenuous mental work that my courses required. But if we're not careful, fun times can become an end in and of themselves. Video games, for example, can either be a refreshing break or an addictive, harmful time waster, dangerous to both your health and your GPA.

Factoid

According to a Pew study, almost half of college students who play video, computer, or online games admit that it keeps them from studying "some" or "a lot" of the time.[1]

In fact, many college students (and post-college adults) have it backward: getting through work as quickly as possible to maximize time for fun, entertainment, and friends. But play was actually meant to equip us for work, not the other way around.

There are two equally serious dangers here: too much play without enough work and too much work without enough play. You may struggle with both of these extremes from time to time, but chances are your temperament inclines you one way or the other. Part of academic and lifelong success will require knowing which danger you're more prone to and creating safeguards to stay balanced, productive, and healthy.

Mistake #7 is living out of balance—working too hard or playing too hard, not recognizing the pithy truth my sixth-grade teacher told me: "There's a time and a place for everything." To thrive at college, you'll need to both work and recreate for God's glory.

You may have heard of working for God, but *recreating* for God? I'll show you what I mean by the end of the chapter. But first, let's look at a couple of examples of work and recreation out of balance.

ALL PLAY AND NO WORK

I had a bright student a few years ago named Mike. An honors student, he was enrolled in one of my classes both for the fall and spring semesters, and I also served as his academic adviser. Mike turned in the first test of my fall class with twenty-five minutes to spare. While the other students sat there sweating bullets, I flipped through the pages of his test. A quick glance was all I needed to discern that he had scored 100 percent.

Congratulating Mike, I told him the good news the next day. I encouraged him that, if he applied himself, he could be very successful in college. But Mike just smiled, seemingly unmoved. Puzzled, I asked him how long he had studied for the test. He said he hadn't studied very long at all, that the test had been easy, just like high school.

I suggested that he challenge himself by trying additional problems not required of other students. I assured him that the material would get more difficult and that the next test

Q: *You speak against skipping classes (which I understand, since you're a professor). But what do you think about situations when you have so much work in one class (perhaps a class in your major or just a generally more important class). What do you think about skipping the less important class to do work for the other class?*

—KATE, FRESHMAN, Creative Writing

A: Confession: I did this myself as a student. I remember a particular course outside my major that met four times a week. I often went once a week—just enough to turn in my assignments and make sure I wasn't missing anything huge. I skipped for the reason you specify: to focus on more important courses.

Ideally, I'd say don't take a class that you'd rather skip than attend. But sometimes you have to take courses that neither interest nor challenge you. And certain courses do take more time than others. So I think there's nothing wrong with occasional skipping, provided you take full responsibility for your decision. Make sure you know the professor's policy. Does participation impact your grade? Participation generally includes attendance, but it often also includes things like raising your hand and having intelligent things to offer. Might you be less prepared for the exams, papers, and other assignments if you miss class? Could you miss out on concepts and conversations that could truly enrich you personally? Remember that you're not just in college to collect grades. But in a busy semester, it's ultimately your call to make—we all have to say no to some things so we can say yes to other things.

would probably not come as easily for him. But he remained unmoved. Joking, I apologized for the material being too easy and promised that by the end of the semester, the class would at least keep him awake. Again, no reaction.

Mike seemed totally uninterested. I wanted to get into his head: What did he hope to get out of college? What was he hoping to do when he graduated? It seemed that Mike himself had no idea.

Mike was not without interests in life. I soon found out that he was the reigning video game champ in his dorm and that games and movies typically kept him up for a large part of the night. In October, he had trouble getting to class on time. By November, he would sporadically miss classes entirely, unable to get himself out of bed. Though he started with a high A, he wound up with a B in the fall and a D in the continuation course that spring. By the next year, Mike was on academic probation and on his way out of the engineering program.

What happened?

Too much play and too little work. Sure, he was bonding with the guys in the dorm and no doubt having the time of his life. But a semester of college cost $10,000 back then, and Mike took five classes per semester, which meant he'd lose $2,000 for every class he had to repeat. Not a wise investment.

Ironically, part of Mike's problem was that high school was too easy. I alluded to this potential problem in chapter 2. It is not uncommon for students to get A's and B's in high school but never learn how to really apply themselves. When Mike found my first test to be relatively easy, he assumed my class would be just like high school. He had never developed the discipline of studying. Unfortunately, by the time the alarm bell went off in his head, the semester was almost over. He became a victim of his own bad habits.

Factoid

Something to think about next time you consider sleeping through a class: If a semester of college costs $12,500 (not counting room and board), and you take five classes, that's $2,500 a class. If the class meets three times a week for fourteen weeks, that's about $60 a class period. About a dollar a minute. (No, trust me, that does not all go to your professors.)

Recreation was not meant to be our default state in life. No, recreation is a *temporary* refreshment from God-honoring work. So whatever you do for enjoyment, see that it doesn't become an addictive distraction. In college, away from your parents, a lot of the structure you had in high school is gone. A lot less time is actually spent in class, so it can feel like you have more time to yourself, to do what you want. But be aware of this inescapable principle: "A little sleep, a little slumber, a little folding of the hands to rest, and poverty will come upon you like a robber, and want like an armed man" (Proverbs 24:33-34).

The pattern is this: Ignore responsibilities, and they'll overwhelm you. But if through disciplined effort you conquer your responsibilities, you'll not only enjoy the fruit of your work (success, strengthened character, improved skills), but you'll be able to truly enjoy recreation without it consuming your life.

ALL WORK AND NO PLAY

Emily was an outgoing, bright, and hardworking student. She regularly told me that she hoped to pass my class, that the coursework was very hard, and that she was continually feeling anxiety about her grade. Each time I'd reply the same way: "Actually, you have an A or A- in the class right now. Just keep up the good work, and try not to worry so much."

> If through disciplined effort you conquer your responsibilities, you'll not only enjoy the fruit of your work (success, strengthened character, improved skills), but you'll be able to truly enjoy recreation without it consuming your life.

Interacting with Emily made me think back to my college days. Actually, I was more like Emily than I'd like to admit. God blessed me with a desire to do well, and I was able to earn a 4.0 GPA in my first semester. But the better I did, the more anxious I became. I started to find myself lamenting the fact that even an A- would knock down my GPA! After every test, every project I turned in, I'd be plagued by . . . anxiety. Worrying. And waiting.

"Uh, Dr. Jones, when are we going to get our tests back?"

Q: *Should weekends be focused more on having fun and leaving most of the schoolwork behind for the week? Or is it better to get ahead on your schoolwork and spend less time having fun?* — JACQUI, SOPHOMORE, Nursing

A: In chapter 2, I offer a sample schedule. My basic thought is that college is a full-time job for a full-time student. A sixteen- to eighteen-credit-hour schedule converts to fifty hours per week when you consider the out-of-class workload. If you don't need to work a side job during the semester, which would be the ideal, the weekend can be devoted to a combination of schoolwork (catching up or getting ahead), sleep (probably catching up), time with friends, and church-related activities.

I don't recommend working all weekend. Take at least two large blocks (five to seven hours) of time off—you'll need it. And you should be able to do that if you're diligent during the week. Work when it's time to work, and play when it's time to play (Ecclesiastes 3:1).

"Dr. Sigmundson, I know you haven't graded our tests yet, but is there any way we can have another chance to boost our grade this semester? I don't think I did well on it."

Now that I'm a professor, I feel sorry for how I badgered those poor guys, because I've heard the exact same lines.

Can you relate? Have you found that working hard to keep up your GPA feels all-consuming? You're not alone. According to a doctoral dissertation on the subject, the average college student in the 1990s was more anxious than 85 percent of college students in the 1950s.[2] And the problem has only gotten worse in the last decade.

What's going on?

The trouble starts in high school, if not earlier. There is overwhelming pressure to succeed; to have the "right background"; to be able to get into the "right college"; to earn high grades, be strong in athletics, music and/or theater; to feed the homeless once a week; to exhibit leadership potential (somehow); and to stay involved at church, all while keeping up with your social and family life and getting enough sleep. No wonder we're a generation of worriers.

Here's an indicator: When you spend more time *worrying about* grades rather than *working on* your courses, grades have become too important.

When that happens, we're working for *man's* approval, not *God's*. We're studying to accomplish a small (and fleeting) man-made honor rather than to discover more about God's world and God's ways. Good grades should be a by-product of excellent work, not a primary and consuming goal. College provides an incredible opportunity to learn to love God with all our minds, to increasingly master math, chemistry, English, and history as bodies of knowledge whose axioms and beauty owe their entire existence to the God of truth and beauty, the God without whom no truth or beauty could possibly exist. We're to seek to please him through our growing understanding of the various academic disciplines, because all truth is God's truth.

> *Good grades should be a by-product of excellent work, not a primary and consuming goal.*

WORK WITHOUT WORRYING: LEARN TO LOVE LEARNING

So how do we study and learn without worrying? We do it by learning to love the *process* of learning—the discovery of new things, the challenge, the growth in understanding that only comes from spending focused time on our course work. Live fully in the moments of your study. When you do, you'll find your anxiety about the outcome start to fade. Ecclesiastes 9:10 says, "Whatever your hand finds to do, do it with all your might" (NASB).

Remember Colossians 3:23-24: "Whatever you do, work heartily, as for the Lord and not for men. . . . You are serving the Lord Christ." Give yourself rigorously to learning, to the development of academic skills, to being a good steward of the intellectual ability that God has given you, even if it's not as great as you wish it was. Your Christ-like attitude and grace-dependent effort please him apart from whatever grade you end up receiving (Philippians 2:13; 1 Peter 4:11).

Don't confuse God and your professor. Here's what I mean: Your professor's job is to help you learn and grade your work. But God is your real boss. He's the One you are to work for, to seek to please, and pleasing him is more important than getting good grades. You can get a C in a class and succeed more in God's eyes than someone more talented who got an A. The professor's job is to grade based on external, objective standards, but God is more pleased by what you do with what you're given than by the raw outcome.

Avoid the temptation to compare yourself to others. Comparison inevitably leads to envy, discontentment, and frustration. Instead, be a good steward of what God has given you. Don't complain, don't whine, don't make excuses. Just do the very best you can, and sleep at night knowing that you did what you could. Leave the rest to God. Later in this book, we'll talk about how your grades can be a good indicator of your gifts and skills and how they can direct you, both before and after graduation, into certain lines of work.

> *Don't complain, don't whine, don't make excuses. Just do the very best you can, and sleep at night knowing that you did what you could. Leave the rest to God.*

Work is fundamentally good; more than that, it is actually a gift from God. Working hard as a student involves vigorously developing your brain, like a weightlifter develops his muscles, so that you are prepared for the good works God has for you down the road (Ephesians 2:10).

But as I mentioned earlier, work, on its own, isn't everything. Recreation is also important. In fact, without it our bodies and brains grow weary and break down. Through recreation, we restore our mental and physical faculties, reflect on and enjoy God's goodness in creation, and develop relationships. In recreation we ought to be refreshed for further labors. In recreation we also say, "It's enough. I've given it my best. I can trust God for the outcome."

As a student, when I worried about grades, I couldn't rest. Worrying saps energy for work and the ability to unplug. A diligent student can let go, take a healthy break, and sleep at night.

So we need to live with balance; it's easy to either play too hard or work too hard. We can't neglect either; each is vitally important. Let's explore the inherent goodness of both work and recreation and the potential pitfalls of loving either of them too much.

THE GOODNESS OF WORK

We've talked about the difference between working and worrying. And I've mentioned the need for recreation. But we haven't yet talked about the *value* or the *inherent goodness* of work, including academic work. Our culture's attitude toward work can be summed up by the bumper sticker, "A bad day fishing is better than a good day at work." If we apply this belief to a college campus, I think most students would agree with the general concept—anyone would rather play than go to class.

In other words, our culture views work as a necessary evil. We all know we *have* to do it, but we'd rather not. Be honest: If your grades didn't depend on it, would you actually go to class? Is class something that just has to be endured between weekend breaks?

All over the world, the main focus for many working people is to earn lots of money, to attain a certain lifestyle or cultural status, to have more toys and leisure, and perhaps to advance to a level where they can exercise authority over others. The Bible, however, teaches us that we are to work (and study) before the face of God as an expression of our love for him and for others and for the *intrinsic value of the work itself.* Our work is to be a creative, meaningful expression of our devotion to Christ.* Our studies in college prepare us for work later. But, for now, studying *is* our work. Earlier, when I talked about working instead of worrying, I mentioned seeking enjoyment in the process of learning. That's studying for the intrinsic value of the work itself.

But don't we often find work difficult or monotonous? We can read the account of the Fall in Genesis 3 and think that God's curse *invented* work: "By the sweat of your face you shall eat bread, till you return to the ground, for out of it you were taken" (Genesis 3:19).

---

* My perspective on work has been shaped by Dorothy Sayers's excellent essay "Why Work?" which appears in her book *Creed or Chaos* (Sophia Institute Press, 1999).

Actually the Fall merely *distorted* our relationship to our work. God had appointed work for Adam and Eve before the Fall (Genesis 2:15). Why? So that his image bearers would fruitfully cultivate the world they inhabited, subduing the earth itself and exercising a responsible dominion over the animal and plant life that God had created for their flourishment and enjoyment. Without a doubt, work was in place prior to that fateful bite of the forbidden fruit.

But God's curse as a result of the Fall meant that going forward, work would not always be satisfying (though it often is; see Ecclesiastes 2:10, 24; 3:13, 22; 5:18-20; 9:9-10). The reality we all know is that work is sometimes painful, even aggravating (Ecclesiastes 1:2-3). In short, fulfilling our God-given mandate now involves occasional mental, physical, and even psychological frustration. It's the new normal.

Before the Fall, God told Adam and Eve to "be fruitful and multiply and fill the earth and subdue it and have dominion over the fish of the sea and over the birds of the heavens and over every living thing that moves on the earth" (Genesis 1:28). The Hebrew term used in Genesis for "subdue" (*kabash*) elsewhere has the meaning of bringing a people or a land into subjection to serve the one subduing it (for example, Numbers 32:22, 29). The idea was that mankind was to make the earth's resources serviceable for humanity.

This includes scientific and technological study—the exploration of physical patterns in nature that God has ordained, the harnessing of which leads to products that improve lives. For example, the fact that wood floats on water can be utilized to construct basic canoes. The fact that every action (force) creates an equal and opposite reaction (codified as Isaac Newton's third law of motion) makes paddling possible, and now you've got a way to cross bodies of water. Designing and constructing roads, cars, and eventually airplanes and helicopters are other examples of putting God's laws to work.

All branches of science and engineering are possible because God has created an orderly world in which certain laws can be discovered and utilized. This principle extends to human and veterinary medicine and all forms of biology and health science: We are exploring the way God made our bodies to work, how to fight disease, how to improve well-being through nutrition, exercise, and the like.

On the humanities side of things, we're exploring truth or beauty more directly (literature, philosophy, art, music), or perhaps studying the history of civilization to understand the societal patterns, laws, and social mores of various cultures and nations over the centuries. Such studies help us understand the consequences of ideas.

In college, studying is our work. It is what we do as an expression of our love for God, our desire to develop and maximize the gifts he's given us, our desire to understand the world around us, and to be prepared for a fruitful, productive life after college.

In college, studying *is* our work. It is what we do as an expression of our love for God, our desire to develop and maximize the gifts he's given us, our desire to understand the world around us and to be prepared for a fruitful, productive life after college.

THE GOODNESS OF RECREATION

Okay, so we know that work is important. And college certainly involves a lot of work. But what about recreation? What's its role? And what does God have to do with our recreation, anyway?

My wife and I once had one of those free two-week subscriptions to Netflix for unlimited movies. They offered to extend it for another two weeks, but we decided to cancel. The persistent lady on the phone wanted to know why, but our reason wasn't on her list. She asked, "Have you enjoyed it?" We said yes and thanked her. "Are you finding the movies you want?" Affirmative. "Are you able to find the time to watch the movies?" Again, yes. "So, why are you canceling?" she asked incredulously.

Our culture's worldview is straightforward: You've worked long and hard, sacrificing your desires to do what others need you to do, and come Friday, you should reward yourself. You've earned it. And when you're sitting by the pool with a Diet Coke and a great magazine, you can remember that *this* is what you were working for. It doesn't get any better than this.

But that way of thinking could not be further from the biblical framework. No, just as we're to work for God— not for money, not for ourselves, and not even to secure the approval of others—so our recreation should be seen from the vantage point of our entire life being lived out before the face of God. Through our time, talents, and possessions we bring a joyful sacrifice to the One whose lovingkindness is better than life (Psalm 63:3), the One whose mercies include oxygen, food, and the occasional Ultimate Frisbee game, though we deserve only punishment for our sins (Psalm 36:7-9; Romans 3:23; 6:23).

Times of recreation are undeserved gifts of God. They should result in a greater love for the Giver, and a deeper humility and gratefulness that accompany a sense of our total dependence upon him. Recreation should also rejuvenate us for the good work that he's appointed for us. Let's look at a few key elements of recreation.

> *Recreation should also rejuvenate us for the good work that he's appointed for us.*

1. Recreation is essential.

Working constantly is—at best—foolish and inefficient, leading eventually to burnout. Never taking time off may also mean we've forgotten that "unless the LORD builds the house, those who build it labor in vain" (Psalm 127:1). It goes hand in hand with anxiety and fear, which are unavoidable consequences of idolizing accomplishment for accomplishment's sake. But we don't have to work from a posture of anxiety. We can work from a posture of rest: doing our best and trusting that the outcome is always in God's hands. In the end, that attitude raises the quality of our work, particularly over the long haul.

Our need for refreshment is a reminder that we are finite creatures, and that only God is infinite, never needing rest (Psalm 121:4). With that perspective we're able to take consecrated breaks for soul and body refreshment. God modeled this for us in creation by resting on the seventh day (Genesis 2:2-3). If rest was fitting for God, how much more for us?

2. Recreation should be intentional.

It is very helpful to set aside times for breaks and even activities to do during those breaks. That way, you're not at the whim of every possible diversion that presents itself. Between texting, Facebook, Twitter, Skype, Wii, etc., the number of potential distractions we face can be overwhelming. We can't let ourselves become servants of recreation, at the beck and call of every fun thing that we could possibly do. Rather, we must optimize our limited time for recreation by choosing it deliberately and wisely.

Consider the difference between recreation and entertainment, a distinction we often fail to make in our use of leisure time. *Merriam-Webster's Collegiate Dictionary* defines recreation as "refreshment of strength and spirits after work." However, entertainment is defined as "amusement or diversion provided especially by performers." Both are diversionary; they take our minds off work. But while recreation is the purposeful attempt to restore or refresh creative energy, entertainment is often more on the mind-numbing end of the spectrum, possibly failing to rekindle mental energy.

That's not to say that all entertainment is bad. It's just a caution to consider when deciding how to spend our limited leisure time. To replenish my energy, I find that what my brain often needs is not the cessation of stimuli, but a different kind (or lower intensity) of mental stimuli. Reading, writing, a nice meal with the family, and exercise generally do much more for me than passively consuming whatever's on TV or the Internet.

Recreation can be solitary, or it can be a means for building relationships. In college, I was a Division III cross-country runner. To this day, I find running to be an excellent opportunity for reflective thought, prayer, and planning. But intentionally recreating with others through things like intramural sports, Ultimate Frisbee, or going on trips is a great way to find refreshment and also build quality relationships. Each has its advantages.

As a student, I found it helped me to use a fun recreational activity as an incentive to get my work done, particularly when I really needed to focus and be disciplined. For example, when a classmate and I each had a paper to write, we'd agree to meet up for tennis after we were both done (tennis was my other sport). Try it. I think you'll find that the fun thing you're looking forward to doing will drive you to work in a focused, productive manner. And then when you go have fun, you won't feel guilty or burdened by the work you didn't do. Rather, your heart will be at peace, thankful for God's help in getting the job done. This tactic works with big projects, too, even ones that take several weeks to complete. First, break down the larger project into several smaller, concrete tasks. Then, go after these tasks one by one, taking time to refresh yourself after each is completed (kind of like what I'm doing as I write this book).

3. Recreation should be limited.

Too little recreation can lead to mental or physical breakdown. People get sick. They have trouble falling asleep, being constantly wrapped up in their work. But too much recreation or leisure tends to distort a gift of God into an idol (something that's too important to us). Our hearts turn inward, and we become immune to the needs around us, let alone the satisfaction of doing our work well. We end up living for pleasure, and the enjoyment decreases over time. We lose our sense of purpose.

Remember our two free weeks of Netflix? We canceled not because we couldn't find the movies we wanted or didn't enjoy them, but because it ate up too much time, and we were being lulled away *from* responsibilities rather than being refreshed *for* responsibilities. We were elevating entertainment to an unhealthy level. So yes, we'll see movies occasionally, but we didn't need a new DVD in the mail each day, demanding to be watched that night.

4. Recreation should restore, not detract.

The attitude we bring *to* recreation should be one of God-dependent, faith-filled thanksgiving—a recognition that we can rest from our labors because, though our effort is important, so is our rest. We humbly recognize that we are finite, and that only God is infinite. But just as importantly, the attitude we take *from* leisure should include thankfulness for the gift of work—in particular for the personal set of responsibilities that God has given us as stewards of his grace (1 Peter 4:10). We should sense that it's right for leisure to represent *temporary* refreshment. And we should be thankful that work is a regular and important part of the Christian life.

There are many different forms of recreation. I've mentioned activities like running, Ultimate Frisbee, and going on trips. Are there any kinds of recreation that are inappropriate? Sure. Some activities are obviously off-limits, such as watching pornographic videos or shoplifting. Other activities, such as spending money on online poker or watching movies with gratuitous violence or reading sexually explicit novels, can be just as damaging. If your brain is fried from calculus, but you could handle a relaxing, uplifting novel, reading it would probably refresh you more than a mindless TV show.

But most forms of recreation are morally neutral, so you're completely free to choose the ones that work best for you, as best fits the occasion. In the limited time you'll have for recreation, my suggestion is to choose activities that you find restorative, that don't become harmfully addictive, and through which you can build sustaining relationships with others. For example, while there's nothing in the Bible that says video games are inherently evil, I have always found them too addicting. So I keep my distance. The same could be said about many TV shows. (Of course, many video games and TV shows today *are* evil, because of the raunchy content.) Know yourself, and set proper boundaries so that recreation restores you instead of enslaving you.

CONCLUSIONS

Work and recreation are each important. As you launch into adulthood, balancing work and recreation (along with service) should become the natural rhythm of your life. College presents a great opportunity to start implementing a healthy balance of these. After you graduate, if not before, your waking hours will likely consist of work, family responsibilities, service activities (church, community, volunteer stuff), and recreation (alone, with friends or your spouse, and eventually with kids). By learning to discipline and budget your time, and to have a healthy, biblical perspective of work and recreation, you're preparing yourself for success in whatever lies ahead while enabling yourself to get the most out of your college experience.

DISCUSSION STARTERS

1. How do you approach your work? Do you see it as drudgery, as something to get through as quickly as possible? In what ways might you need an attitude adjustment with regard to work?

2. How much time a week do you spend in recreation? What things really refresh and recharge you? Do any of your recreational activities ever become detrimental?

3. While some students recreate too much, others are consumed by work and find it difficult to relax. Which error are you more prone to? What will you do to protect yourself from that error?

4. Consider whether you need to make one or two resolutions to be more God honoring in your work and recreation.

PART 4
ACADEMICS MATTER

COMMON MISTAKE #8:
Being Too Passive or Too Cocky

> *Thrive Principle: Wisely Select a Major*

WE SHIFT OUR attention now to what many think of as the most important aspect of college: academic development. In a sense, academics are the heartbeat of the college experience. As important as character formation and relationships are, it's college and only college where you can get a well-rounded education that prepares you for a variety of professions in the modern economy. Many employers exclusively hire college graduates because they want employees who know how to think, figure things out, and communicate with clarity and professionalism. Moreover, a college degree implies a measure of discipline and maturity. It says you had the ability, determination, and perseverance to finish what you started and achieve a level of competence in a particular academic field.

The fact is that while 70 percent of high school graduates in America immediately go on to college, 30 percent drop out after their first year, and half never graduate. A diploma means you made it.

Factoid
According to the Bureau of Labor Statistics (U.S. Department of Labor), as of October 2009, seven out of ten high school graduates go on to college.[1] However, 30 percent of college and university students drop out after their first year, and half never graduate. Nonselective colleges graduate, on average, 35 percent of their incoming students, while the most competitive schools graduate 88 percent.[2]

But the diploma itself is not what has value; it's the accomplishment that the diploma reflects—what the diploma signifies—that matters. In the next few chapters we'll talk about how to make the most of your academic preparation. Taking classes in a variety of departments will allow you to explore your interests and discover both what you enjoy and what you're really good at. And choosing an academic major will allow you to dig deep in a particular area, taking your God-given talents and honing them into significant skills that can someday help you earn a living.

Mistake #8 is going about choosing your major in one of two wrong ways. There may well be more ways to do it poorly, but these are the most common. The first is being too passive, sitting on the sidelines for a couple of years, just taking a bunch of semirandom courses, afraid to commit. This kind of timidity sometimes comes from thinking that there is just one right answer and that to get it wrong would be disastrous. Not only could there be more than one great major for you, but changing majors is not the end of the world. Better to try something and then have to shift gears if it doesn't work than to never try something at all.

> Better to try something and then have to shift gears if it doesn't work than to never try something at all.

The second wrong way is the exact opposite: being too confident, charging ahead either without much thought or in blatant disregard of the informed opinions of those who know you best. Students who do this underestimate how much hassle it can be to change majors, and they insufficiently value a sober assessment of their talents. But first, let's explore the value of what many call a broad, liberal arts education.

LEARNING HOW TO THINK: THE BENEFITS OF A BROAD, LIBERAL ARTS EDUCATION

People change jobs and even career tracks with increasing frequency in our day. Statistics on this vary, but everyone agrees that it is more and more common.* So what you study may not end up being what you do, or at least not what you do

---

* According to one report, people in their twenties go through an average of seven jobs. (Robin Marantz Henig, "What Is It about 20-Somethings?" *New York Times Magazine*, August 18, 2010.) I'm not convinced all of this job switching is necessary or wise, but I do think some of it is probably an inevitable, amoral by-product of a changing economy.

for more than a few years. Life happens. That doesn't mean your choice of major is unimportant. What it does mean is that regardless of your major, having a diverse educational background is a good investment, given the uncertainty of what the future holds.

Part of why I say this is that I notice students asking questions like "When am I ever going to use this stuff?" They want to know when their paychecks are going to depend on their ability to draw a free body diagram or to cite the major turning points of World War II. And it's a natural question to ask when you're choosing courses, or when you are enduring a course you don't particularly enjoy.

The answer is that you may use it directly or (more likely) you will use it indirectly. You are in college to learn how to think so that you can, for the rest of your life, increasingly love God with a well-trained mind, a mind that can analytically break down an argument, discover logical fallacies, communicate effectively, and be able to manipulate numbers and spreadsheets (all remarkably practical skills, my stay-at-home wife, a Stanford graduate, tells me).

Regardless of your major, part of college involves learning to appreciate some of the great works of literature, music, and art, and to be able to write well in a variety of contexts—persuasive essays, research papers, and technical reports. Another part of college is learning how to give the occasional speech, because almost no job is immune to public speaking. Last but not least, you're in college to gain experience working on projects with teammates you might not choose as

Q: *Have you ever suggested that a student take a year off to work out his or her goals or to not go to college altogether?* —JOSHUA, RECENT GRADUATE, English/Philosophy

A: I've known people who have taken a year off after high school to go on mission trips. They started college at nineteen with much greater maturity than they had at eighteen. They may not have made it right out of high school. The reality is that not everyone has the maturity at age eighteen to undertake a rigorous academic program. Some students are better off delaying the huge price tag on what would be a lousy investment.

And there are some people who simply don't need traditional college for what God has wired them to do. In his book *God at Work*, Gene Veith tells the story of a college student who, though dedicated, simply couldn't pass his courses. Exhausted, he took a semester off. He got a job doing what he loved—working on cars. He excelled and became highly respected at the garage, earning more money and taking on more responsibility. He kept thinking he should quit and go back to finish college. He was apologetic to others, but he shouldn't have been. He had found his calling.

Our culture says that some careers are more prestigious than others, but as Christians, we should not accept the world's perspective on degrees, money, and status. To God all legitimate vocations have equal dignity.

friends; that's life, you know—you don't always choose your coworkers. You want to graduate as a well-rounded, intelligent, articulate, flexible person, someone who can work in a variety of environments, and who has strong problem-solving, communication, and people skills. Whether you want to be an engineer, a social worker, or a junior high teacher, these abilities will come in handy.

You are in college to learn how to think so that you can, for the rest of your life, increasingly love God with a well-trained mind.

So remember that a lot of what you're picking up in class is going to enable you to think and live well. Solving physics problems will help you think analytically, which will help you spot weaknesses in your company's sales plan. A history class is not about memorizing a bunch of useless dates, places, and events; it's an opportunity to understand how the past shapes the present, to become conversant on political issues in our day so as to better understand the changing world we live in, to differentiate between historical facts and the opinions of commentators, and to articulate your own perspectives in a clear, coherent manner.

Of course, some majors naturally require more specialization, which will mean more "in major" courses and perhaps fewer "nonmajor" courses. While an English major might require forty credits of English courses, a nuclear engineering major might require seventy "in major" credits, plus a bunch of math, chemistry, and physics. That means the English major will have more opportunities to take courses in other areas, pursue a double major, or simply take fewer overall courses.

This speaks to a larger point: Some majors are inherently broader than others. Being a pre-med major just means that you're committed to taking a few specific classes. Beyond those limited course requirements, you can take whatever you think will help you on the MCAT or in medical school (while, of course, completing the requirements of whatever major you select). A major like health science is meant to lay a broad foundation to allow students to pursue a variety of fields like dentistry, physical therapy, or physician assistant work upon graduation. Conversely, I once spoke to a sophomore aeronautical engineering student who was thinking about switching universities and majors. He was bummed because none of the courses he took would transfer into any other major at the other university. He had chosen a narrower major.

Both broad and narrow majors have their advantages and disadvantages. With a broad major, there's plenty of room to change your focus without losing a lot of time. The disadvantage is that you are more likely to need additional schooling after graduation because it is harder to differentiate yourself within the job market. By contrast, I studied ceramic engineering, which you've probably never heard of. At the time there were only about thirteen colleges in the nation that offered bachelor degrees in the field. Alfred University (where I went) was the most well known. Doing a good job in college meant getting a job was pretty easy. It's not like there were a ton of jobs in my field, but there sure weren't that many graduates either. So I took more of a risk, in a sense. Had I wanted to switch majors, it would have been harder to do so. I would have had the same problem as the sophomore aeronautical engineering student. Consequently, what I tell students is that if you go into a narrow major, you need to be more certain about your choice because there's a higher price that will come with switching.

Factoid

Did you know that just over a third of students at public universities graduate in four years? Meanwhile, slightly more than half of full-time freshmen will receive their degree within five years.[3]

But getting back to the benefits of a broad, liberal arts education, I think taking a variety of courses is important even for those with narrower majors like mine. Philosophy professor Arthur Holmes puts it this way: "The question to ask about an education is not 'What can I do with it?' but rather 'What is it doing to me, as a person?' Education has to do with the making of persons."[4] Do you get what he's saying? There's a personal, transforming impact of education. It enriches your life and expands your horizons. Don't just demand that everything you learn be immediately useful in a tangible sense.

Being well-rounded helps in unexpected ways. I learned

how to write primarily in philosophy and English literature classes. I built on these skills when I needed to write technical reports and engineering publications. Through an honors program, I took classes in music, creative writing, and even chess, while also attending theatrical events and concerts in major venues. All of these expanded my horizons and enriched my life. Look for these kinds of opportunities regardless of your major. Chances are they won't come as easily after you graduate.

Speaking of opportunities, take time at college to enroll in one or two classes that simply fascinate you. My wife took a class on Shakespeare and another on the impact of the plague on medieval Europe. Neither fulfilled a requirement or seemed to have an immediate bearing on her life, but both provided a larger perspective on history and culture, not to mention refreshment, variety, and great memories. I audited a seminar class on U.S.–Iraq relations in the spring of 2003 during the lead-up to the much-debated war in Iraq. Each week there was a different speaker and a different perspective on the upcoming war—some for it, some against. It was amazing.

By the same token, if you hear that a particular professor is really good, try to take a class from him or her if at all possible. Regardless of the subject, you'll learn a ton from a good teacher whose enthusiasm will help you learn to love learning for a lifetime, which is the right attitude for a Christian in God's world. We want to go through life with our eyes wide open, continually learning more.

DON'T BE TOO TIMID: MAKE A DECISION

God knows what you'll end up majoring in. You may not, at least not yet. But it's an *amoral* decision, so God doesn't reveal to us in the Bible whether we should go with history, architecture, or English. With amoral decisions, we are free to choose within the parameters established in God's Word. In selecting a major, you don't need to put out a fleece like Gideon to get an answer from God (Judges 6:36-40).†

The topic of "knowing God's will" has always been a hot button for young adult Christians. We all agree that God's moral will is revealed in the Bible: Flee sexual immorality (1 Thessalonians 4:3-7), maintain an attitude of thanksgiving and prayerful dependence on God (1 Thessalonians 5:16-18), obey your parents (Ephesians 6:1), tell others about Jesus (Matthew 28:19-20), don't steal (Ephesians 4:28), tell the truth (Ephesians 4:25), and so on.

We also agree that God has a personal, specific will for our lives, a will that covers our amoral decisions like where to go to college, what to major in, whether we'll marry and whom, what we'll do after college, etc.—see passages like Jeremiah 29:11 and Romans 8:28. God is orchestrating the events in and surrounding our lives for our good, and he holds our future in his hands.

Here's the controversy: Some Christians think we can

---

†Some people put forth Gideon as a model of godly faith, since (unlike some biblical characters, like the men of Israel in Joshua 9:14) Gideon was careful to consult God on his big mission to deliver Israel from the Midianites. But if you look at that passage in context, you'll see that Gideon was actually *testing* God, which is why he's so apologetic in verse 39. God had already told Gideon what to do. God ends up playing along as a *concession* to the weak faith of Gideon. We need to remember that just because something happened in the Bible doesn't mean we need to imitate it. As someone cleverly put it, not everything the Bible *describes* is *prescribed*.

Q: *I have had many hardworking and involved friends who really struggled to land on a major. Many of them felt that they had a few mild academic interests or strengths but no particular major really was standing out. What would you suggest for people who cannot seem to find a major that really resonates with them as they pass on to their sophomore or junior years?*
—KELVIN, JUNIOR, Physics/Engineering

A: That's a really tough one. It is common for academically gifted students to have difficulty landing on a major because there are so many things that they do well and which genuinely interest them. For other students, they may not necessarily be super-talented; they're just kind of wishy-washy. I would start by encouraging them to worry less about future employment and more about loving their classes and doing as well as they can in them. That in itself will open doors post-graduation. Employers want intelligent workers who know how to think and learn. Such employees are often lifelong learners, picking up new skills as the occasion demands. In the first half of college, someone without a clear passion could take a variety of classes in different fields rather than worrying about employment.

But that still leaves the problem of landing on *some* major. In short, I'd encourage them to pick the hardest major that they enjoy, that they can do reasonably well in, and that can allow them to graduate fairly quickly (to minimize debt). They'll have really pushed themselves, which will lay a good foundation for whatever comes next.

(and therefore should) discern God's personal, specific will for our amoral decisions in advance so that we can make the "right" choices and stay in "the center of his will," experiencing God's greatest blessing.

Others think we cannot know God's personal, specific will for our amoral decisions in advance of making them. We discover it step by step as we live. God's will is that we live holy lives (following the Bible's moral guidelines for Christians), becoming more like Jesus every day. We use our minds to make wise, informed decisions on amoral matters, asking God to guard our hearts from sinful motivations, but ultimately owning our decisions, knowing that God will play out his story for our lives through these decisions (over which he is sovereign).

So which is it? Can we know God's personal will for us—like whether we should major in math or chemistry—in advance of making that choice? Do we need to wait for him to specifically tell us before we make a decision? I don't think so. The problem with this view, besides the fact that Scripture never encourages us to pursue this kind of knowledge, is that it's highly subjective.

First, as a rule, I don't think it's wise to expect God to lead our decisions the way he led Moses and David from being anonymous shepherds to big-time prophet/miracle worker and king, respectively. These guys had very special roles to play in God's redemptive plan. Likewise, the apostle Paul was sometimes led in extraordinary ways (Acts 16:6-10). But *generally* Paul seems to have gone about making decisions the same way God expects us to: by exercising sound judgment and planning (e.g., Acts 20:16; 1 Corinthians 16:5-9).[‡]

Second, if God expects us to discover and select the "right major" in advance, does the same logic apply to other decisions? Is there only one right man or woman for us to marry? One right job after graduation? How about summer internships? How about whether to play paintball or football with the guys in the dorm? Which parking space to choose?

> ### Factoid
> A majority of students in all colleges and universities change their majors at least once in their college careers; and many change their majors several times over the course of their college careers.[5]

But wouldn't it bring more peace to "know" you are doing exactly what God wants you to do? Theoretically, sure. But people who believe that God grants this knowledge in advance offer only subjective ways of being certain, which leads to endless second-guessing of our decisions, especially if things don't work out as we had hoped (which is often the case). We end up thinking maybe it wasn't really God's will. Maybe we didn't pray enough. Maybe what we thought was an open door was a temptation from the devil. Maybe our motives weren't pure.

[‡] For a book-length defense of this perspective, see *Just Do Something: A Liberating Approach to Finding God's Will* by Kevin DeYoung.

Well, our motives are never perfectly pure. We can probably find fault if we look in the mirror long enough. But God has a better way than our continually analyzing impressions. He's only revealed his moral will for us, not his personal will (Deuteronomy 29:29). We can experience peace when we're obeying God's moral will (Romans 8:6), and God chastises us when we don't (Hebrews 12:6-7). We're not told the future, so even our planning should recognize that God may decide otherwise (James 4:13-16).

Thinking you can know God's personal will in advance magnifies the stress it claims to remove. Trusting in God's control brings peace and rest. God wants us to walk in his ways more than we do. It's not that we can't make mistakes; we can, and sometimes they're painful. But God uses even our mistakes (and everyone else's) to work out his perfect plan for us (Romans 8:28), which is that we become more like Jesus regardless of what our majors are, where we live, what jobs we take, or whatever other amoral decisions we make.

> *Thinking you can know God's personal will in advance magnifies the stress it claims to remove. Trusting in God's control brings peace and rest.*

I'm not suggesting we shouldn't pray about big decisions like which major to choose. Nor am I suggesting that there are no bad options. It would have been really bad for me to major in voice or painting. The disaster would soon have been apparent in my GPA. We should pray for wisdom (James 1:5); God wants to help us make wise decisions with biblically informed motivations. We should seek the advice of wise, trusted counselors, particularly those who are older and more mature (Proverbs 11:14; Hebrews 13:7). And we should ask God to open our eyes to things in his Word—things that may reveal sinful attitudes or motivations on our part, like wanting a particular major just because we can make a lot of money with it (1 Timothy 6:10) or acting in fear of what others may think (Proverbs 29:25).

In short, we should ask God to help us obey his moral will, to do the things that the Bible tells us are pleasing to him. Beyond that, we make the best decisions we can and trust God to bring glory to himself whether we're math majors or English majors or nursing majors. Every legitimate major and profession can be used as a platform to bring glory to God.

WEIGHING THE FEEDBACK OF OTHERS

Does this mean you can press ahead choosing *any* major you want? Not necessarily. Of course your interests are important—it wouldn't be smart to pick a major you don't like. But you'll also want to look at your *gifts*: What are you good at, and what do wise people in your life, people who care for you, think you're good at? In what areas have you had success?

In choosing your major, you should be realistic. If you got C's and D's on essays in high school, and you don't enjoy reading, that probably eliminates a bunch of majors that require a lot of reading and writing, like English, journalism, history, or philosophy. If you were not very good at math and don't have enough interest in the subject to get better, you'll be hurting in a math, physics, or most engineering majors, even though one of those may be what you want to pursue. Check out what's required.

What does it all mean? If you like a major, and it seems doable based on your high school experience, go for it. But be open to feedback from your professors that may indicate that another course of action could be better for you.

Suppose you want to be an aeronautical engineer. You grew up making model airplanes and imagining the flight patterns of your handiwork. You're hard working and disciplined, but you fail calculus and have no idea what's going on in physics. You get a tutor and spend time with your professors during office hours, but nothing seems to do the trick. You take both courses twice, but still don't pass them. What's going on? God may be mercifully limiting your options. Check with your career services office on campus. There are probably other ways to pursue your love of airplanes. (We'll talk more in the next chapter about how grades help reinforce or weaken our sense of calling.)

THE CONCEPT OF VOCATION

This brings us to the concept of *vocation*. Ultimately, and long term, you're trying to find your vocation. Our word vocation comes from the Latin *vocatio*, which means "a summons or a calling." Even today we talk about vocational training opportunities, like specialized schools where people can become chefs, auto mechanics, or plumbers. But other fields, like teaching or architecture or writing, can also be spoken of as vocations, as callings.

Christians used to speak of *callings* as sets of responsibilities to which we are called by God. For example, you are a son or daughter to your parents, and if they are helping you pay for college, they probably expect certain things from you (like that you'll actually go to class and study). Being a son or daughter is a calling. If you work ten hours a week at Starbucks, that's a calling. You need to be making venti caramel mochas at your appointed times.

Everything else we've been saying in this chapter has been about recognizing your gifts and interests and choosing a field of study. But the word *calling* implies a caller —namely, God. When we talk about a calling, we're talking about something that comes to us from outside ourselves. You see, although we go about trying to recognize our gifts and interests—an important process—it is God who ultimately calls us to a certain line of work. Our role is to respond to him by recognizing, receiving, and pursuing this calling. And if we look, we can see that even our desires for certain kinds of work, and our life experiences that have led us to pursue certain interests, are orchestrated by God.

Think about the analogy of a marriage. It is not enough to want to marry someone. In most cultures, that person has to want to marry you, too. It takes two to tango, as they say. On the one side, our interests and passions, combined with our God-given talents and hard work, lead to the formation of skills and competencies (activities or services we can offer to others in exchange for pay). What's the other side of the coin? Some organization or entity needs to be willing to hire us, to pay us to apply our skills. Your calling comes from outside you.

So though you choose a major you like, and though you weigh the feedback of others in making that choice, only time will tell what God has in store. I may think I'm good at basketball, but failing to make the team will reveal otherwise. Likewise, many freshman college students think they're going to medical school, only to have their GPA or MCAT score tell another story. So you sense God's call and choose a major based on your interests and gifts and the feedback of others, but your grades will tell you if you can handle that major. You also need to remain sufficiently interested in that major to take all the required classes. And after you graduate, someone needs to hire you.

Factoid

Of those college freshmen who aspire to become medical doctors, less than 10 percent actually do.[6]

So now that you're freaking out, let's ask the pertinent questions: What if you graduate and you can't get the kind of job you want? Does that mean you aren't very skilled in that particular field? Maybe or maybe not. In the most highly competitive fields, it is possible to be quite good and still not get paid. Think of how many good baseball players never make it to the big leagues. A good friend of mine in high school was a phenomenal athlete—the best I ever knew. He made it to the minor leagues but just never got that big break. With sports, after a certain age, you can pretty much throw in the towel. Likewise, plenty of good writers don't make a living just from their writing. The same can be said about theater or music.

However, the majority of college majors prepare you for a variety of jobs—some more than others. Earlier in the chapter I talked about narrow and broad majors and how each had their pros and cons. In more narrow majors there are fewer jobs, but fewer graduates, so less competition for those jobs. In broader majors there are more jobs, but also more graduates with that major. All that said, if you do a decent job in your major, finding a job is usually what happens if you go after it in the right ways, which we'll talk about later. My point here is just to say that choosing a major based on your interests and your perceived gifts, incorporating the feedback of others, is only the beginning of the journey. God will either confirm your sense of calling (with grades and open doors) or redirect you.

And coming back to those competitive fields like professional sports, even those can lead to open doors if you get creative. You might never play professional baseball, but you can coach high school ball and teach physical education (though you may have to also endure teaching driver's ed). You might not become a Broadway actress, but you can go to graduate school, get a master's degree in fine arts, and teach theater at the college level. So go for it, but balance idealism with realism.

Of course, there may be many things you like to do that you don't get paid to do. Most people have one salaried vocation and several nonsalaried avocations. An avocation is a pastime, a hobby, something you do on the side. College is a great time to pursue new things, some of which can become lifelong hobbies that bring you all kinds of enjoyment and new friendships, but not necessarily income. Lots of people like drawing or painting; very few get paid for it.

RECOGNIZE YOUR CALLING

Here are some practical guidelines for how to go about deciding on your major and recognizing your calling. You can start this even when you're in high school. First, narrow down your interests, passions, and gifts:

Interests/Passions

- What do you like to do?
- What have you done in your life just because you wanted to? How did it go? Do you want to do more in that area?
- What academic subjects interest you? What topics?
- If you could do anything you wanted for work, and if making money didn't matter, what would you do? Be as creative as you'd like. (You can get practical later.)

Gifts

- What do people who know you well (your parents, your pastors, your mentors) say you are good at? What actual jobs can they see you doing? (Here's the practical part.)
- What successes have you had so far in life, even modest ones? (Particular classes, projects, club activities, music, theater, sports, etc.)

Next, look for overlap between the first list and the second. If you think you have a strong interest in something that you have never actually done, find a way to try it and see how it goes. Okay, by now you should have a fairly short list. Perhaps rank them to force yourself to think of which represent the stronger combinations of your passions and gifts.

Work the list down to a handful of majors. Go online and read about these areas. Talk to your parents and professors about this list, and ask them what they think. Also talk to people who work in these fields, both people who've been in those fields for many years (perhaps your parents, or their friends, or older friends from church, or the parents of your friends) and those who've only been out of school for a few years (since fields evolve). Ask them what it's like. What do they like about it? What do they actually do in a typical day? Can you ever observe them at work or maybe help them, even if they can't pay you? What sorts of jobs are available if you choose this major? Will it take you a long time to get a stable position? What can you expect three years out? Are you likely to travel a lot in this field (can be a plus for a while, but most say it gets old, particularly when you get married and start a family)?

What if there are several majors you think you can success- fully pursue? Make a wise, informed decision. If you are will- ing to work hard and think that graduate school might be of interest, a double major may be right for you, as long as your GPA can handle it—graduate schools look at GPAs a lot more than employers do. But look carefully at the degree plans. Double majoring in two related fields with some over- lap, like engineering and physics or philosophy and English, may not mean a lot of extra classes, but pursuing both math and theology certainly will. Internships and other sorts of work experiences can also help you narrow down your inter- ests. We'll get to those in chapter 10.

There is no need to rush or panic if you aren't sure of a major your freshman year. Just take as wide a variety of classes as possible with the best, most dynamic professors. Your first year is a good time to get some of the general, core class requirements taken care of. Keep going through the exercises regarding your interests, passions, and gifts, and aim to make a decision by your sophomore year.

TWO REALITY CHECKS

Some students struggle because their parents want them to go into a particular field, but their hearts just aren't in it. It is not uncommon for the parents in these cases to be motivated either by prestige and economics (they want Junior to be a doctor, lawyer, or engineer) or tradition (they're hoping their child takes over the family business, etc.). What do you do in this situation? First, I think you need to honestly talk to your parents. Don't put it off and think it will go away. It may not. When you talk, be open to concerns and questions that may not have occurred to you. Take seriously every reasonable caution they raise.

It would probably help to present to them some alternative majors that you're considering. Doing so will show them that you are taking your decision seriously. If neither of those leads to a resolution, ask them if their economic support for your college education is dependent on you pursuing a specific major. If it is, and you're absolutely not interested, tell them you'll take some time off to work. Pay them rent in exchange for living at home while taking some general education courses at a community college. That strategy will show them you are serious about your responsibilities and that you don't want to take advantage of them, but that you still intend to pursue your education in an area where you think God may be leading. It will also buy some time for the Lord to unite your hearts as you earn their trust and respect (see the principle of Proverbs 16:7).

In the absolute worst case, you might have to pay for your college education entirely on your own, taking on the full mantle of adulthood a bit earlier than you anticipated. Ultimately, you're responsible to *God*, not to your parents, for what you do with your life and the professional aspirations, gifts, and opportunities that God gives you.[§] But chances are you'll win them over as they see your sincerity, maturity, and willingness to shoulder responsibility.

One last warning: Be mindful about debt. If you have student loans, have realistic expectations about when you'll be able to pay them off. Find out what entry level positions earn for your major, and with your parents' help, calculate how quickly you could pay back your loans. It would probably be wise to earn as much money as you can over breaks and during the summer and to pay for at least part of college while you're in school if at all possible. You don't want to be enslaved to years of massive debt after graduation, particularly if you anticipate personal plans (such as child raising) could direct you out of the workforce for a season, or if you think God is calling you into a lower paying field. Again, balance idealism with realism.

CONCLUSIONS

You can love God with all your mind by being fully present in your studies, knowing that God is preparing you for what lies ahead in ways you cannot fully comprehend. Most of what you learn in classes will benefit you indirectly in the years to come, which is why a broad-based liberal arts education is so valuable. Wherever possible, take classes from teachers who can infect you with a love for learning. In choosing a major,

---

[§] As we discussed at length in chapter 5, while you should always honor and respect your parents, the Bible does not command *adult* children to obey their parents. Of course, if you're financially dependent on Mom and Dad (and you probably are, to some extent), then you've not yet completed your transition to adulthood. That's what makes it messy.

carefully consider your interests, passions, and gifts, as well as the feedback of others about your strengths and how suitable you might be for certain lines of work. Move toward the decision with intentionality, an accurate self-assessment, and a wise consideration of the pros and cons, but recognize that the selection of a major is only the beginning of a journey. In the years that follow, God will confirm or redirect your sense of his calling in various ways. In fact, that's the topic of our next chapter.

DISCUSSION STARTERS

1. How did you go about choosing your major? Do you think you exhibited intentionality? How did you consider the feedback of others?

2. What did you think about the idea that we cannot know God's personal will in advance?

3. What do you think about the concept of vocation—the idea of God's call on your life coming from outside you?

4. Do you have any expectations about your abilities or future prospects that may ultimately prove unrealistic? Would it leave you devastated, or could you trust God to create other avenues for you to serve him?

COMMON MISTAKE #9:
Living for Grades

> *Thrive Principle: Recognize That Growth Requires Challenge*

I LOVED GOING TO my 9:00 a.m. philosophy class. It was a refreshing break from the tedium of my freshman engineering classes. I could sit and listen to Dr. Simmons describe the thoughts of Plato, Hume, and Kant, perhaps occasionally raise my hand and join in, or just soak up the ideas. I enjoyed reading the assignments, taking notes, and really trying to understand the material.

I felt ready going into the first in-class exam. I had gotten solid A's in English my last year of high school, so I thought I had come a long way as a reader and a writer. We had to respond to three essay questions in one hour. Twenty minutes each—no problem. I walked out of the room full of confidence. The exam had even been fun.

A week later, Dr. Simmons handed back the exams. To my surprise and horror, he had the audacity to give me a B-. *He must have made a mistake*, I thought. I quickly scanned the test for his red-penned remarks, preparing to rebut his concerns and press my case. Didn't he know that I was an A student? What was wrong with the guy?

No grade change was made. Dr. Simmons explained that my essays were simply mediocre and that his standards were apparently higher than those of my high school. And with that, my love for learning philosophy was quickly overwhelmed by disappointment, frustration, a sense of injustice, and anxiety over my GPA. I would go on to hate that joker's class for the next few weeks.

JOY IN THE JOURNEY

Is the point of college academics to learn or to get good grades? You can guess my answer, I hope. The joy, as they say, is in the journey.

It's easy to count down the days until class is over and to make good grades your primary or even exclusive objective. The semester ends, and you breathe a sigh of relief if you get the grades you wanted—or freak out if you didn't. Before you know it, the next semester is underway, and the cycle starts all over again: You're living in fear of every test, project, and major assignment. The higher your GPA, the more the anxiety builds, because any slip-up can cause your GPA to come tumbling down.

When I went to college, our grades weren't even posted

online. I generally waited two or three weeks to get them in the mail. There were times when I worried daily over what would come in that envelope—something over which I had absolutely no control.

Don't try to rush through phases of your life as if the point is just to get through. Find joy in what you're doing *right now*. With your studies, jump in with both feet. Focus on learning, growing, and getting better. Don't freak out about grades. Live in the moment.

> Don't try to rush through phases of your life as if the point is just to get through. Find joy in what you're doing right now.

But sure, I know grades are important. That's why I'm taking this chapter to share with you some study strategies I learned the hard way. I think these will help you learn more and (yes) boost your grade-point average. I also want to share with you some of the hows and whys of grading, so that you'll have a healthy appreciation for the process. Mistake #9 is living for grades instead of working for them. There are *so* many reasons not to live for grades, but I wasn't aware of any of them when I was in your shoes! Of all the mistakes in this book, this is the one I was most guilty of. My grades were way too important to me. I really want to help you avoid the needless stress and anxiety that followed me by day and kept me up at night.

Let's start here: First of all, while it's important to maintain a solid GPA, the grades on your transcript are not necessarily going to make or break your career prospects. Truly.

Most employers just have a minimum (like maybe a 3.0 or 3.3); beyond that, they'll make hiring decisions based on letters of recommendation, past experiences (internships, projects, etc.), and the interview process. In fact, I'm pretty sure recommendations and experiences almost always trump grades. They also look for improvement, as it shows maturity, so doing better your sophomore or junior year helps. The other big factor is that alumni tend to go back to their alma mater to hire—they interview people who have a decent GPA and make decisions based on half-hour interviews. They know what a "good" GPA is at that school because they went there.

Those who live for grades tend to be more stressed and on edge. They're more likely to think their professors are unreasonable, making comments like "Dr. Hayward is just not fair. She doesn't know how hard I tried." Far from empowering you, thinking this way only makes it more difficult to do well.

Yet as students we all complain and blame from time to time. I know I did. And like I said in chapter 3, some professors are truly unreasonable and don't care. But for the most part, I was wrong when I thought I got ripped off. I deserved a B- on Dr. Simmons's exam. I needed to learn *how* to study—not just to work hard, but to work *smart*. And college was supposed to be harder than high school. It sure was more expensive.

STUDYING IS ESSENTIAL, EVEN WHEN NOTHING IS DUE

In chapter 2 we talked about working when it's time to work. I suggested making a detailed schedule, putting times for study into your schedule, and devoting two hours of studying out of class for every one hour in class. Okay, so what should you actually *do* during those study hours?

There are two immediate and significant differences between high school and college: class attendance and the homework policy. In high school, you generally saw your teachers five days a week. In college, you'll see them in class two or three times a week. There are MWF classes, TuTh classes, and occasionally classes that meet once a week, usually in the evening for a few hours. If you can avoid it, don't take one-night-a-week classes if the subject is demanding, because it's usually difficult to learn a challenging subject with only one day per week of exposure to the teacher. Better to spread it out.

Of course you'll only see your professors if you actually *go* to class, and *nobody will ever make you go. Ever.* But we already covered that. So let's assume you read chapter 2 and that you're going to class. The other difference you'll discover is that you may not have homework due each time class meets. It may be due once a week (say, every Friday) or once every two weeks, or never. And whatever the homework policy, the homework probably won't be worth much of your actual grade.

What's up with that? Many of you will often *wish* that

Q: *Do you have any advice on how to study while taking a class so that the material will stick with you longer after the class is over?* —KELVIN, JUNIOR, Physics/Engineering

A: Study regularly instead of cramming. If you have a three-credit class for which you plan to work six hours per week, I'd spread out those six hours over three to four days rather than one or two. With each exam, make cheat sheets with the key information. This pushes the content into long-term memory, and it also gives you something handy to go back to later if you need the specifics.

It is not uncommon to forget the details of any class. Our memories only retain so much. What matters is that you learned how to think about physics or calculus or European history or anatomy. Or that you learned how to appreciate American literature and to write coherent papers. You know where to go to find the details when you need them, and (most important) your brain has been trained to think along the lines of that particular subject.

homework counted more because, as long as you do it (and you can get help from your classmates or professor), you generally score very high on it. But it doesn't count for much because it's intended to be practice. It's the tests, papers, and projects that really count. And the higher you go in your education (sophomore, junior, senior years, and graduate school), the more it's done that way.

So let's say you have a three-credit class. It meets MWF for an hour each time. I doubt you'll actually have six hours of homework a week for that class—at least not in the sense of what the professor or graduate student will actually collect. It will probably be more like three to four hours, depending on how fast you are with the activities assigned (reading in a history, English, or philosophy class; problem sets in a math, physics, or engineering class; memorizing vocabulary in a foreign language class, etc.).

So what do you do with the remaining two to three hours that you've scheduled for study? You start getting ready for the quizzes or exams. If a semester is fifteen weeks, most classes will have a quiz or test (a.k.a., midterm) at least every five weeks, if not more often. Sometimes there will be just one big midterm halfway through the semester.* Either way, if you wait until the week of the exam to study, it might be too late. In my experience, cramming *can* work in some classes (been there, done that), but it usually produces only

---

* Once in a while, there are classes that don't have quizzes or exams; there's just homework, essays, and projects. Assuming these are three-credit classes, you'll probably be able to work less than six hours a week outside of class during most of the semester, but then you'll have to kick it into high gear (maybe up to eight hours a week) when you need to write an essay or complete a project.

short-term learning, and therefore should be avoided, though it's better than doing poorly on a test.

If a class is *skill based*, as opposed to *knowledge based*, cramming almost never works. Have you ever played a musical instrument and had an upcoming recital? If you were scheduled to play a challenging piano concerto by Mozart at a recital on September 15, would it work to wait until the fourteenth, stay up all night practicing, and show up at the recital with a pair of Red Bull cans? That might work if you had to spit out a bunch of memorized facts and figures *about* the concerto. But *playing* the piano is a skill; even if you're naturally talented, it takes practice (even if you *are* Mozart—his dad worked him!). It's the same way with organized sports: You practice every day so that your skills are sharp for the Friday night game. In fact, most coaches work their players harder in practice than in the games. That way the games seem easy. Apply the same motto to your studying. If you're prepared, the tests won't seem overwhelming. And if you're not overwhelmed, you'll be able to relax and even enjoy the process of taking the test, which will help you do even better.

What we've been talking about here is working *smart*. You already know you need to work *hard*. Let's get specific with some strategies.

In class

When you're in class, take a lot of notes. The act of writing helps your brain learn. Try to organize your notes as you're taking them, but prioritize keeping pace with the professor. PowerPoint is increasingly popular; in fact, students in my classes purchase my notes at the beginning of the semester (about six hundred PowerPoint slides printed out on about one hundred sheets of paper and bound together in a note-book). So they have it all in front of them in class. But I still encourage them to write their own thoughts directly into their course readers to reinforce their learning.

What do you do when the professor says something you don't understand? Raise your hand to ask a question. Some professors won't be willing to address more than two to three questions per lecture, particularly if the class is large; but it's worth trying to ask one, at least until you figure out their willingness to interact. The smaller the class, the more likely your professor can take your question immediately, particu-larly if it's quick and to the point.

But you shouldn't be the *only* one who ever asks questions, because you'll be viewed as holding up the class. That view might not sound fair—your questions may be very good; and just because your classmates are silent doesn't mean they understand what's going on. But fair or not fair, that's how it generally will be interpreted. So do raise your hand, but be mindful of others and the professor.

As a professor, I love questions from students. I want to stop and answer each one in great detail. Most professors I know feel the same way. But the reality is that we need to get through a certain amount of material that day, that week, and over the course of the semester. If we don't, you may think you're getting a break, but you're actually getting ripped off. Think about it; you *paid* good money to be taught all the material. It's not like you're going to get a partial refund on your tuition.

So what do you do when you *can't* immediately ask a question? Well, I used to draw a little square box in the column of my notebook, right next to the point in question. The box reminded me to figure this out later either by thinking about it, reading about it, or by talking to a friend or the professor right after class. It's always preferable if you can get the professor's attention for about ninety seconds after class, because your friends might not yet understand it either, or—and this happens—your friend confidently gives you the *wrong* explanation. Been there.

Out of class

Strive to trace the flow from the specifics of a given assignment, passage of reading, or homework problem, back to the underlying concepts in that course. In a math, science, or engineering class, think about how the problems relate to one another. In a liberal arts course, think about how the assigned reading relates to the other readings, or the themes of the particular novel, era of history, or philosopher or philosophical topic you're studying. You want to go from the particulars to the big picture, from the trees to the forest. For example, in human biology, you have a circulatory system, a digestive system, an endocrine system (hormones and glands), an immune system, etc. Each system can be studied individually or as a whole (how the systems relate to each other).

In one of the classes I teach, I cover two chapters on the properties of stationary electric charges (charges at rest) and two chapters on the properties of charges in motion. Each chapter has five or six sections. I tell students, "First master the individual sections, then look at how the sections within a chapter are related, then look at how the two chapters on stationary electric charges are related to each other, and then look at how all four chapters are related, if at all. On a test covering all four chapters, the first key for you would be to categorize each kind of problem: charges at rest or charges in motion? Then, you can break the problem down further and solve it using the appropriate methods for that kind of problem."

In Dr. Simmons's philosophy class, we studied Socrates, Plato, Kant, Hume, Hegel, and maybe a few others (it's been awhile). After that B- on the first test, I learned to study each philosopher's main ideas. Then I compared and contrasted them with one another. Dr. Simmons also suggested I write out practice essays—taking no more than twenty minutes to write out a philosopher's main arguments for something, then a critique of those arguments, after which I'd offer my own opinion and reflection. I did these exercises with a stopwatch in a private room in the library. I learned to explain ideas clearly, even when I didn't agree with them. I also grew in my confidence to contribute my own thoughts to the discussion, to go beyond merely parroting back what was in the assigned reading.

That last aspect is a distinguishing feature of an A student, so it's worth saying a bit more about it. Merely regurgitating what's in the book can get you an A in an easy class, or in many high school classes, but most college professors will expect more. Knowing the facts, figures, definitions, and the like is necessary and important. But you should be able to apply this information *to a new situation*. In essay exams, professors want to see how *you* think, not that you can merely parrot the thoughts of others (though if you can't even do *that*, you're looking at a C or D).

The exams in the physics courses I teach are mainly problems. Some of the problems are harder than others, and there's always one problem intended to stretch the student. That problem does *not* require concepts the students haven't been taught. But it *does* require them to *apply* what they've learned in a new and perhaps unusual situation. If they're A- level students or better, they'll be able to do it. In fact, that's how I find out who the A- and A students are. As for those who think that having such problems on tests isn't fair, my response is that I cannot lower academic standards and maintain my integrity as a professor. Without more challenging problems, the most capable students have no way to accurately and fully distinguish themselves. All students who wish to improve are welcome to come to office hours or pursue help at the tutoring center (a.k.a., academic services). I once had a student adamantly tell me that I needed to slow down until *every single student* was ready to go on, even if that meant not covering all the material that semester. In addition to being inconsiderate to the more capable students, such an approach would leave the entire class unprepared for any future courses that built and depended upon that content.

Regardless of the class, the point is this: You don't need to wait until *all* the material is covered to start getting ready for the test. The best students do this bit by bit as the class moves through the material. It's a good idea to go over everything the week of the test, but it shouldn't feel like you're trying to learn it all for the first time. You're just putting the final pieces together and solidifying them in your mind, going over the material again and again, mastering it. By this stage, I was working off my cheat sheets.

Cheat sheets

Getting ready for tests can be stressful. A little adrenaline can be good; it gets us going, gives us energy. But it needs to be channeled and controlled so that it helps us rather than cripples us. A cheat sheet is a tool that several friends and I used to get ready for tests, and it really helped. Let's say it's been five weeks since the last test, and it's time for another midterm exam. Five weeks means fifteen classes for a MWF class. Let's suppose you took four pages of notes per class. That means you have sixty pages of in-class notes and maybe sixty pages of content from the textbook, all of which is fair game for the test. That's a lot of stuff.

So try this: As you're going through the material, condense your notes (which your brain is learning even as you're condensing) onto one cheat sheet (front and back of a standard, 8.5" x 11" paper). You aren't rewriting your notes.

That would be very time consuming, generally not worth the trouble, and it certainly wouldn't all fit on one page. You are *organizing* the material and *pulling out* what's most important. Behind ten lines of writing on your cheat sheet there are ten pages of detailed notes in your notebook.

I liked to do this on unlined paper, because I would create boxes of content and even use multicolor pens to make things stand out. The goal is for everything to be easy to find if you were allowed to take that paper into the test with you. Try to do it all on one sheet for a typical midterm exam, but use two sheets if you really need to. When it comes time to study for the final exam, you'll have several of these sheets ready to go, covering the entire semester.

For some tests, you *will* be allowed to bring this sheet with you. This sometimes happens in math, science, and engineering courses (like mine). But even if you are allowed to bring it, you now start studying from *this sheet*, and not from your notes. You've already studied your lecture notes (you were keeping up with them in your out-of-class study times during the weeks leading up to the exam); now you're focusing on your condensed notes. This is *not* a substitute for doing lots of problems in problem-based courses; rather, this is a tool for mastering concepts (something essential in *all* classes).

Other learning/test-preparation strategies

Different classes may require different methods. In problem-based courses, doing lots of problems is a must. Check the back of the chapter in your textbook. There are usually lots of problems there that were not assigned, but that you can do. Answers to the odd-numbered problems are probably at the back of the book, so you can check your answers. And your professor or TA might be willing to check even-numbered problems, if you can't find them on the Internet, which my more resourceful students seem to do.

For other classes, you might benefit from making diagrams or flash cards. I used flash cards in foreign language classes that required lots of memorization. As I mentioned with the cheat sheets, some people use different-colored highlighting pens, with each color representing a different kind of information. I like to write summaries for books while or immediately after reading them to help me internalize the major themes of the book, whether fiction or nonfiction. That kind of thing helps in a variety of liberal arts classes, as does practicing essay writing in a timed environment to simulate a test (like I did in Dr. Simmons's class). The simulated test thing works with math and science classes, too. You can pick out a few good problems from the back of the chapter(s), find a quiet place, and try to finish them in an hour.

The night before the exam, instead of an all-nighter, you can go to bed early.

Office hours

Some students really understand the concept of office hours; others don't. My Stanford-graduate wife admitted to me that she completed college not knowing what office hours were. (She let me say that in the book.) So this section's for her.

Office hours are set times when professors sit around their offices furiously catching up on e-mail, grading, and other work-related items hoping no students show up. Okay, that last part's a joke. We're not twiddling our thumbs—we *are* doing stuff—but we're hoping students come with questions. Most never do. If a student is really understanding the material and never needs extra help, that's one thing. But if they're struggling, it's foolish not to ever use office hours.

Colleges have rules for how many office hours faculty are required to have. At large universities, those hours are probably the only times you can ever find your professors. At smaller colleges, your chances of finding them at other times are better. However, the most respectful thing is to come during official office hours because those are the times they've designated to help students like you. At other times, they may not want to break from what they're doing, and though they may help, they technically have no obligation to be available for you. Oh, and office hours are posted on the syllabus. If you really want to annoy your professors, ask them repeatedly when they have office hours. You'll impress them if you *know* when they are and come at those times.

If you go to see a professor during office hours and there are other students there, most professors (and students) don't mind if you listen to the professor answer questions from others. Oftentimes their struggles are similar to yours. Some

Q: *When students improve over the semester, do teachers notice? If I start out getting B's, but by the end of the semester I'm getting A's, do professors keep that in mind? Is it better to improve than to start off doing well?* —GRACE, FRESHMAN, Finance

A: Yes, professors certainly notice, unless your class size is several hundred, in which case you're probably just a number on a computer. And it *might* make a difference in terms of how your grade is computed—it depends on what percent of your grade is determined by early versus later assignments. In some classes, 60 percent or more of a student's final grade is determined in the last two weeks of the semester. In other classes, the assessment is more uniform over the semester. Something like the former is more common in my experience, both as a student and a professor.

It also depends on a professor's "forgiveness" policy. Some professors "discount" the weight of a student's lowest exam. For example, if each of three exams is worth 15 percent of a student's grade, the prof might make the lowest exam worth only 5 percent, or perhaps even drop it. I make my final exam count more if a student does particularly well on it.

So all things being equal, it is best to start strong *and* end strong. But improvement is generally noticed, and professors sometimes reward it by rounding up, particularly if a student ends the semester on the borderline between two grades.

students come to office hours with another classmate or two just to hear the professor answer other people's questions.

What if you really want to see your professor, but none of his hours work for you? Make an appointment. E-mail is usually best for that. Send him three time slots that work for you, and he'll pick one in his reply. That's a lot better than saying, "Hey, I'm busy during your office hours; when else can you meet?" Help him help you.

How grading is done (the inside secrets)

Even though learning should be your main focus, it's good to have an idea of how you'll be graded. It's wise to try to optimize your grade, while not being neurotic about it.

So how is grading actually done these days? There are two standard methods of grading: Grading against a set scale (for example, 90-100 percent is an A; 80-89 is a B; 70-79 is a C; 60-69 is a D; 0-59 is an F) and grading on a curve. With a curve, the professor picks a class average grade (historically a B- has often been used). Then he picks a rule to decide how broad to make the curve. The top group of students receive A's (an exact percentage, perhaps twenty-five, is sometimes selected by the professor or her department). The next group of students receive B's (maybe 35 percent), and so on. This method is easy to implement and is often used for large classes, anywhere from fifty to several hundred students.

One problem with this method is that it can encourage unhealthy competition. Let's say there are one hundred

Q: *How do professors assign grades? Do they figure out where their students are at and then adjust? Or do they just have a strict grading scale and stick to it, expecting students to work their way up?* —LUKE, FRESHMAN, Worship Arts

A: It's the second option. Sorry! Though each class has a different set of students, professors have a sense of what quality of work is reasonable to expect. The possible exception to this principle might be when a professor is teaching a course for the first time. That said, an introductory course typically taken by or designed for freshmen will be graded much more leniently than an upper-division course in the same subject.

people in the class, and the top 25 percent will get A's. The top twenty-fifth and twenty-sixth students are fighting over that spot. No matter how high their actual test scores are, only one of them will get an A. Even if they're only a fraction of a percentage point off from each other, one would get an A- and the other a B+. I've heard of students at some schools hiding books from their classmates to get an extra edge. Pretty ugly.

The beauty of grading on a curve is if there's a challenging test and all the scores are low, in one sense, it doesn't matter. *The top 25 percent of the students are still going to get A's.* But that also presents a problem. For the best students, the drive to be the "best you can be" can be supplanted with the lesser goal of merely being better than others.[†] Regardless of their actual scores, the top 25 percent of the students will get A's, the next 35 percent will get B's, and so on. If the class as a whole is weak or just plain lazy, the bar is lowered, and an A becomes less meaningful.

Grading on a curve has often led to grade inflation, because the professor can just "curve up" the grades, making 70 percent the cutoff not for a C- but for a B-. Don't like how students did on the test? Curve it up. Believe me, this is an easy trick, and it always makes students happier. That doesn't make it right. Generally, I'm a fan of a set scale. When you take courses with set scales, you know exactly how you need

---

[†] This attitude reminds me of a pair of John Wooden quotes: "When you give total effort—everything you have—the score can never make you a loser. And when you do less, it can't somehow magically turn you into a winner." And "Don't measure yourself by what you've accomplished, but rather by what you should have accomplished with your abilities."

to do to make a certain grade, and you can calculate your own grade throughout the semester. You can also decide how much a course means to you. You may decide, *I've got a solid B in Chediak's course, and realistically no shot at an A. But I do have a good shot at an A in my history class. I'll invest more time getting ready for my history final.* That's totally respectable, and I'm never insulted by such thinking. In addition, if everyone does an awesome job, the entire class can get A's and B's. The flip side is that if everyone does a lousy job, everyone can end up with D's and F's.

The problem with a set scale is that a professor's tests from year to year may not be *exactly* equal in difficulty (unless he or she uses the same tests, which only works until the students figure it out). So if students in 2011 do better than in 2010, it could be because the tests were easier. Still, that's the lesser of two evils, in my view. I try to make tests of equal difficulty from year to year and let the set scale force me to give my students the grades they earn, even if my bleeding heart wants to give them higher grades.

Of course it's also important with a set scale to make exams at least reasonably difficult. If every student earned an A semester after semester, outside observers would probably question the meaning of that A grade. Generally there should be a distribution of grades. The professor's job is to differentiate the students—the letter grade is a measure of whether a student's performance is excellent, good, average, below average, or unacceptable. That being said, what I really like about the set scale is that sometimes I have very strong classes. Those classes wind up with higher grades overall than weaker classes. It wouldn't be that way with a forced curve since specific percentages of the class would get A's and B's no matter what.

How a professor plans to grade should be on the syllabus. If you're not sure, respectfully ask him or her during office hours.

GRADES CONFIRM CALLING (OR NOT)

Why bother telling you all that? First of all, I want you to have a healthy respect for the grading process. Your professor has a job of distinguishing between various degrees of achievement. If everyone got A's, people would be suspicious. Grading is useful only to the extent that it is meaningful. And to the extent that grading is meaningful, it helps you confirm your calling. If you want to be an engineer or an accountant or a doctor or whatever, the last thing you want is for your professors to give you inflated grades, getting you through college with an unearned 3.6 GPA, only to graduate and find out that you are not prepared to be as successful in your chosen discipline as you might have thought—especially if you have $50,000 to pay back in student loans.

The idea that "you can accomplish anything you set your mind to" is pervasive in today's American culture. In fact, to even question it almost feels wrong, doesn't it? Many of us were raised being told we were special, winners, talented, and capable. And there's something right about parents and teachers wanting children to feel good about themselves. I mean, you'd really question the parent who repeatedly puts down his or her kids, telling them how pathetic they are. It'd be miserable to go through life with your head down, assuming you'll fail at everything you do. That mind-set often becomes a self-fulfilling prophecy: If you think failure is inevitable, then it probably is.

But our society has swung the pendulum to the other extreme. There's something unhelpful about growing up in a world where every team in Little League gets a trophy and every player on the soccer team gets a winner's ribbon just for showing up. The intention in the "everybody is a winner" philosophy is to make sure nobody feels bad. The loser isn't penalized, but winning isn't celebrated. And getting a trophy means less if everyone gets one. Where's the motivation to win if everyone's a winner? *Accomplishment* is not appropriately recognized; in fact, not even *effort* is encouraged, since all participants are treated the same way, regardless of how hard they tried.

And there's a bigger problem. By constantly being affirmed, regardless of what you've actually done, your generation has learned to confuse self-confidence (which we naturally acquire from praise) with actual ability or accomplishment. Yet just because we think we're good at something doesn't mean we are. In fact, sometimes it's the people who

> *There's something unhelpful about growing up in a world where every team in Little League gets a trophy and every player on the soccer team gets a winner's ribbon just for showing up.*

think they're the best who actually are the worst! A recent study found that 39 percent of American eighth graders were confident of their math skills, compared to only 6 percent of Korean eighth graders. There was just one problem: The Koreans actually did much better than the Americans on math tests.[1]

Why is it important to recognize and encourage accomplishment? Because the desire to be excellent, to accomplish *anything* (earn a high test score, set a record in sports, etc.) is meant to bring out the best effort in *all* participants. While the outcomes may be unequal, because not everyone is equally gifted, or gives equal effort, or has equal exposure to the best kinds of help and support, the pursuit itself is meant to make every person better. Effort is encouraged.

Accomplishment vs. effort

Okay, so when we recognize accomplishment, we encourage effort by all. But accomplishment and effort are different: Some people accomplish a lot with little effort, and others try very hard and accomplish little. Life isn't fair.

When people get A's in a class, or win a sporting event, or earn any kind of award, an accomplishment is being observed. The person may or may not have tried hard. Professors (or referees, or judges) reward accomplishment, but God looks at the heart and is either honored by the effort or dishonored by the lack of effort. What pleases God? "Whatever your hand finds to do, do it with your might" (Ecclesiastes 9:10).

Those who lost a competition or ended up with a C+ are still "winners" in another sense, *if they gave their best effort.* God sees the heart. If a Christian does something to the best of her ability for God's glory, with a humble, obedient heart, it pleases God, even if she got a C+ in calculus or lost a tennis match or a swim meet. God is pleased when we do, as Oswald Chambers said, our "utmost for his highest." God is saying, in effect, "Give it all you got! You may get an A, B, C, D, or F, but you do the very best you can with the abilities and opportunities you have."

Doing your best at something, and maintaining a cheerful attitude, pleases God, but it's not necessarily the same as doing something well. Our job as professors is to measure how well you do or know certain things. We judge accomplishment and assign letter grades, which essentially is how the world and your future bosses will judge you after you graduate. The university where I work keeps paying me because they think I do a good job. If they didn't, they would need to find someone else, *even if I was trying hard.* When you get a full-time job, they probably won't care if you work forty or fifty or sixty hours a week. They'll care about what you get done, not how hard you try. It's accomplishment that allows them to sell their products and services and be successful. If your iPhone didn't work, you wouldn't care how hard Steve Jobs and his buddies tried—you wouldn't want to pay for it.

Can you do "anything you set your mind to"? I would not say *anything.* But it's also true that you don't know how well you might do at something until you try with maximum effort and focus. Learning to stretch yourself often comes with growth in maturity and character, like we discussed in an earlier chapter. Based on my high school grades, my freshman adviser in college said to me, "Aim for a 3.0 GPA." She was trying to help me, not insult me.[‡] It is good to set realistic expectations. But by God's grace I did a lot better than a 3.0. What happened? I had goofed off for most of high school, but by the time I got to college I had grown up a bit, at least with respect to my work ethic. I took that level of dedication into college and was able to exceed my adviser's expectations.

That won't always happen. Some people put forward a lot of effort but accomplish very little in a particular area. If that happens in calculus, maybe they should pursue something else instead.

Healthy and unhealthy competition

Doing anything well requires a combination of God-given talent, a good attitude, hard work, and smart work (using the best methods to learn a particular discipline). The latter includes exposure to good teachers, mentors, and coaches. Part of a good attitude is recognizing that others may be more talented than you. In fact, they may not even work very hard and *still* be better than you. I remember working my tail

---

[‡] You might be curious to know that the average college GPA has risen from the 2.5 or 2.6 range in about 1960 to well over 3.0 today. See Valen Johnson, *Grade Inflation: A Crisis in College Education* (Springer, 2003).

off in some classes to do well while a friend of mine would seem to just show up and ace the tests. It can be aggravating, but you can't let it get to you. We can only do our very best for God. Getting hung up on comparison with others will just mess you up.

Love does not envy those who accomplish more or boast over those who accomplish less (1 Corinthians 13:4). Instead, channel comparison with others into making you stronger by learning from those who are better and helping those who may be weaker. I started playing recreational tennis when I was fifteen years old. I tried out for the team the next year as a junior in high school. I played my heart out for three weeks and was the last cut; the team could only carry twelve guys, and I was number thirteen. Having gotten so close, I played a lot that summer. I even got some lessons. I went back out for the team my senior year and made it. The coach told me frequently that I was his hardest working player, yet I almost never got to play in the matches. Why? Because only the top eight guys got playing time. Most of them had grown up going to elite tennis camps; six of our players were ranked among the top players in the state of Illinois. Although some of our star players were lazy during practices, they'd still easily beat me. I had to *choose* not to let that get me down. I was getting better, and (unfortunately) some of them were failing to reach their potential. When I got to college, I was one of the best players on our Division III team. That wouldn't have happened had I not been able to play with great players in high school.

But others didn't have to not reach their potential so that I could reach mine. If everyone had worked hard, we *all* would have been advancing toward our potential. Healthy, vigorous competition lifts all participants. It is only jealousy and pride that cause us to want others to "go down" at the expense of our "going up." With sports, college, and life, if we just do the very best we can for God's glory, with a good attitude, we can have the satisfaction that we pleased him, regardless of the external results or how we are ranked relative to others. Wisely channeled effort (working smart) plus dedication (working hard) will lead to our becoming as accomplished as we can be in a certain area. Of course, this is more than just a college pursuit; it's a lifelong goal.

> *Healthy, vigorous competition lifts all participants. It is only jealousy and pride that cause us to want others to "go down" at the expense of our "going up."*

Remember the parable of the talents (Matthew 25:14-30)? You know the story: The guy with five talents made five more, and the guy with two talents made two more. Yet Jesus commends them in the exact same way: Both were faithful with "little," he says. It wasn't how much they received but what they did with it that mattered; two and five were both "little." But notice the guy with one talent got scolded; he, too, had "little," but he didn't do anything with it.

I sometimes wonder if the one-talent guy was too busy not only worrying about the "hard" master (vs. 24) but also comparing himself to the two-talent and five-talent guys.

That kind of comparison brings self-pity and is deadly, yet I've seen it over and over and have been tempted to it myself. "I shouldn't be a math major because I'm not as good as Joe. Better to not even try." No, better to do your very best, even if you're never as accomplished as Joe. Learn from Joe, imitate him, and you'll be doing your best with what God gave you.

So whether your professors grade according to a set scale or on a curve, be motivated to do your very best and, as a by-product, to earn the highest grade possible. But don't freak out or endlessly badger your professors about every point. Submit yourself to the grading process, trusting that God is in control and is using it, imperfect though it may be.[§] Through it God begins confirming (or not confirming) the sense of calling you had when you chose your major. That student who chose aeronautical engineering but repeatedly failed calculus and physics is being redirected by God through the feedback of his grades. Meanwhile, the student who decides on accounting and pulls a 3.2 GPA in her first year while landing an internship with a nonprofit is being confirmed in her sense of God's calling.

> *With sports, college, and life, if we just do the very best we can for God's glory, with a good attitude, we can have the satisfaction that we pleased him, regardless of the external results or how we are ranked relative to others.*

[§] That doesn't mean you can't respectfully approach your professors if you think they made a grading error. We talked about interacting with faculty in the relationship section of this book.

OTHER FACTORS CONFIRM CALLING (OR NOT)

Though I've said a lot about the role of grades, I don't want to give the impression that grades are the *only* factor in confirming or redirecting you in your sense of God's calling. Your interests may develop and change over time, particularly in your first year or two at college. You may hear more about what athletic trainers do and decide it's not for you. Many people start off thinking medicine or law, and later decide to go another direction (both of those fields require many years of expensive education at the front end).

Or you may do an internship in a major and hate it. One of my all-time favorite students, Jake, started off in civil engineering. I helped him land an internship in that field after his freshman year, and he hated it. He switched to electrical engineering, got a different job the next summer, and loved it. He's since earned both a bachelor's and a master's degree in electrical engineering and works full-time in that field.

INDECISIVENESS

Having just explained that it's okay to shift gears to a new major or perhaps a new emphasis within a major, I want to sound a note of caution. Before making a switch, consider your rationale, and count the cost. There's an idea out there that when we figure out what we were made to do, it will always be an enjoyable experience, that "work" won't ever feel like "work," that it will all come naturally with no sense of struggle. Not true. I can assure you that almost everyone has a tough day at work from time to time. The reason we call it "work" is because it takes work and it isn't always easy (Genesis 3:19; Ecclesiastes 1:2-3).

I love teaching and writing, but both take discipline and perseverance. I generally like going to work, but my job isn't perfect. There are things I just have to make myself do. But the struggle is ultimately rewarding and a good exercise of my skills and temperament. While there's nothing else I'd rather be doing as a career, I don't *always* feel like doing it.

We have to talk to our emotions on bad days, on days we're not really "there," and strengthen our resolve in the knowledge that God has placed us there; we ultimately work for him (Psalm 42:5; Colossians 3:23-24). We live in a culture that seems to believe in quitting when the going gets tough. We place a high premium on immediate gratification and the avoidance of pain. We're not that surprised when people leave marriages, churches, or jobs for something they think might be more satisfying. It seems permanence is far less common in our day. But just as you shouldn't choose your major flippantly, don't leave it flippantly. You're not locked in (like a marriage); you can change it. Just examine your heart, and discuss your thinking with some older adults who care about you and can speak into your life. There were times when I felt like bailing on my major, usually in the middle of a nasty course with a hard-core, no-mercy professor. But sometimes we just need to keep rolling, and things will get better in due course.

Proverbs 28:19 says, "Whoever works his land will have plenty of bread, but he who follows worthless pursuits will have plenty of poverty." These "worthless pursuits" can include gambling and other forms of get-rich-quick schemes, which tend to only enrich those who suck others into them. But they also include jumping from one thing to another, switching majors every other year, or jumping from job to job, never really developing strong, highly marketable skill sets. People in their twenties these days go through an average of seven jobs.¶ I know things happen, but you have to wonder if all those changes are all necessary or beneficial. Over the long haul, this pattern, not surprisingly, does not generally lead to wealth. As of 2005, only half of Americans in their mid-twenties earned enough to support a family.**

CONCLUSIONS

Learning how to learn is a huge aspect of college, and it will really prepare you for life. In fact, when I got my first job with IBM, most of what I needed for that job I learned on the job. They hired me because they believed that I could learn it, because I had demonstrated that I was able to learn things in college. Good study skills will help you not only work hard, but work smart. Through the process of receiving grades and the maturation of your professional interests (as

---

¶ Robin Marantz Henig, "What Is It about 20-Somethings?," *New York Times Magazine*, August 18, 2010.

** I recognize that there are some legitimate reasons for this. For example, more people are spending more time preparing for careers via higher education, not just at the undergraduate but at the graduate level. The process is both time consuming and expensive. Still, one wonders if all the job transitions twentysomethings experience might also have something to do with it.

you become more informed and gain new experiences), God confirms or redirects your sense of his calling. Where are you in this process? Keep doing your utmost for his highest, and trust that he will continue to direct and lead you, come what may.

Learning how to learn is a huge aspect of college, and it will really prepare you for life.

DISCUSSION STARTERS

1. Do you struggle with anxiety about your grades? How do you deal with it?

2. What can you do to cultivate greater joy in the journey of learning and less anxiety about the outcome?

3. What can you do to work smarter, not just harder?

4. How have you had to battle jealousy of others who seem more academically gifted than you? How have you had to battle pride toward those who seem less academically gifted than you?

5. I wrote, "If we just do the very best we can for God's glory, with a good attitude, we can have the satisfaction that we pleased him, regardless of the external results or how we are ranked relative to others." Does this feel liberating or deflating? Do you think your answer to that question may reflect whether you're living for God's praise or the praise of others?

6. Where do you think you're at in the process of confirming your sense of God's calling regarding your major?

COMMON MISTAKE #10:
Wasting Opportunities

> *Thrive Principle: Use Your Downtime Wisely*

LET'S REVIEW WHAT we've said so far about thriving in our academics. In choosing our major, we're paying attention to our interests and our strengths (or gift set) while weighing the feedback of others. We've recognized the concept of vocation—that God is the one who ultimately calls us into certain lines of work (through the way he's wired and gifted us) by the means of other people affirming our work and "calling" us to do it (giving us a job).

In the early stages when we choose a major, we're trying to sense God's call, given our interests and past successes. As we progress academically, we're continuing to evaluate our call by examining our progress in our majors—not only our grades, but also the extent to which our interest in our majors grows or decreases. I mentioned my student Jake who switched from civil engineering to electrical engineering. My wife, Marni, started out pre-med, but as she learned more about the profession, decided she didn't want the expense and commitment of medical school. She completed her degree in human biology with significant coursework in business, spending a lot of time her senior year launching and managing the campus's student-run clothing store.

After she graduated, she went into the business world instead of the scientific or medical world. Her extracurricular activities had every bit as much to do with her preparation as her academic work. Through her interest and success as a store manager, God called her into the business world via AT&T, who hired her into their leadership-development program. She was later promoted into family management, where she now reigns as queen in our home.

In this chapter, we'll talk about how important it is to not waste anything. College is full of opportunities—twenty-four hours a day, seven days a week. There are certainly distractions to be avoided, but there are also many wonderful ways to develop your interests, gifts, and skills outside the classroom. Under the banner of "extracurricular activities" I want to talk about things like internships, short-term missions, student government, and other groups like that, as well as athletic or musical commitments. In addition, many of you will have part-time jobs to keep you busy outside the realm of your academic work. Some of you may even need to have full-time jobs to pay tuition, which seems to keep rising every year. Extracurricular activities are important and formative, but they can overwhelm your class attendance and study time if you're not careful.

Last, I want to discuss something else that can overwhelm you: finances. Though every student's situation is different, for many of you, this is the first time you have to manage your earnings, savings, and expenses apart from the direct supervision of your parents. Whether you're splitting rent in an apartment with friends or just covering your entertainment and clothing expenses while living in the dorms, managing money is an important skill, and one that everyone must develop.

Let's get to work.

INTERNSHIPS

Having an internship under your belt might be the single best way to improve your chances of finding full-time work in your field after you graduate. If a graduating senior with a 3.3 GPA and internship experience were competing for a job with another graduating senior with a 3.7 GPA but no internship experience, chances are the student who had an internship would get the offer. The hiring company could be IBM and the previous internship with AT&T—it makes no difference. Any internship is better than no internship.

Merriam-Webster's Collegiate Dictionary defines an *intern* as "an advanced student or graduate usually in a professional field (as medicine or teaching) gaining supervised practical experience (as in a hospital or classroom)." While it is usually easier to get an internship when you're more advanced in your field, the truth is that you can start looking for them during your freshman year.

An internship is any job that is related to your academic work in some way. It can be with a local business, school, or laboratory. It can be at another college or university, either near your hometown or clear across the country. It can be doing research with a professor at your own school, either in a laboratory (setting up or performing experiments) or a library (investigating some aspect of an ancient civilization).

Although some programs allow you to take a semester off school, most internships are done over the summer. Nevertheless, the time to start looking for them is late fall and no later than early spring. Most agencies will select their interns by March or April. Some smaller groups might decide in April or May, but that's more unusual. If there's an online application process, fill it out early. Seek some sort of confirmation that your application has been received; it doesn't hurt to use the phone for this—sometimes it even results in a quick, on-the-spot interview. If you haven't heard, check back in February or March. Ask them when they anticipate making a hiring decision. Show respect for their process and give them the time they need, but a bit of persistence doesn't hurt. It shows them the internship is important to you, and it demonstrates initiative.

Q: *This coming summer I need to take two or three classes in order to complete my transfer credits for my engineering studies at the next school I am going to. Would pursuing an engineering internship at the same time be counterproductive or too ambitious?*

—KELVIN, JUNIOR, Physics/Engineering

A: I was an engineering major myself, and I worked several internships during my college years. I once took an easy speech class at a community college while doing an internship just to get the requirement out of the way. Keep in mind that summer classes often move more quickly than semester courses because the schedule is somewhat compressed. Taking two or three of them in one summer while doing an internship sounds pretty ambitious, unless the courses are particularly easy. It would be a good idea to find out how much time the internship will require. Will it be a forty-hour-a-week commitment? Is there a possibility of putting in overtime? You'll also want to consider your other commitments. Will you be doing your own shopping and cooking? In my opinion, you'd be better off keeping your off-work hours open for social-izing, relaxing, and other forms of physical and spiritual mainte-nance, if you can pull it off.

What are some ways to prepare for an internship interview?

- Research the organization or group, and know a few things about them, especially before the interview.
- Don't overload them with questions, but do prepare one or two good questions.
- In the course of conversation, don't hesitate to reveal things you found out about them in your research. It's a way of honoring them because it shows them you cared enough to prepare.

As I describe in the appendix on the college selection process, colleges and universities come in different flavors. Some are more research oriented, and others are more teaching oriented. A quick way to tell is to notice how much (or little) time the faculty actually spend teaching in a classroom. The range is generally one to four classes per semester. The less teaching your faculty do, the more they're being driven to do research. This means there's a greater likelihood that, if you do a really good job in one of their classes, you might be asked to join them on one of their projects. It also means that less of their job performance rides on how well they teach.

If you feel a strong rapport with a professor, ask him or her after class one day if there might be any opportunities. Let your professor know that you'd be interested in work along the lines of what you're doing (or did) in the class you took with him or her, or on something else. Remember what I said about academic skills being transferable and enabling?

If your professor knows you to be a good student in one area, he or she will often figure that you could be successful doing a variety of things within the general field.

There are paid and unpaid (volunteer) opportunities. As you might expect, there are a lot more things you can do if you're willing to work for free. With a few rare exceptions, even paid internships pay less than other jobs you could get. The fact that you could make more money on tips as a waiter or waitress is irrelevant. You don't accept an internship for the money; you do it for the experience. It's an honor to be asked—someone thinks you have potential in your field of choice. That said, internships in industry (for private businesses or large, established companies) generally pay more than those in universities. Also, my friends who teach history and English agree that there are probably more paid internships in fields like engineering and computer science—fields in which students more immediately gain what are perceived to be highly marketable skills. I've seen engineering students receive paid internships after their freshman years. However, not all internships are equally valuable. Look at the actual *tasks* they need you to do and what *skills* you'll develop in the process. Running the accounting books for three months and keeping track of a two-million-dollar budget will help you grow a lot more than just filing papers in an office. Still, a foot in the door is a foot in the door. Something is better than nothing.

You don't accept an internship for the money; you do it for the experience.

So how do you *get* an internship? I've already mentioned approaching your faculty, particularly if you've done well in one of their classes. In addition, some schools have a staff member or office that functions as a liaison between the college and its external constituencies—businesses, laboratories, hospitals, and nonprofit personnel who might hire you part-time at first or full-time when you graduate. If you're at a small college of three to four thousand students, this office is probably campus-wide, meaning that the same office seeks to help all the students in all the academic majors. If you're at a large school of ten thousand or more students, chances are each department or college within the university has its own office.

I went to Alfred University, and we only had about 2,400 undergraduate students, yet my engineering department had its own internship office, which was a huge blessing.* You can also research internships yourself on the Internet or ask upperclassmen if they have any recommendations. Lastly, don't hesitate to tap any contact you know in a particular field. Respectfully inquire with your parents, friends of your parents, your pastors (they often know lots of people, and what they do), and your professors.†

I was thankful to have the chance to do an internship every summer. I was encouraged by being able to make a

---

* If you've not yet decided on a college, it wouldn't hurt to check out what they have in the way of an internship-liaison office. They may even keep statistics on the percentage of students who acquire internships and/or full-time jobs prior to graduation.
† As an aside, this is a good way to start finding people who might advise and mentor you in various ways as you launch into adulthood.

contribution. My summer jobs from one year to the next were in different areas, which is also something I'd recommend. Once you graduate, whatever you do full-time probably won't involve moving from job to job every three months, so using summers to get different types of experiences related to your major is a good idea (though it's also really nice if wherever you worked after one summer wants you back the next summer—you can always fall back on that position if nothing else pans out).

But internships aren't the only way to spend your breaks, and summers aren't the only breaks you have. Most schools have three to four weeks off at Christmas/New Year's and a weeklong spring break. Let's look at some other opportunities, ones I wish I had pursued.

MISSION TRIPS

If you're at a Christian college, it probably offers all kinds of mission trips, mostly in the summer. Staff and even faculty might also participate. Third-party organizations and campus fellowships like InterVarsity and Campus Crusade for Christ also sponsor trips. Why go on a short-term mission trip? Aside from the awesome bonding and priceless memories you'll form with your teammates, there are many other reasons.

Ideally, you'll go to a place in the world where there is real need. Perhaps you've never seen poverty on a massive scale. Being able to serve in any capacity in such a context changes *you* at least as much as it helps the people you're serving.

For starters, it will encourage you to appreciate the material blessings you enjoy on a regular basis. But it will also help you understand that many people who lack material blessings are often happier than those who have them. I've spent time in parts of Mexico and El Salvador outside the resort areas, and it had that effect on me. Moreover, you'll have a chance to give a small portion of your life away and experience what Christ promised when he said that "it is more blessed to give than to receive" (Acts 20:35). Hopefully giving to missions work throughout the world will become a lifelong pattern, freeing you from the manacles of materialism that hold so many in our country.

Mission trips tangibly connect you to a cause greater than yourself: the advancement of the rule and reign of Jesus Christ. It's easy to lose sight of that priority in a culture where self-absorption is the rule and people chase after things that won't last (keeping their existence small and ignoble). For some of you, a short-term mission trip will be a prelude to a full-time career overseas. I have an engineering friend who has traveled throughout Africa using his skills to help hospitals get up and running. Others will teach English overseas or strategically take full-time secular jobs within their vocations in areas of the world that have little Christian presence. Or perhaps you will remain in the West after graduation, but be more mindful of the needs of the world and more equipped to strategically invest in full-time missionaries in parts of the world for which you have developed a special affection.

One suggestion: Avoid taking these trips during the

Q: *My mom and I have a difference in opinion about summer breaks. For the upcoming summer, I've been toying with the idea of working with some sort of Christian organization that leads groups in serving in certain communities, but these positions are often unpaid. My mom (the accountant she is) wants me to work in a paid position, even if it's a menial job. I think the experience of my choice would be more valuable than any money I would earn. How do you weigh in on this issue?*
—KATE, FRESHMAN, Creative Writing

A: In an ideal world, if money were no object, I agree that it's preferable during college to choose growth experiences without regard to income. But realistically, you owe it to your mom to find out why she wants you to earn money. Hear her out. Is she counting on you to provide for your living expenses in the academic year so you don't have to work while managing a full load of classes and extracurricular activities? If so, honor your mom by getting a job. She's protecting your ability to focus on your classes without accumulating too much debt. And chances are, your parents are already footing a hefty bill.

If you do end up working for pay over the summer, there are other times when you can get involved with Christian organizations doing service and even international mission projects. Look for opportunities during spring break or between semesters or possibly during a January term, if that's something your school offers. College is a great time to expand your horizons and learn about the needs in different cultures and communities, but it's also important to consider your family's budget.

academic year. Summers, Christmas breaks, and spring breaks provide plenty of times to have these life-shaping experiences. There's no need to let them cut into the eight or nine months of the fall and spring semesters. Remember that you're also serving the Lord when you faithfully attend classes, do your homework, complete course projects, and study for exams.

STUDENT GOVERNMENT, SPEECH AND DEBATE TEAM, AND OTHER ACADEMICALLY ORIENTED GROUPS

If you're at a big university, there may be literally hundreds of student organizations. Some are artistic or cultural in nature, others are political or professional (honors societies and the like). The remaining categories are religious, service oriented, or academic. Being a part of a strong Christian organization, particularly if you're at a non-Christian university, is a great way to make like-minded friends and to thrive in your faith (as we discussed in an earlier chapter). We've already talked about service-related activities and mission trips, so let's say a few words about academically oriented groups.

Involvement in an academic organization is probably second only to internships with regard to experience that prepares you for the full-time job search. Whatever your major, chances are your campus has an organization or club for members of that major. Start there. Go to the meetings; find out what they're up to. These groups may know the inside scoop on how to get internships within your major. For example, they may be involved with inviting speakers to

campus—speakers who hire summer interns or have connections with others who do.

Speaking of speakers, aside from any immediate professional benefit, going to lectures by political and business
leaders is usually worth it. Whether you agree with them
or not, you'll definitely learn something from folks like Al
Gore, Steve Jobs, Condoleezza Rice, or Bill Gates. If you're at
a secular university, your Christian organization can invite a
well-known, engaging speaker to debate a famous atheist. At
many schools, the Christian and atheist organizations work
together to make this sort of thing happen, and it's a great
chance for Christians to exhibit love, grace, and respect to
classmates who don't yet have a saving relationship with Jesus
Christ.

Other campus organizations provide opportunities to
develop specific skills. For example, running for student
government can give you leadership experience and a taste
of politics. The speech and debate team is a natural fit for
those of you interested in legal or communications-related
work such as journalism, law, or politics. Running the student bookstore or joining an investment club is a great way
to develop business, management, or investing skills. On the
math/science/engineering side of things, there are math teams
and professional associations in every branch of engineering
and science you can imagine. Some campus chapters of these
professional associations are very active in spearheading projects, entering regional or national competitions, or developing resources like old exam files for the courses required

within the major. The more you know about what the groups are doing, and the more you are a part of them, the more you stand to benefit from the inside information and networking these groups inevitably facilitate.

SPORTS, MUSIC, AND THEATER

There are two ways to participate in music, theater, and athletics. If you join an intramural or recreational group, you're participating for fun. If your involvement is at the university level, you may have a scholarship that *requires* you to do a certain activity. For example, some students get a few thousand dollars of tuition reduction, if not a full-ride scholarship, just for being part of a musical group or the university's swim team. If that's your situation, I would view it as a job: Basically, you're getting paid to perform. It's a firm obligation if you want the scholarship money. But there's a big difference if you're doing the sport, musical, or theatrical activity just for fun. With intramural sports, you could go or not go depending on what else you have going on that week. It's a good refresher and a relationship builder, but you're not supercommitted.

With music or theater, however, be careful. You generally can't get out of practice. I've seen many students take a big hit to their GPAs in a semester by accepting a lead role in a play or musical. Nothing against theater; I like going to watch them perform. I'm just saying count the cost because there is a much bigger commitment involved than with intramural sports. Get the facts on how much you're expected to practice before you commit. Put the hours into your master schedule like we talked about in chapter 2, and make sure it will work. If it's very important to you, perhaps take a lighter load that semester so you're not overwhelmed. This is another occasion to balance idealism and realism. You can only do so much.

PART-TIME (OR FULL-TIME) JOBS

The trends say that more students than ever are working jobs as they go through college. Times are tough, money is tight, and college just keeps getting more expensive. How much should a student work while taking classes?

Remember in chapter 2, where I talked about time management and how college and high school are different? One of the things I pointed out was that in college it may look like you have a lot more free time, but you'll need to do more work outside class than in high school. On average, the expectation is two hours out of class for every one hour in class. And that's *on average*, which means that some students will need to do more (I did for some classes) and other students will get away with less (like my genius friends). Okay, so if you're taking a load of sixteen credits (four to five courses), that means you're putting in thirty-two hours outside class. Right there, that's forty-eight hours a week. I posted a sample weekly schedule in chapter 2, and it had forty-eight hours marked for academic work, plus two hours a week for chapel, which may or may not apply for you.

But I didn't say anything there about a part-time job. Basically, if you have a part-time job, it should eat into your time with friends or for other recreation, not your academics. Now you *do* have the time, if you make a schedule and discipline yourself to use it wisely. But ask yourself how many total hours a week can you really work without sacrificing your health or your sanity. It's no good if you're sick or burned out.

Some part-time jobs are really low key and may even let you get some studying done. Working behind a desk in a library or answering phones in the evening for campus security may allow you to spend most of your on-duty time studying. That's a sweet deal. If you work ten hours a week, perhaps you'll get seven hours a week of studying done. That's really only three extra hours a week to factor into your schedule of commitments.

The other highly desirable part-time job, in my opinion, is the kind that lets you build on your academic training. For example, most schools have some sort of academic resource center that hires strong students in various subjects to provide tutoring in those subjects. The job pays minimum wage or slightly more, but it's a great way to develop even greater mastery of a subject you already like and in which you do well. Likewise, professors often hire teaching assistants to help with grading and other functions. It doesn't pay much, but it can be a great way to develop a relationship with a professor (from whom you can later ask for a recommendation letter).

Then there are the I-really-need-to-make-money jobs. My guess is that you know better than I where to find them. I would just caution you not to sacrifice your academics merely to have a lot of spending money. Better to focus on your classes, do cheaper things for fun with your friends, and avoid eating out too much. College is a season of training. The better you do, the more it will launch you into post-graduation opportunities.

I know a student who works as a waiter in a fairly ritzy club. He makes really good money for a student. But they work him twenty to thirty hours a week during the semester, plus the commute is forty minutes each way. As a result, he's often exhausted, unable to finish his homework, and pulling straight C's when he could be pulling B's. But when I try to get the guy to work less and put more effort into his courses, he just reminds me how much money he rakes in at the club. Maybe he's got a really tough situation and absolutely needs the money. But I fear that he's hurting his credibility with future employers who won't really care how good he is at serving dinners, desserts, and drinks. And let's say he really *does* need the money. It'd probably make more sense for him to defer his education, live at home, and save up the money he needs to go to school full-time without having to work.

Perhaps some of you are working full-time while going to college. You don't need me to tell you that's the absolute toughest way to do it. I realize it simply must be done sometimes. In your case, I would not recommend taking a full-time academic load because your chances of failing a class or dropping the ball on a major responsibility or family obligation are quite high—unless you're unusually bright, or your classes are unusually easy, or your full-time job gives you *lots* of time to study. Take perhaps two or three classes fall, spring, and summer if you need to get your degree as quickly as possible. Leverage whatever classes you can take at a community college to save money. Some schools have two summer sessions if you really want to keep things moving. Take classes all year long if you can, but don't ever take more than two or three at a time. That's just my suggestion. You'll probably still be putting in sixty-hour weeks (or more). It's not ideal, but if you're determined to get that degree, and you probably are, it can be done. Hats off to you.

For everyone else, my strong recommendation would be that you do as little nonacademic work during the semester as possible. I know that might sound unrealistic. But think about it: A semester is fifteen weeks, plus finals week, at the most. That's thirty-two weeks total, counting both fall and spring semesters. There are twenty other weeks in the year that you could work. If you take two weeks off, that's eighteen weeks; put in forty hours in each of those weeks, and you'd earn just over $7,000 a year assuming you earn ten dollars an hour. And jobs with tips generally pay even more. Earning $7,000 a year is like earning $600 a month. That can pay for quite a bit of recreation, clothes, and non-dorm food. During the academic year, devote yourself to studying as much as possible, and allow yourself enough downtime to form and maintain strong friendships.

And, hey, you may not need as much spending money as you think. The fact is that many of your classmates are going into serious debt to pay for the things they enjoy but may not need. Remember the story of Daniel from chapter 5?

FINANCES

I hope your parents have discussed the subject of money management with you, at least a little bit. Maybe you had a high school job and were required to pay for your own clothing, like my wife was. Or maybe you went into college as completely ignorant as I was. At least I was helped in some ways by my miserly instincts.

The first thing you need to know is that credit card companies target *you* every year, usually at the beginning of each semester. You'll be encouraged to sign up for a MasterCard, a Visa card, an American Express card, and a Discover card. And if that's not enough, individual stores like Best Buy also have their own credit cards so that you can buy a new laptop computer but not have to pay for it until next June. Credit card companies used to come to campuses and give out free pizzas and T-shirts at the beginning of the semester, enticing us students to sign up, but that practice appears to have since been made illegal.[1] These weren't charity missions. My friends and I represented big business to them. And so do you.

Here's why: The minimum age to own a credit card is eighteen.[‡] You're the perfect demographic: You have material needs and wants, but generally not much cash flow. With one little swipe of a plastic card, you can have it *now*. The sooner they get you to start using their services, the more likely they

---

‡ My understanding of the law as of 2009 is that if you're less than twenty-one years old, you need someone over twenty-one to cosign the application unless you can verify that you are bringing in a sufficient monthly income. There are lots of reasons why parents may not wish to cosign credit cards for their children. Others might be willing to do so. That's a big discussion for another book. Verses like Proverbs 17:18 highly discourage cosigning arrangements; the basic issue is that if parents cosign, they are liable if you don't pay your bills. They may trust you (and be willing to train you). Or they may say, "Hey, you can wait until you're twenty-one."

are to have you for life. And since you're young, studies show you're more likely to mess up, which can make them even more money.

Notice that the cash-back incentive plans and advertising campaigns are both geared to make credit card use a regular part of your life. Need gas? You can get 3 percent off with a credit card. Want to eat at a restaurant? Lots of cards have point systems that let you build up frequent-flier miles or future discounts. And the TV commercials for credit cards tend to show people pampering themselves—entertaining friends in restaurants, traveling to picturesque destinations, buying gifts for loved ones, etc. Many credit cards even let you get cash advances—cash you didn't earn—allowing you to buy "cash only" merchandise.

As you might know, the monthly bill they send you indicates two amounts: the total amount owed and the much smaller minimum payment. What happens if you only make the minimum payment? You continue to owe them the remaining amount, and they tack on 15 to 20 percent interest. *That's* how they really make their money. The amount owed just snowballs to the next month (when you buy more stuff). The interest compounds; you end up owing interest on the interest. Before you know it, you're way over your head in debt. And guess what: Employers these days will probably check your credit score when deciding whether to hire you.

Employers these days will probably check your credit score when deciding whether to hire you.

Factoid

A recent study showed that one in every four college
students "rarely or never" pays his or her credit cards
in full every month.[2]

Here's a list of five financial mistakes you don't want to
make:

- not paying bills on time
- maxing out credit cards (they do have monthly limits)
- not making full payments
- using payday loans
- borrowing from credit cards

All of these lead to interest rates you don't want to deal with.
It's like borrowing ten dollars from me today, but having
to pay me twelve dollars tomorrow. Over and over again,
hundreds of times. And here's the scary thing: 75 percent of
college students have done one or more of these five things
in the last six months. One in eight students made four or all
five of these errors in that time.[3] How are you doing?

What's the right way to handle finances? Start with a
monthly budget. Just like you need a complete schedule to
maximize your time management, a monthly budget is essential for good money management. A budget tells every dollar
where to go. And if you don't tell those dollars where to go,
you'll be wondering where they all went. By the way, this

problem only gets worse when you have more dollars and more places for them to go.

Thankfully, making a budget is easier than you might think. All you need to know is how much you earn or receive over a given period of time and that you're spending less than that. Your income could come from a variety of sources: part-time job(s), a stipend from your parents, a scholarship, etc. Put each income source on its own line in a spreadsheet like Microsoft Excel. Add them up to see how much you have to work with. Of course you don't need to spend it all, but you can't spend more than that, because no matter what anyone else tells you, *that's all you have.*

A budget tells every dollar where to go. And if you don't tell those dollars where to go, you'll be wondering where they all went. By the way, this problem only gets worse when you have more dollars and more places for them to go.

Now identify every category of expense in your life: food, clothing, laundry, gas for your car, phone, entertainment (movies, video games, iTunes downloads), medicine, toiletries, books, school supplies, as well as Internet, gas, and electricity (if you're living off campus). List as many categories as you can think of. The next step is to create a "target" column to set maximum monthly amounts for each of these categories. Do your best. If you need to tweak the amounts later, that's okay. I would also recommend that you allocate an amount to give and an amount to save; these are good habits to start forming now. They'll take discipline to implement both now and later.

Next, for a full calendar month, record every expense in your spreadsheet under a column labeled "actual." At the end of the month, you'll compare the "target" column to the "actual" column. If you must use a credit card, use only one—it's easier to keep track of. But use it *as little as possible.* And pay every bill in full when it's due (credit card, gas, electric, Best Buy, etc.). This is absolutely crucial. Especially when you're starting, spend as little as possible to make sure you have enough money to pay all your bills at the end of the month. Okay, after one month of implementing a budget you should have something like this:

INCOME		
SOURCE	**AMOUNT**	
Job at Denny's	$ 350	
Money from Grandpa	$ 150	
TOTAL	**$ 500**	

BUDGET		
EXPENSES	**TARGET**	**ACTUAL**
Food	$ 100	$ 96.75
Clothing	$ 75	$ 83.68
Toiletries/Laundry	$ 25	$ 21.35
Phone	$ 50	$ 49.88
Internet	$ 25	$ 24.95
Entertainment	$ 50	$ 72.05
Gas for Car	$ 25	$ 23.06
Giving	$ 50	$ 50.00
Miscellaneous	$ 50	$ 60.78
TOTAL	**$ 450**	**$ 483**
AMOUNT SAVED	**$ 50**	**$ 17**

For this student, the actual total did not match the target total because while she aimed to spend $450, she actually spent $483. As a result, she was only able to save $17 instead of $50. You'll notice that she had set a goal of giving 10 percent of her income and saving another 10 percent. These are good figures to start with for both categories.

After you've done this for a month, think through how you actually spent your money. For example, were there certain things you spent money on that you now regret? Is any category out of whack? What will you do differently next month? In the example I gave above, the student is pretty much under control. She spent more in a few areas, but a bit less on gas and food, and she simply wasn't able to save as much. Next month she can make a few reductions to her spending so that she can boost her savings. That way she'll be ready when Ashley asks her to be a bridesmaid and she needs to chip in for a dress and a bridal shower.

College is a great time to learn to live within your means, delay gratification when necessary, and to give and save regularly.

College is a great time to learn to live within your means, delay gratification when necessary, and to give and save regularly. And don't forget to take advantage of student discounts and to look for deals on fun activities!

CONCLUSIONS

Don't waste good opportunities in college. Prioritize and develop your academic skills, but also take advantage of extracurricular growth opportunities like internships, mission trips, student organizations, and special events. Some are more about academic development, others more about spiritual and relational development. All are important. Also aim to grow in your time and money-management skills so that you'll be successful in the responsibilities God assigns you, both in college and beyond. "For we are his workmanship, created in Christ Jesus for good works, which God prepared beforehand, that we should walk in them" (Ephesians 2:10). Let him shape you into a vessel uniquely equipped for a life of faithfulness, in accordance with how he's gifted you, and for his global purposes to spread his name and fame throughout the earth.

DISCUSSION STARTERS

1. If you've had an internship, how did that experience influence you? Did it shape your professional goals? If you have not had an internship, do you plan to pursue one?

2. If you've been on a short-term mission trip, how did that experience influence you? How do you hope that it continues to affect you ten years from now?

3. What extracurricular activities have you chosen to pursue and why?

4. Do you work a part-time job? Do your academics ever suffer as a result? What steps can you take in order to prioritize college but not go broke?

5. Do you use a credit card? Have you made any of the mistakes I mentioned: not paying bills on time, maxing out the card, not making full payments, using payday loans, or borrowing from credit cards?

6. Have you ever tried to use a budget? How'd it go? What did you learn about yourself?

Conclusion

Don't Waste Your College Years:
Get Ready for the Real World

WE'VE EXPLORED FOUR areas of college life: general issues (maintaining and growing in your faith, adjusting to college from high school), relationships (with peers, professors, the opposite sex, and Mom and Dad), character (integrity, balancing work and play), and academics (choosing a major, working for grades, and internships/extracurricular opportunities). Now let's put it all together: What does it look like to get ready for the real world? And how do these four areas of college life interact and relate with one another?

JOSEPH (AND SAMANTHA)

Joseph is halfway through his senior year. A biology major with a strong grade-point average at the University of California at Los Angeles, Joseph is starting to think seriously about the MCAT (the admissions exam for medical school). His freshman year was tough but good. He was confronted with immoral situations and opportunities in the dorms and professors who looked down on Christianity. But he found a strong church and a great group of Christian friends. Over breaks he devoured books on how Christianity and science were mutually reinforcing. Through standing firm to intellectual and moral attacks, his faith grew stronger and deeper. He learned not only how but why to take a stand and go against the flow.

He procrastinated at times his first year, but then learned to plan ahead and get his work done in a regular, systematic fashion. Studying for tests became less consuming, and after freshman year he never again had to pull an all-nighter. During his first two years, professors knew he was intelligent and wanted to hire him as an assistant, but they regarded him as somewhat flaky. He was a great student, they thought, but would be a pain as an employee, as he was generally high maintenance. But as his study habits were becoming more disciplined, he also grew in recognizing the importance of dependability and providing value. He learned to bug his professors less and work more independently and resourcefully. As professors saw this, their resistance to hiring him was overcome, and one of them picked Joseph as a research assistant.

Notice for a moment the relationship between character and academics. Joseph was a smart guy—God gave him plenty of intellectual talent, and his previous education had served him well. His character wasn't terrible—it wasn't like he was a lying, mischievous, dishonest person. But he was a procrastinator, and he didn't exhibit maturity. Rather than get things done, he tended to bog down his professors with questions and excuses. Those character deficiencies limited his academic progress, as they short-circuited potential opportunities. But let's get back to Joseph's story.

In high school, Joseph had coasted. His friends weren't bad influences, but they didn't really push him to be stronger. But one of the best decisions Joseph made in his freshman year at college was to choose a church and a strong network of Christian guy friends. He didn't just get "lucky" in finding this church; he checked out several churches and asked people for advice. He and his new friends were able to challenge one another and create a counterculture against the tide of the dominant dorm scene. Together, they helped one another to focus on their classes, to set and maintain a study schedule, to be careful with their finances, and to get enough sleep. But they also pushed one another to be faithful in their spiritual disciplines and to carve out time, especially during breaks, for significant reading—stuff that expanded their minds and helped them grapple with the intellectual challenges to Christianity. After their sophomore year, several of them went on the same mission trip. But they also had a lot of fun together. Bob taught Joseph how to water-ski. Joseph and Darren took a windsurfing class and spent many Saturday mornings catching the waves. They would each graduate with lots of great memories.

Joseph's choice of friends had a direct bearing on his transition to college from high school, on his balancing work and play, and on his spiritual growth. No doubt it also had a role in his character development, his increased maturity over his first three years, which led to his professional development through the opportunity of a research assistantship (granted on the basis of academic ability and character).

Joseph met Samantha a year ago through their campus fellowship. He was drawn to her maturity, the way she took her work seriously but didn't let it become all-consuming. Samantha played clarinet in the orchestra and tutored at a local high school. They had a number of mutual friends, and both of them stayed busy enough that their relationship never developed an unhealthy preoccupation. They each had known people who got burned by getting too close to someone too quickly, and they wanted to avoid that. Yet they knew they had a strong, growing connection and that with each of them graduating the next year, it was something worth thinking about.

With regard to his parents, Joseph was growing in functional independence. Thanks to a plan they had mapped out together, Joseph would graduate with only $10,000 to pay back in student loans. He was planning to take a year off before medical school, get a job, and live on the cheap so he could pay it all back before starting to take out new loans. He knew his parents wouldn't be able to provide any more financial help, and he was okay with that. He was planning to move back home to facilitate paying off that $10,000, but that wouldn't work if he proposed to Samantha. He knew he needed to balance taking financial responsibility for his future, a realistic perspective on debt, and the possibility of marrying Samantha.

Joseph is an example of a well-integrated Christian young man who is thriving at college. His experience hasn't been marked by perfection, but by continual growth. He is having a great time in school, but his life isn't defined by the need to have fun. As he looks out over the horizon, he knows the future may be challenging, but he's been well trained and he's thoughtfully approaching the big decisions with an informed, balanced perspective.

Instead of having a big wedding, Joseph and Samantha asked their parents to use what could have gone into a fancy dinner to pay off what was left of Joseph's and Samantha's college loans. Joseph ended up working for a couple of years before medical school. They had even built up a little nest egg so that they weren't completely overwhelmed when Samantha found out she was pregnant. The maturity, competence, and wisdom that Joseph and Samantha had developed in their college years had equipped them for launching well into post-college life.

Let's contrast them with Nicholas.

NICHOLAS

Like Joseph, Nicholas had a great time in college. But unlike Joseph, Nicholas was defined by the need to have "the time of his life." *You're only in college once*, he figured. *I've got the rest of my life to grow up and get serious.* He made good money as a waiter and bought a monster entertainment center that was the envy of every guy in the dorm. The surround-sound system alone took a whole day to wire up and could fill the entire building with music or movie audio.

Toward the end of his freshman year Nicholas settled on an interdisciplinary studies major because the course requirements seemed less than in other majors. He thought he might do something with communications or marketing. But Nicholas's real "major" seemed to be hanging out with friends and having a good time. Weekend trips, getaways, video game sessions until two in the morning, you name it.

In spite of his job, Nicholas had racked up some serious debt by the middle of his sophomore year. He apologized profusely to his parents, and they bailed him out so it wouldn't keep hurting their credit rating, since they had cosigned on the card. Nicholas was smart and was able to keep up a 2.6 GPA in the midst of his festivities. That kept him off academic probation and his parents (mostly) off his back.

Nicholas's friends didn't have a lot of ambition either. It's not that they were *bad* influences; they just weren't *good* influences. They all were Christians, which they each took as an indication that their salvation was secure, meaning they didn't need to be intentional about the way they lived their lives. As for intellectual challenges to Christianity, Nicholas and his buddies just shrugged those off. Didn't Jesus say that we should have the faith of children? He saw no need to grow deep in his understanding of what he believed, why he believed it, how he should live because of it, or how he could best spread it to others.

When it came to girls, Nicholas was glad to hang out

with a bunch of them. They'd see each other at various parties, campus events like football games, or Christian ministry events that Nicholas often attended. He'd sometimes feel a strong connection to one of them, but didn't want to take the awkward step of telling her how he felt. He didn't really understand the point. After all, he could just ask her to do things with him without making some sort of big speech and weirding her out. As long as he was a nice guy, he figured he'd always have girl and guy friends, and that was all he needed. Even as graduation rolled around, the thought of getting married someday seemed *way* in the distance and totally uninteresting. He needed to get a job and at least figure out how he was going to keep paying for all his stuff if his parents ever cut the purse strings. In the meantime, he was planning on moving back in with Mom and Dad, rent free. They were giving him the basement so he could have plenty of space to set up his entertainment system.

A STUDY OF CONTRASTS

Joseph and Nicholas may seem extreme. But I've known both of them. Which one of these guys most closely resembles you? What Joseph really had going for him is that his life was *integrated*. His Christian faith informed his desire to be a good student, to be productive and fruitful in his work, to develop godly character traits, and to balance his work and his play. His good work, in turn, opened doors for him to get research experience—an opportunity that made a difference with his application to medical school.

Nicholas failed to live in light of verses like Colossians 3:17, which says, "Whatever you do, in word or deed, do everything in the name of the Lord Jesus, giving thanks to God the Father through him" and Ecclesiastes 9:10, which reads, "Whatever your hand finds to do, do it with all your might" (NIV).

Joseph chose wise companions, knowing that "bad company corrupts good character" (1 Corinthians 15:33, NIV) and that "whoever walks with the wise becomes wise" (Proverbs 13:20). The result was a group of friends who encouraged his spiritual and intellectual growth, and from among which he met his future wife. Nicholas's friends could be worse, but they sure could be better. Likewise with regard to his parents, Joseph is growing up while Nicholas is merely growing older.

Which will it be for you? Which way are you going right now? What changes do you need to make?

TWO OUT OF FOUR

Looking back on my college life, I'd give myself a two out of four: I did well in two of the four areas of this book. My life wasn't as integrated as it should have been. On the one hand, I didn't chuck my faith, and in general I grew closer to God. I didn't treat college like high school but rather adjusted quickly to the workload, getting after my assignments and projects. I excelled academically and had a bunch of great internships. My résumé upon graduation looked pretty solid.

But I was weaker with regard to character and relationships.

On the work-life-balance scale, I had fallen off on the work side. Looking back, I wish I had sought after and cultivated stronger relationships. I had friends, but I wish I had invested more in them rather than squeezing out every point in my classes. I tell my students now that there are trade-offs everywhere in life.

I recommend setting a time limit on your studies; after that, take whatever grade you get on the test, paper, or assignment you're completing. That was the best you could do *all things considered*. What do I mean by that? It might not have been the best you could do if studying was the only thing on planet Earth that mattered to you. But it's not. So maybe you get a B+ instead of an A-, but you had a series of wonderful, encouraging times with great friends—friendships that, because of shared experiences, are more likely to last.

At the same time, others will tend to err on the opposite side. You would benefit from setting time limits on your recreation, entertainment, and Facebook use. Know yourself and your tendencies. All four of the areas we discussed matter greatly to God, and all will influence your happiness and success after you graduate.

THE TRAJECTORY OF LIFE

Set yourself on a trajectory for responsible, fruitful Christian adulthood. Take a moment and jot down some things that you want to be true of your life five years from now. Do you want to be known as someone who is dependable and trustworthy? Humble and kind? Gracious toward others? One who works hard and gets things done, resisting the temptation to procrastinate? One whose life is marked by the fruit of the Spirit (love, joy, peace, patience, kindness, goodness, faithfulness, gentleness, and self-control)?* One who has deep and wonderful friendships? One who is discreet and intentional with the opposite sex? One who is growing in the grace and knowledge of the Lord and Savior Jesus Christ (2 Peter 3:17-18)?

Now identify a few changes you need to make to get there. It might help to break your life down into the four areas I used for this book (faith, relationships, character, and academics). That little old phrase is only too accurate: "Sow a thought and reap an action; sow an act and reap a habit; sow a habit and reap a character; sow a character and reap a destiny." The "reap what you sow" principle is biblical (Galatians 6:7) and inescapable.

One of my favorite quotes in a movie is said by Russell Crowe's character, Maximus, in the classic film *Gladiator* (2000): "What we do in life echoes in eternity." Even if you're still a freshman, right now counts *forever*, because not only will you live forever (in the eternal joys of heaven or the eternal miseries of hell) but your influence and reputation will help or not help countless others. Even beyond your generation, consider that your future children, and in turn their children, will be profoundly shaped by the man or woman

---

* Galatians 5:22-23

you are becoming. You are ancestor to people not yet born. How will they remember you?

You are on the launching pad of life. The decisions you make now will have long-term ramifications. The more deeply ingrained your good habits, the easier it will be to maintain them. The more deeply ingrained your bad habits, the harder it will be to alter them. But with God's help you can alter them—resolve now to do so. You don't have to waste your twenties, as so many in our culture are doing.

> *The decisions you make now will have long-term ramifications. The more deeply ingrained your good habits, the easier it will be to maintain them. The more deeply ingrained your bad habits, the harder it will be to alter them.*

Proverbs 4:18 says it this way: "The path of the righteous is like the light of dawn, which shines brighter and brighter until full day." The word *path* here refers to the moral orientation of your life: To live in an upright manner brings greater clarity, beauty, and winsomeness to your life, allowing you to make better decisions that, in the long haul, lead to your success. This is true relationally, even among those who might not naturally like you: "When a man's ways please the LORD, he makes even his enemies to be at peace with him" (Proverbs 16:7). And it's true professionally: "The plans of the diligent lead surely to abundance. . . . The hand of the diligent makes rich" (Proverbs 21:5; 10:4). That doesn't mean God promises you enormous wealth as long as you obey him. It means that *in general* diligence leads to professional and, therefore, monetary blessings. The opposite way leads to confusion: Proverbs 4:19 says, "The way of the wicked is like deep darkness; they do not know over what they stumble."

Thrive in the life God gives you; every day is a gift to be lived out fully for him. Don't waste your college; aim to thrive in every aspect of it. Your college experience matters to God because every aspect of it either reflects the fact that Jesus Christ is your supreme treasure or that your heart in some area is captivated by the world's values. Of course, none of us is perfect, but as nineteenth-century author Charles Bridges says, "Christian perfection is the continual aiming at perfection."[1]

To live in an upright manner brings greater clarity, beauty, and winsomeness to your life, allowing you to make better decisions that, in the long haul, lead to your success.

Or in the language of Philippians 3:13-14, "Forgetting what lies behind and straining forward to what lies ahead . . . press on toward the goal for the prize of the upward call of God in Christ Jesus." The prize is the perfect fellowship with Christ that awaits us in heaven. I'll meet you there. Until then, let's push ourselves, with God's help, to be more like Jesus every day, to represent him well on this earth, to be salt and light, living in a way that makes him look precious. Let's do college that way. Let's do life that way.

APPENDIX 1

The College Selection Process

THE COLLEGE SELECTION process can be a stressful experience for both students and parents. There are all kinds of handbooks out there on the subject, and I won't try to reproduce all they say. I'll just give you a short breakdown on two significant criteria that will probably influence your college decision: academic considerations and the issue of attending a secular vs. a Christian college or university.

My perspective is shaped by my own story: I attended public school all my life, became a Christian in high school, and attended a secular university at both the undergraduate and graduate levels. While I've done some teaching at a secular university, I've been a full-time professor at a Christian college for the last six years.

Clearly, there are many subjective factors that I won't get into here, like how you feel walking around the campus, the dorms, the dining hall, the surrounding town, distance from your family, etc.

Also, more college students today are starting at local

community colleges and then seeking to transfer to traditional four-year schools. Just a couple of remarks about that: This can be a very cost-effective way to go, but before you try it, investigate whether there may be any unanticipated snags. For example, some large state universities may limit the percentage of transfer applicants they'll consider. Other schools make it difficult to transfer in the units from the community college, which can end up costing you an extra year. Look for a community college with a proven track record of students who have gone the route you're considering. Get as much as you can in writing, as registrar and academic advising personnel may change during the course of your studies.

With that, let's jump into the academic and secular vs. Christian considerations.

ACADEMIC CONSIDERATIONS

What's the best way to assess a school's academic credentials? There are so many ways that it's easy to get lost. Lots of parents place a great deal of confidence in indexes such as the *U.S. News and World Report*. While these can be helpful, be aware that schools play plenty of games to artificially boost themselves on these kinds of scales. You can also look at the entrance requirements, things like ACT and SAT scores. I'd look at those more than high school grade-point averages, which are increasingly meaningless due to grade-inflation trends. The selection ratio is also worthwhile: Take note if they accept everyone who applies. Of course, that won't mean that all the students at that school will be weak. But it will put pressure on the faculty to not lower academic standards simply to retain students. The success of the school's graduates also speaks to a school's reputation.

Adjuncts

Another question worth asking is the percentage of classes taught by adjunct professors. Adjunct professors are inexpensive for colleges; they're paid by the credit, and very little at that. Almost every school uses them for some of their courses (particularly lower division). Besides the issue of cost, another rationale behind this policy is that it limits the school's commitment or liability. Adjuncts are hired on a semester-by-semester basis, whereas full-time faculty enjoy the expectation that their positions are permanent, which is even more secure if they have tenure. By letting adjuncts teach a certain percentage of the courses in a particular discipline, the school can delay hiring a full-time professor until the need is significant and they are confident they won't have to subsequently lay off the position (a process which can have legal implications). In addition to their teaching duties, full-time faculty are expected to serve on committees and perform varying amounts of research in their academic discipline as well as perform other kinds of service. Not surprisingly, they generally make better teachers than adjuncts, which is why they were offered their positions in the first place. So check the percentage of classes taught by adjuncts.

Class size

Small schools have an advantage over large schools in that they have smaller class sizes. This tends to facilitate better learning. Also, many large universities farm out their large freshman and sophomore courses to adjuncts or teaching assistants, both of whom tend to be less experienced, as I mentioned above. On the other hand, large universities often afford more opportunities in terms of specialization and concentrations. For example, whereas smaller schools may offer three engineering majors, larger schools may offer ten. In other fields, you might find many concentrations within the majors that might not be available elsewhere (like a major in the "history of Latin America" rather than simply "history").

Research driven or teaching driven

Some schools push their faculty to do a lot of research, whereas others emphasize teaching. One quick way to tell what they're doing is to find out how many units per year faculty are required to teach. At the University of California at Berkeley, where I did my graduate education, faculty generally taught one course per semester. As you might have suspected, U.C. Berkeley places a lot of emphasis on research, and therefore graduate students (on average) get more attention than undergraduates. At many other schools, professors are responsible for closer to three or four courses per semester. These schools place less emphasis on research and a greater burden on teaching. That means the faculty at those schools put more time and effort into their courses and are more accountable to their students.

That said, it is worth noting that *some* professors at research-driven universities are phenomenal teachers. Moreover, their research informs their teaching, so they're likely more fluent on the latest developments in their respective fields. Additionally, these schools are more likely to make research opportunities available to well-qualified students. The flip side is that with more students comes more competition for those spots.

Another statistic to consider is the retention rate: What percentage of freshman students advance to the sophomore year at that institution? This figure is a measure not just of how much the students like the place but also of whether or not they are able to achieve at least a modicum of academic success.

In a nutshell, if you're looking to really get to know your professors on a more personal level and have a generally more intimate college experience in a place where it's harder to get lost, a small college makes more sense for you. If you want to have a whole maze of academic and social opportunities to choose from, and don't mind receiving less personal attention, a larger university may be right for you. I do think that larger schools require a greater degree of self-discipline, if for no other reason than that there is so much going on and greater academic anonymity. At a small school, like California Baptist University, where I teach, I notice every student who's absent and will often send an e-mail if he or she misses a few consecutive class sessions. I let the student know that

I'm concerned about his or her academic progress. That's probably not going to happen at a large state school.

I chose to go to a small school for my undergraduate. It really helped me academically, as I'm not sure I was ready to learn in humongous classes (lecture halls of several hundred are not uncommon at large universities). But for my graduate studies I'm really glad I went to a big school, since my graduate class sizes weren't very large (about twenty-five to thirty) and I was able to take advantage of a wide variety of research opportunities that wouldn't have been present at most smaller institutions.

Secular vs. Christian

I'll try to make what I say here as evenhanded as possible. The truth is, this is an issue that many well-intentioned Christians have strong opinions on. Just as Christians debate the merits of homeschooling, Christian schooling, and public schooling, so Christians debate the merits of a Christian versus a secular college education.

Christian schools are private and generally more expensive than secular *public* schools, but not necessarily secular *private* schools. That said, I've seen cases in which high-caliber students have received significant scholarships and other kinds of aid from Christian colleges that resulted in the final price tag being on par with nearby state universities. So don't let the initial sticker price shock you.

Private, non-Christian schools (or top-tier public universities) are sometimes perceived to be more academically prestigious than their Christian counterparts. But some Christian colleges and universities are quite rigorous and seek to provide both an enriching intellectual and spiritual experience. Clearly, Christian colleges differ with respect to academic rigor: Some are highly selective and demanding, and others are less so. That can be said of secular schools also. But secular colleges draw students almost exclusively on academic and professional grounds, as they self-identify almost entirely on those terms.* Christian schools, in contrast, tend to draw students on the basis of both academic and spiritual considerations. Since I already discussed academic rigor, let's jump into some of the *nonacademic* reasons (as I see them) why you might want to consider Christian colleges. I'll give you four.†

1. There is an undeniable attack on the Christian faith in secular academia, especially at the more elite, selective, and prestigious institutions.

---

* Some Christians I've known make the case, as high school seniors, that they want to go to a secular university in order to share Christ with others. Though unquestionably an admirable intention, I honestly wonder if some of those who speak this way feel compelled to justify their decision in terms of evangelism, as if speaking about Jesus were the only way we could honor Christ. As I deal with elsewhere in this book, this represents a truncated view of the God-honoring nature of our regular day-to-day work. Most Christians spend most of their lives doing something other than talking about Jesus—and there's nothing wrong with that. After graduation, God calls most of us to be faithful and exemplary accountants, doctors, lawyers, history teachers, and journalists. So why wouldn't we take this into account when we select a college or university? Every legitimate academic pursuit (and profession) done for God's glory brings him honor and accomplishes his purposes. I'm not saying you can't go to a secular college. I'm saying don't feel you have to employ evangelism to justify going to such a college. Get a strong foundation for your life's work. And if you happen to do that at a secular college, then by all means, yes, share Christ with others in appropriate ways. But I don't think that should be what fundamentally drives you to choose a college. You should be considering your own needs and goals. If you feel called to college ministry, that is always something you can return to after you graduate. First get a strong foundation for your life's work.

† The reasons I list are similar to the ones James Dobson unpacks in his chapter "Choosing a College" from his book *Life on the Edge* (Word, 1995).

There are many Christians in the ranks of secular academia, and we should be thankful for them. They sense God's call to their particular posts, and their work is important and God honoring. Nevertheless, it's a documented fact that your likelihood of meeting atheists or agnostics among secular university faculty is far more likely than your finding them in the wider population.[1] The result is that many Christians in secular academia feel pressured to keep quiet about their faith for fear of ridicule or termination.

Their fears are not unfounded; many secular academicians regard Christians as naive and unsophisticated simpletons in need of re-education.[‡] Some are brazen in their efforts to enlighten Christians in the virtue of "tolerance," by which they mean the denial of absolutes (i.e., relativism). On ethical or religious matters, I'm not allowed to think you're wrong, and you're not allowed to think I'm wrong. Rather, "what's true for me need not be true for you."

The secular academy would have us believe that religious "truths" are private: They have no root in historical events (such as Jesus Christ's resurrection from the dead) and have no implications for non–Christ followers (rendering evangelism not only unnecessary but arrogant—why should you

---

[‡] One unfortunate result is that they may give less "air time" to Christian thinkers throughout history—for example, in a philosophy, literature, or history curriculum. I recall learning that the Puritans were a bunch of mean-spirited, out-of-touch people who liked to talk about God sending people to hell all the time. Never mind the fact that they often spoke and preached of God's love and compassion and the importance of doing good to others. Similarly, an atheistic philosophy professor may gloss over the contributions of Augustine or Aquinas. In fairness, it may also be the case that some Christian professors at Christian institutions fail to interact with the leading non-Christian thinkers. That would be something to investigate about the institution prior to attending, along with the qualifications of the individual faculty (their educational backgrounds, career experience, contributions to their disciplines, etc.).

tell others to change the way *they* think and live to the way *you* think and live?).

But true tolerance does not require the denial of absolute truth; indeed, the claim that there are no absolute truths is a claim to absolute truth. No, true tolerance involves treating people with kindness and respect *while believing them to be wrong on some particular matter.* Since Christianity presupposes theological and moral absolutes, ethical relativism and Christianity cannot coexist.

2. The moral climate at many secular institutions is hostile to biblical Christianity.

Religious relativism goes hand in hand with ethical relativism. Morality based on relativism says that just as no religion can claim to be the only way to God, so no system of personal morality is to be revered above others. For example, "safe" sex is the standard, politically correct mantra. It means "wear a condom so you don't contract an STD or create an unwanted pregnancy." Relatively little consideration is made for the emotional damage that sexualized relationships and breakups cause. The view that sex is special and to be reserved for marriage is considered prudish, repressive, and unhealthy.

Along these lines, in an effort to simplify student housing assignments, many secular universities have long since gone to coed dorms, where a room with two girls may be next door to a room with two guys. The natural extension was coed bathrooms (with individual shower stalls and curtains), which are rapidly becoming the norm. I think it's safe to say that most eighteen- to twenty-two-year-old men find the knowledge that attractive, naked women are showering behind curtains just a few feet away to be alluring to say the least. Meanwhile women who express discomfort with such arrangements are regarded as prudes, as one such woman even called herself in a *Go Ask Alice!* advice column.[2] It's unsurprising that promiscuity is rampant in such environments and that even aggressive behavior such as stalking and acquaintance rape are not uncommon.

3. Christian colleges and universities tend to hire only Christian faculty.

Some schools are doctrinally narrower than others in this regard, but the principle of hiring only Christian faculty is something of a staple for Christian institutions, at least those in the Council for Christian Colleges and Universities (CCCU), of which there are 110 in North America with 75 affiliate institutions in 24 countries. The college years are an impressionable time for young adults. Many will question the faith of their upbringing and perhaps outright abandon it for a season. Studies indicate that about 70 percent of young adults who attended a Protestant church regularly for at least a year in high school will stop attending church regularly for at least a year between the ages of eighteen and twenty-two.[3]

I'm convinced that there are some people who will make it at Christian schools but not elsewhere. They'll graduate at twenty-two with a maturity they didn't have at eighteen. And even if they aren't as solid at twenty-two as their parents would have liked, they may never in the workplace, or in the culture at large, experience the *concentrated* anti-Christian influence found at many secular university campuses. There is an undeniable advantage of being under the watch and care of Christians during the pivotal college years.

4. At many Christian colleges and universities, the majority of students are professing Christians.
Some Christian schools require that every student sign a statement of faith; others are open to the attendance of non-Christians (as a means of exposing them to the Good News of Jesus Christ). Particularly with the former, but even with the latter, you'll be interacting with mostly Christian students. Significant, impactful, and even lifelong friendships can be forged in this once-in-a-lifetime environment.

It is also not surprising that many who attend Christian colleges meet their husband or wife in that context. In general, Christians marry somewhat earlier than their non-Christian counterparts, and have (at least theoretically) a higher view of marriage and sexual fidelity, so it is not surprising that students at a campus full of Christians are more inclined to tie the knot. Finding a godly spouse is a huge blessing that will bring you strength, stability, and deep happiness over the long haul.

As you can tell, I think the Christian higher education scene has distinct advantages. That said, I want to emphasize that whether to go to a secular or Christian school is a matter of Christian liberty. You may live near a large public university and already have a great church situation. And a nearby Christian school might not have the academic program that most interests you.

Each student needs to weigh the pros and cons in his or her particular situation, given personal and academic aspirations, geographic preferences or limitations, available resources, etc. It's definitely the kind of decision you should discuss with your parents and for which you should pray for wisdom. And it's definitely worthwhile to talk to people who know you and have actually attended the institutions you are considering, particularly if they share your values and aspirations.

APPENDIX 2

Do You Own Your Christian Faith?

When I turned sixteen, I started borrowing my parents' cars. I could go to work, see my friends, and come home. It was great. The most I ever had to do was fill them up with gas. If they needed new brakes or tires, my parents took care of it. About halfway through college I took a semester off and went to work in Tennessee for eight months. My parents bought me a car. *Wonderful*, I thought. Until I started paying for all the maintenance. Oil changes, brake pads, tires, everything. Borrowing was better than owning. It had all the perks, and none of the responsibilities.

If you were raised in a Christian home, chances are you started borrowing the Christian faith from your parents on the day you were born. That was appropriate for a time. But as you move into manhood or womanhood, what your parents and pastors are hoping for is that you take ownership of your faith for yourself.

In this appendix, I want to talk to those of you who were raised borrowing your faith, but are not yet sure if you own it for yourself. Maybe some unexpected rebellion in your heart is spilling out. Maybe you're trying things you never dreamed of trying because "you're only in college once." You sometimes wonder where things stand between you and God. Here's the hard truth: Some of you in this category will graduate from college and, in the near future, graduate from God. Of those who leave, some will come back—maybe when you're married and have kids. And others will be gone for good.[§]

I pray college will be the time in your life when God really gets a hold of you, solidifying your faith and empowering you to make great strides toward godliness in your actions, thoughts, and motivations.

How can we explain this? The answer is found in 1 John 2:19 (NIV): "They went out from us, but they did not really belong to us. For if they had belonged to us, they would have remained with us; but their going showed that none of them belonged to us." It is possible to think you are a Christian but to later abandon Christianity. If you ultimately abandon your faith, you prove you never really had it in the first place. You were just fooling yourself (and maybe everyone else). You never internalized or owned the Christian faith. You were merely borrowing someone else's faith. You returned it when it was no longer interesting or useful to you.

But I sure hope that won't be the case for you. I pray

[§] Studies indicate that about 70 percent of all Protestants will stop attending church regularly for at least a year between the ages of eighteen to twenty-two. Of those who do, only two in three return to regular attendance sometime in the next ten years. This data is from a 2007 LifeWay Research study, found here: http://www.lifeway.com/article/165949.

college will be the time in your life when God really gets a hold of you, solidifying your faith and empowering you to make great strides toward godliness in your actions, thoughts, and motivations.

Some of you are borrowing the Christian faith, but you *think* you own it. Time and testing will reveal that your faith is a facade. Others of you really *do* own the Christian faith, but you're not sure that you do. Time and testing will reveal that your faith is the real deal. What both of you need is to *be* saved, *know* that you are saved, and know that you are saved *for the right reasons.*

Christians talk about "getting saved." What does that phrase mean? It means escaping (or being saved *from*) the consequences of our disobedience to God. It also means being freed to obey God from a new heart, from an internal desire to love and please him—to do his will with the right motivation, not to earn his favor but in response to having already received it for all eternity. We're told it requires a new birth (John 3:3, 5; 1 Peter 1:3), because we're born into this world dead to the things of God (Ephesians 2:1-3). The Old Testament speaks similarly of our need for a "new heart" and a "new spirit" (Ezekiel 36:24-28), namely, one that is responsive and warm toward God rather than lifeless and cold.

Blind confidence is dangerous. In 2 Corinthians 13:5, the apostle Paul says "Examine yourselves, to see whether you are in the faith. Test yourselves." The apostle Peter, after acknowledging that when God saved us he gave us everything we needed to grow in godliness, exhorts us to "make every effort to supplement your faith with virtue, and virtue with knowledge, and knowledge with self-control, and self-control with steadfastness, and steadfastness with godliness, and godliness with brotherly affection, and brotherly affection with love." Why? "For if these qualities are yours and are increasing, they keep you from being ineffective or unfruitful in the knowledge of our Lord Jesus Christ" (2 Peter 1:5-8). We learn more about the importance of these qualities in verse 10: "Therefore, brothers, be all the more diligent to make your calling and election sure, for *if you practice these qualities you will never fall*" (emphasis added). To make our "calling and election sure" is to ensure that we are "in the faith" (2 Corinthians 13:5). We gain this assurance over time by living an increasingly godly life. As we see the fruit, we grow confident that there's a root. And our confidence is well-founded.

> Good works don't save us, but those who are saved always produce good works.

There are headlines out there that say things like "Born Again Christians Just As Likely to Divorce as Are Non-Christians." Or surveys that report unflattering percentages about how few "Christians" give to their churches or faithfully abstain from sexual intimacy before marriage. But what those surveys fail to realize is that merely saying you're born again doesn't make it so. The proof is in our lives. Everyone who practices righteousness has been born again (1 John 2:29), and nobody who continually lives in sin can have been born again (1 John 3:9).

If you were accused of being a Christian, would there be enough evidence to convict you? Good works don't save us, but those who are saved always produce good works. We're not talking about *perfection* here. We're talking about *direction*—the tenor, the thrust, the overall aim of your life. Is your deepest desire to please God? Are you aware of a fight against sin in your life? Are you making war with those habits, attitudes, and motivations that you know displease God?

> We're not talking about perfection here. We're talking about direction—the tenor, the thrust, the overall aim of your life. Is your deepest desire to please God?

We can't *become* God's children by performing good works. But if you trust him, then you'll love him because you'll regard him and what he did to be precious. And if you love him, then you'll obey him. And if you don't, then you don't really trust him or love him.

Please don't get me wrong. There's a false gospel out there that has this formula:

Faith + Works → Salvation

But the Bible teaches this formula:

Faith → Salvation + Works

Works are the *fruit* or the *evidence* of salvation.

EVIDENCES OF SALVATION

1. Internal vs. external motivation

Joe and Sam both go to church on Sunday. Joe is truly worshiping. Sam is singing, but he's wondering if people are looking at him and whether he's clapping at the right times. The sermon begins, and Joe opens his Bible. He's eager to hear a word from God. Sam opens his Bible also. He knows that's what he's supposed to do. Hopefully he can stay awake and not embarrass himself.

If you were to see Joe and Sam at church, you probably couldn't tell who's who. It's possible to do all the right things for all the wrong reasons. It's possible to look the right way on the outside and be way off on the inside. But being saved, being born again, comes with a new internal motivation to please God from the heart. Let's look at three aspects.

a. Spiritual affections vs. going through the motions

An "affection" is a feeling, a fondness, a disposition. You probably have affection for your parents and close friends. If they died, you'd be really sad—you wouldn't have to pretend or put on a show.

Matthew 13:44 reads: "The kingdom of heaven is like treasure hidden in a field, which a man found and covered up. Then in his *joy* he goes and sells all that he has and buys that field" (emphasis added). The person who has found salvation has more joy in it than in all his possessions combined. Is Jesus precious to you? Do you delight in the treasure of salvation?

There should be an element of delight in God, or at least the longing to delight in God. These go together, since none of us delights in God as much as we should.⁵ But to some degree, Psalm 27:4 is the prayer of every Christian: "One thing have I asked of the LORD, that will I seek after: that I may dwell in the house of the LORD all the days of my life, to gaze upon the beauty of the LORD and to inquire in his temple."

In 1 Peter 1:6 we read, "In this [your salvation, and the future glories of heaven that await you] you rejoice, though now for a little while, if necessary, you have been grieved by various trials." Peter was writing to people who were undergoing intense suffering, but he confidently writes, "*you rejoice.*" How could they rejoice? Because they truly believed that to have Jesus and to suffer hardship was better than to enjoy comfort and not have Jesus. These kinds of priorities lead Christians to do things that the world views as foolish.

b. Prayer: talking to God vs. performing for others

If you've grown up in the church, chances are you know how to pray. You grew up with prayer before every meal, and perhaps before every class at school. You have a theological vocabulary. You know which phrases to piece together and are sure to end with "in Jesus' name, Amen." But when you

---

⁋ There are some well-meaning Christians who say that love for God is an act of the will, not an emotion. What God commands is obedience. Positive feelings (affections) for God are peripheral—great if you have them, but not necessary. I disagree. I believe that God commands us to pursue joy in him in the midst of all other expressions of obedience. The Christian's pursuit of delight in God is pervasive, not peripheral, in the Scriptures. We are not only to do justice, but to love mercy (Micah 6:8). We are not only to perform acts of mercy, but to do so with cheerfulness (Romans 12:8). We are to *joyfully* suffer loss (Hebrews 10:34), give *cheerfully* (2 Corinthians 9:7), and find *joy* in the joy of others (2 Corinthians 2:3). Yes, God commands us to obey him, but the scope of his commands includes our affections. For a book-length defense of this position see *Desiring God* by John Piper and other works by him.

pray are you really talking to God? Do you have any sense of connecting with him? When you don't pray, do you sense something is missing and long to be with God? Do you find yourself thinking of your life in terms of your need for God, your dependence on God, and your gratefulness to God?

If we *never* seek to commune with the God of the universe, on what grounds can we claim to call him our Father? The Holy Spirit takes up residence in every Christian. And one of the things he does is move us to come to God and call him "Daddy" (Romans 8:15). Now we can grieve the Spirit through prayerlessness (Ephesians 4:30; 1 Thessalonians 5:17, 19), but that will only invite God's corrective discipline for Christians (see Hebrews 12:3-11). It won't—it *can't*—last. Prayer is a fruit of God's grace in our lives, and God will work within us to cultivate it.

Many of us don't pray because we feel too busy or too tired. But those are reasons why we need his help—those indicators are actually *invitations* to pray. Other times we don't pray because we feel guilty or embarrassed by our insignificance or sinfulness. Again, God already knows that, so we can come as we are. As Paul Miller writes in his excellent book *A Praying Life*, "You have to begin with what is real. Jesus didn't come for the righteous. He came for sinners. All of us qualify."[1] Let your desperation draw you to God.

c. Pleasing God vs. pleasing authority
Everyone wants to please authority. That's hardwired into us. There's an immediate payoff from pleasing authority,

whether it's a tangible award (money, praise) or the avoidance of punishment.

But pleasing God is different. We can't see him, and we
don't hear him audibly. We hear him in the Scriptures. Those
who belong to him long to please him because we see his
precepts as appropriate and reasonable and because we have
deeper fellowship with him and joy in him when we do.
We're moved to find out what makes God happy, and then
to do it. We want to do what's right even when nobody is
watching.

I remember spending a week at a Christian camp when
I was twelve years old and not yet a Christian. They had a
mini-golf course that cost a dollar per game. Our cabin was
out that way, and we noticed that the clubs and balls had
been left out, but there was no attendant. There was just a
sign saying to leave the money in the can if we decided to
play. In my brilliance, I announced to the cabin that we
could play for free because nobody would know that we
had not paid. The guys chuckled. The counselor leaned over
to me and told me that God was watching *even if nobody
else was.* A Christian lives for God's praise, not the praise
of others.

Earlier I mentioned the battle with sin. Galatians 5:17
reads, "The desires of the flesh are against the Spirit, and the
desires of the Spirit are against the flesh, for these are opposed
to each other, to keep you from doing the things you want
to do." Do you sense this battle within you? At the age of
twelve I didn't. The golf clubs and balls were there. This was

not a problem; it was our lucky day. I sensed no struggle. Why not? I didn't have God's Spirit living inside me, fighting against the sinful tendencies of my flesh. If you sense this battle within you, that's an indication that God's Spirit is inside you, calling you to fight against your sinful desires and inclinations. Are you committed to the battle to be continuously killing sin so that it's not killing you (Romans 8:13)? Is it your desire to "make no provision for the flesh, to gratify its desires" (Romans 13:14)?

2. Identification with Jesus

A Christian is not ashamed of Jesus. We identify with him and with those who are his. There are two questions to ask here. First, are you willing to undergo ridicule for believing in Jesus? This is big. Have you ever chickened out in a situation where you knew that if so-and-so were to realize you were a Christ follower, he or she would laugh at you? I know I have. But God has helped me to move in the other direction: to willingly accept the disapproval of others in order to publicly identify with Jesus.

And second, do you identify with *God's people*? Or are all of your closest friends people who want nothing to do with Jesus? If so, have you asked yourself why that is? It may be that their values are a better representation of your *actual* values—not the values you theoretically absorbed from your parents and home church, but your actual values—those things *you* personally cherish and hold dear.

I'm not saying Christians shouldn't have friendships with non–Christ followers. We should be salt and light wherever God places us, seeking to influence others toward God by our words and actions. But if we truly belong to God, we will seek connections and friendships with those who share a desire to live in a way that pleases God.

Are the Christians you know flawed? Join the club—you're just like them. In your upbringing, you went to a church because your parents went there. You conformed to their expectations. That was natural, and it was good. But as you take ownership of your faith, you must seek out a faith community for yourself, knowing how necessary it is for your soul, and so you can be an encouragement to others.

ACTION PLAN

Come to own your faith during your college years. Don't be content to coast on your parents' faith or to do what's right just to keep up appearances with your friends. Make Jesus Christ the treasure of your life, your highest priority, so that others can see you walk to the beat of his drum. Pray for the character qualities in 2 Peter 1:3-6, then ask your close friends to help you look for them. Live from the inside out. And you'll find deep rest in the knowledge that you belong to him and will never fall away, having been born again "not of perishable seed but of imperishable" (1 Peter 1:23).

FOR FURTHER READING

1. John Piper, *Desiring God* (Sisters, OR: Multnomah, 2003).

2. John Piper, *Finally Alive* (Tain, Scotland: Christian Focus, 2009).

3. Karl Graustein and Mark Jacobsen, *Growing Up Christian* (Phillipsburg, NJ: P&R Publishing Company, 2005).

4. R. C. Sproul, *Can I Be Sure I'm Saved?* (Orlando: Reformation Trust, 2010).

5. Jonathan Edwards, *Religious Affections* (Carlisle, PA: Banner of Truth Trust, 1997).

Acknowledgments

I COULD NOT HAVE written this book had I not been given the privilege of being a professor these last five years. I am grateful to those who have given me that opportunity and for my many wonderful colleagues at California Baptist University, including Todd Bates and Chris Morgan, who gave helpful feedback on a chapter; Natalie Winter, for sharing some of her findings on how millennials think; and John Montgomery, Dan Wilson, Berniece Bruinius, and Anthony Donaldson, who among others were kind enough to express general interest in this project.

But my perspective on this subject was probably first shaped by my own professors. For my first teaching assistant at Alfred University who, as a Christian, was tough but fair, thank you. I've forgotten your name but not your lessons. Thanks for removing my preconceived notion that Christians should exhibit more mercy than justice in their grading standards. I'm also grateful to Paul Strong and Bill Dibrell at Alfred for pushing me to be a better thinker and writer.

Thanks for giving me fair (low!) grades and then helping me get better. And I'm grateful to my parents, without whom I could not have attended college. What an amazing privilege to be able to dedicate a season of life to learning and preparation. Thank you.

I appreciate Tullian Tchividjian and Alex Harris looking at my first proposal for this book and expressing encouragement. Your kind regards gave me the confidence to keep going. I am grateful beyond words to those who read and supported the proposal in its final form: Kenneth Boa, Colin Creel, David Dockery, Rick Holland, Sally Lloyd-Jones, Russell Moore, Burk Parsons, Ray Pritchard, Alexander Strauch, Sam Storms, Bruce Ware, and (once again) Tullian Tchividjian. Your kind words were very much appreciated. And I appreciate everyone who took the time to review and commend this book to others.

I am grateful to Erik Wolgemuth for his good work as my literary agent and for providing amazing help in organizing, focusing, and fine-tuning the book's proposal, as well as "shopping" the book. Thanks, too, for your first-rate feedback and support on numerous issues along the way.

I am very thankful for the student reviewers who served as outstanding sounding boards, providing a number of excellent suggestions and improvements to the shape, scope, and content of the manuscript: Kate Caldwell (Emerson College), Joshua Harris (Calbaptist University alumnus), Alyssa Chen (University of California–Berkeley, my other alma mater—go Bears!), Jacqui Cox (Calbaptist University),

Grace Perkins (Miami University), Luke Jackson (Colorado Christian University), and Kelvin Adams (Pacific Lutheran University). Calvin Lu was kind enough to provide substantive interaction with the book's themes, as were my former students Brendan King and Kit Joos.

I'm grateful to Jim Newheiser for interacting with me about Christian parents of young adults. I appreciate Karl Graustein and Brian Borgman corresponding with me on the topic of "churched kids" taking ownership of their faith. And I appreciate my friends Alvin and Kim Davis for interacting with me on the book's cover and title, and for their general encouragement and support. I'm grateful to friends like Brent Parker and Eric and Jocelyn Chi, who for years now have encouraged me in the sometimes arduous task of writing. A special word of thanks goes out to Ted Slater and Burk Parsons for allowing me to publish articles over the last three years—a process that helped refine my writing.

At Tyndale, I am grateful for the many excellent editorial contributions on all aspects of this project from Stephanie Voiland, Erin Marshall, Erin Gwynne, and Jon Farrar. The content and style of this book are a lot more engaging because of your good work. I'm also grateful for April Kimura-Anderson and Vicky Lynch for their support on the marketing and publicity side of things. Thanks for all you do.

I want to thank my family, starting with my wife, Marni, for her patience with my work schedule and for reading and rereading numerous drafts of this book and for enduring many conversations about it. I also thank my children, Karis,

Jonathan, and baby Abigail, born a week after I submitted the first draft. Thank you for letting me work at home, for reminding me when dinner was ready, and for telling me when you wanted to go swimming.

Above all, I am thankful to Jesus Christ, who saved me and called me to a holy calling, not because of my works but because of his own purpose and grace (2 Timothy 1:9). The trials and long hours notwithstanding, it's far easier to write a book than to regularly live a godly, exemplary life before a watching world. The former is done; I'm still working on the latter. I pray that by God's grace my life and this book will be used of God in some small way to help Christians thrive at college, maximize their God-given potential, embrace full-orbed adulthood, faithfully develop their talents, and take their places as salt and light in God's world, living for a cause far greater than themselves. *Soli Deo gloria.*

Notes

PREFACE

1. Jack Tobin, *They Call Me Coach* (New York: McGraw-Hill, 1988), 95.
2. Originally spoken in his sermon to the Baptist Association meeting in Northampton, England (May 30, 1792), http://www.wmcarey.edu/carey/expect/expect.htm.

INTRODUCTION: SURVIVING OR THRIVING? MAKING COLLEGE THE BEST YEARS OF YOUR LIFE (SO FAR)

1. Alex Harris and Brett Harris, "The Myth of Adolescence (Part 1)," *The Rebelution* (blog), August 19, 2005, http://www.therebelution.com/blog/2005/08/myth-of-adolescence-part-1.
2. Derek Kidner, *Tyndale Old Testament Commentaries*, vol. 17, *Proverbs* (Downers Grove, IL: IVP Academic, 2008).
3. Many large classes at state universities have "forced bell curves," which virtually guarantee such outcomes.
4. "Adult Children Moving Back Home: Don't Let 'Boomerang Kids' Derail Your Goals," *New York Life*, http://www.newyorklife.com/nyl/v/index.jsp?vgnextoid=d0bd47bb939d2210a2b3019d221024301cacRCRD.
5. Leonard Sax, "What's Happening to Boys?" *The Washington Post*, March 31, 2006, http://www.washingtonpost.com/wp-dyn/content/article/2006/03/30/AR2006033001341.html.

COMMON MISTAKE #1: CHUCKING YOUR FAITH

1. Neil Gross and Solon Simmons, "How Religious Are America's College and University Professors?" (working paper, October 5, 2006) and *U.S.*

Religious Landscape Survey, The Pew Forum on Religion & Public Life, February 2008.

2. C. S. Lewis, *The Weight of Glory* (New York: HarperOne, 1976), 140.

3. G. K. Chesterton, *The Collected Works,* vol. 16 (San Francisco: Ignatius Press, 1988), 212.

4. The poll was published at *Religion News Blog,* http://www .religionnewsblog.com/19142/religion-trends-3.

5. "LifeWay Research Uncovers Reasons 18 to 22 Year Olds Drop Out of Church," LifeWay Research, http://www.lifeway.com/article/165949/.

COMMON MISTAKE #2: TREATING COLLEGE AS IF IT WERE HIGH SCHOOL

1. "Significant Sleep Deprivation and Stress Among College Students," *Medical News Today,* August 10, 2009, http://www.medicalnewstoday.com/ articles/160265.php.

2. The research was conducted at Ohio State University by Aryn Karpinski, comparing the GPA figures of Facebook users to non-users. Karpinski also found that 79 percent of Facebook-using students "believed the time they spent on the site had no impact on their work." This research was reported in Jonathan Leake and Georgia Warren, "Facebook Fans Do Worse in Exams," *The Times,* April 12. 2009, http://www.timesonline.co.uk/tol/ news/uk/education/article6078321.ece.

3. Jonathan Leake and Georgia Warren, "Facebook Fans Do Worse in Exams."

4. Katie Hafner, "Texting May Be Taking a Toll," *New York Times,* May 25, 2009. The anxiety stems from not wanting to be left out of the loop, or the fear of not replying promptly enough to friends.

5. Adam Gorlick, "Media Multitaskers Pay Mental Price, Stanford Study Shows," *Stanford Report,* http://news.stanford.edu/news/2009/august24/ multitask-research-study-082409.html. Also on this theme is Nicholas Carr, "Is Google Making Us Stupid?" *Atlantic,* July/August 2008.

6. William Deresiewicz, "Solitude and Leadership," *The American Scholar,* March 1, 2010, http://www.theamericanscholar.org/ solitude-and-leadership/print.

This speech was given to the plebe (the equivalent of "freshman") class at the United States Military Academy at West Point in October 2009. The text of the speech is at the link below. The subject of the speech was leadership and solitude. Deresiewicz made the case that leadership involves clear, original thinking and such thinking requires sufficient solitude.

COMMON MISTAKE #3: NOT BEING INTENTIONAL

1. James W. Sire, *Discipleship of the Mind: Learning to Love God in the Ways We Think* (Downers Grove, IL: InterVarsity Press, 1990), 29–31.
2. Adam McHugh, *Introverts in the Church* (Downers Grove, IL: InterVarsity Press, 2009), 41.

COMMON MISTAKE #4: DISTORTING DATING AND ROMANCE

1. Robin Marantz Henig, "What Is It about 20-Somethings?" *New York Times Magazine*, August 22, 2010, http://www.nytimes.com/2010/08/22/magazine/22Adulthood-t.html?_r=2&ref=magazine.
2. Mark Regnerus, "The Case for Early Marriage," *Christianity Today*, July 31, 2009.
3. Institute for American Values, *The 2008 Marriage Index Report*. Also, Robin Marantz Henig, "What Is It about 20-somethings?"
4. Data is from the Centers for Disease Control as reported by Bradford Wilcox in "The Real Pregnancy Crisis," *Wall Street Journal*, May 22, 2009.
5. Mark Regnerus, "The Case for Early Marriage," *Christianity Today*, July 31, 2009. And yes, as much as I hate to use this language in my book, oral sex and mutual masturbation are forms of sex, contrary to what some college students may suggest.
6. "Abortion Common among All Women," Alan Guttmacher Institute, 1996, http://www.guttmacher.org/media/nr/prabort2.html.

COMMON MISTAKE #5: REFUSING TO GROW UP

1. "2009 College Graduates Moving Back Home in Larger Numbers," *CollegeGrad.com*, July 22, 2009, http://www.collegegrad.com/press/2009_college_graduates_moving_back_home_in_larger_numbers.shtml.
2. Hara Estroff Marano, *A Nation of Wimps: The High Cost of Invasive Parenting* (New York: Broadway, 2008), 183–84.
3. Hara Estroff Marano, "A Nation of Wimps," *Psychology Today*, November 1, 2004.
4. G. Stanley Hall, *Adolescence: Its Psychology and Its Relations to Physiology, Anthropology, Sociology, Sex, Crime, Religion and Education* (New York: Appleton, 1904). It's a long story, but the changing economic conditions and the rise of compulsory high school education are what led to a phase in which young people were all together, and to a large extent removed from the intergenerational society and workforce. This led to the "adolescent" stage, which has now been expanded because having a college degree today is almost the equivalent of having a high school degree forty years ago.

5. Melissa Korn, "Students Take Chances With Finances. Gulp," *Wall Street Journal*, May 8, 2009.

6. Both of these examples are adapted from Jim Newheiser and Elyse Fitzpatrick, *You Never Stop Being a Parent: Thriving in Relationship with Your Adult Children* (Phillipsburg, NJ: P&R Publishing, 2010).

COMMON MISTAKE #7: LIVING OUT OF BALANCE

1. Jane Weaver, "College Students Are Avid Gamers," *MSNBC.com*, July 6, 2010, http://www.msnbc.msn.com/id/3078424.

2. Jean Twenge, *Generation Me: Why Today's Young Americans Are More Confident, Assertive, Entitled—and More Miserable Than Ever Before* (New York: Free Press, 2007).

COMMON MISTAKE #8: BEING TOO PASSIVE OR TOO COCKY

1. "College Enrollment and Work Activity of 2009 High School Graduates," *United States Department of Labor*, April 27, 2010, http://www.bls.gov/news.release/hsgec.nro.htm.

2. Mike Bowler, "Dropouts Loom Large for Schools," *U.S. News and World Report*, August 19, 2009, http://www.usnews.com/articles/education/best-colleges/2009/08/19/dropouts-loom-large-for-schools.html.

3. Jeanne Sahadi, "College in 4 years? Try 5 or 6," *CNNMoney.com*, June 22, 2004, http://money.cnn.com/2004/06/21/pf/college/graduation_rates.

4. Arthur F. Holmes, *The Idea of a Christian College*, Revised Edition (Grand Rapids, MI: Eerdmans, 2002), 25.

5. Randall S. Hansen, "Choosing a College Major: How to Chart Your Ideal Path," *Quintessential Careers*, http://www.quintcareers.com/choosing_major.html.

6. Jean Twenge, *Generation Me: Why Today's Young Americans Are More Confident, Assertive, Entitled—and More Miserable Than Ever Before*.

COMMON MISTAKE #9: LIVING FOR GRADES

1. This report was cited in Jean Twenge and Keith Campbell, *The Narcissism Epidemic: Living in the Age of Entitlement* (New York: Free Press, 2010).

COMMON MISTAKE #10: WASTING OPPORTUNITIES

1. Connie Prater, "Obama Signs Credit Card Reforms into Law," *CreditCards.com*, May 22, 2009, http://www.creditcards.com/credit-card-news/obama-signs-credit-card-law-1282.php.

2. Melissa Korn, "Students Take Chances with Finances. Gulp," *Wall Street Journal*, May 8, 2009.

3. Ibid.

CONCLUSION: DON'T WASTE YOUR COLLEGE YEARS: GET READY
FOR THE REAL WORLD

1. Charles Bridges, *Commentary on Proverbs* (Carlisle, PA: The Banner of Truth Trust, 1998), 51. Charles Bridges (1794–1869) was one of the leaders of the evangelical party in the Church of England. He was the vicar of Old Newton, Suffolk, from 1823 to 1849.

APPENDIX 1: THE COLLEGE SELECTION PROCESS

1. Neil Gross and Solon Simmons, "How Religious Are America's College and University Professors?" (working paper, October 5, 2006) and *U.S. Religious Landscape Survey*, The Pew Forum on Religion & Public Life, February 2008.

2. "Concerned over Co-ed Bathrooms," *Go Ask Alice!* http://www.goaskalice.columbia.edu/3277.html.

3. "LifeWay Research Uncovers Reasons 18 to 22 Year Olds Drop Out of Church," LifeWay Research, http://www.lifeway.com/article/165949/.

APPENDIX 2: DO YOU OWN YOUR CHRISTIAN FAITH?

1. Paul Miller, *A Praying Life* (Colorado Springs: NavPress, 2009), 33.

Pine River Library District
P.O. Box 227
395 Bayfield Center Drive
Bayfield, CO 81122
(970) 884-2222

www.lmpl.org